What Makes Us Moral?

OTHER PHILOSOPHY TITLES FROM ONEWORLD

Descartes, Harry M. Bracken, ISBN 1–85168–294–5
Did My Genes Make Me Do It?, Avrum Stroll, ISBN 1–85168–340–2
God: A Guide for the Perplexed, Keith Ward, ISBN 1–85168–323–2
Kierkegaard, Michael Watts, ISBN 1–85168–317–8
Modern French Philosophy: From Existentialism to Postmodernism,
    Robert Wicks, ISBN 1–85168–318–6
Moral Relativism: A Short Introduction, Neil Levy, ISBN 1–85168–305–4
Nietzsche, Robert Wicks, ISBN 1–85168–291–0
Philosophy and Religion: From Plato to Postmodernism, Max
    Charlesworth, ISBN 1–85168–307–0
Political Philosophy: An Historical Introduction, Michael J. White,
    ISBN 1–85168–328–3
Postmodernism: A Beginner's Guide, Kevin Hart, ISBN 1–85168–338–0
Sartre, Neil Levy, ISBN 1–85168–290–2
Spinoza, Richard H. Popkin, ISBN 1–85168–339–9
Wittgenstein, Avrum Stroll, ISBN 1–85168–293–7

What Makes Us Moral?

Crossing the Boundaries of Biology

Neil Levy

ONEWORLD

OXFORD

WHAT MAKES US MORAL?
CROSSING THE BOUNDARIES OF BIOLOGY

Oneworld Publications
(Sales and Editorial)
185 Banbury Road
Oxford OX2 7AR
England
www.oneworld-publications.com

ISBN 1–85168–341–0

Cover design by Mungo Designs
Typeset by Jayvee, Trivandrum, India
Printed and bound in India by Thomson Press Ltd.

Contents

Preface

Man in his arrogance thinks himself a great work, worthy the inter-
position of a deity. More humble and I believe true to consider him
created from animals.

Darwin, *Notebooks*

What are we, we human beings? Are we animals, or angels, or something in between? Science has an answer to this question, or at least the
beginnings of an answer. We are animals. We are a unique species, to be
sure – but there's nothing special about *that*. Uniqueness is nothing
special; all species (all individuals, for that matter) are unique. And in
many ways, we're not that different from other animals. Our basic body
plan, and the great majority of our genome, we share with many other
animals. Behaviorally, genetically and morphologically we are most
similar to the apes, our close cousins. We are more closely related to
chimpanzees, with which we share an ancestor who lived a mere five
million years ago, than chimpanzees are to orangutans. Indeed, there is
a case to be made for the claim that we are a type of chimpanzee: the
third chimpanzee, as Jared Diamond styles us (since we already recognize two distinct species of chimpanzee).[1]

But this answer itself raises many questions. What does it mean to
be a modified ape? What does it imply for our hopes, for our morality,
for what we can achieve and dream of achieving? A great many people
– call them Darwinian fundamentalists – take the claims of evolution
to have deflationary implications.[2] That is, they take it to show that we
are radically mistaken in our self-image. We are not the exalted

creatures we take ourselves to be; we are something quite different, something much less noble. As science gradually uncovers the mechanisms of our behavior, we shall discover – are already discovering – just what it means to be merely an animal. Our vaunted morality is mere disguised selfishness, and our exalted free will is just so much hot air. Instead, the deflationists claim, we are driven by irrational instincts, just like every other animal. Reason and emotion are revealed to be nothing more than chemical processes in the brain, love to be a product of hormones, choice to be illusory, and morality to be bunk.

To those who would deny these claims, the Darwinian fundamentalists respond by pointing triumphantly at the successes of genetics and of evolutionary theory. As our knowledge of the human genome increases, we are learning how our traits – our height, our hair color, but also (and more threateningly) our intelligence – are (allegedly) "encoded" in our genes. Moreover, at the same time we are acquiring the ability to decipher the genome, evolutionary theory is providing us with the story of how it came to have its present form. The evolutionary history of a species is recorded in its genome, in a way that is somewhat analogous to the manner in which the history of a people is recorded in the artifacts they leave behind them. Evolutionary theory is of more than mere theoretical interest: it can illuminate the genome, by providing hypotheses concerning the kinds of adaptations that are likely to be encoded in it. Evolutionary science thus provides the geneticist with hints as to what to look for in the genome, and perhaps even where to look.

These twin sciences – or, more accurately, these two groups of sciences, since there are many sub-disciplines of each – are providing us with an unprecedented understanding of the nature of life on this planet, and promise a greatly expanded ability to predict and intervene in the course of that life. Though many people continue to be skeptical about some of the evolutionary sciences, this skepticism is usually the product of nothing more than superstition and obscurantism. In its general outlines, the theory of evolution is massively well confirmed, and its truth is accepted by most major religions. The promise and power of the new life sciences is, therefore, indisputable.

We must accept that we are a kind of ape. We must accept that we have evolved dispositions, emotions, bents and propensities, that our evolutionary history has shaped us, making us into a kind of animal with a characteristic set of behaviors. But does this imply that we ought to accept the deflationary view of the Darwinian fundamentalists? Do the sciences of genetics and evolution really imply that morality is bunk and free will is illusory?

How are the evolutionary sciences supposed to imply the deflationary conclusions drawn from them by the Darwinian fundamentalists? Genetics, for instance, is often supposed not only to explain the development of normal and abnormal physical traits, but also to explain our psychological dispositions and propensities. In our genome will be found, not only the story of how, say, cancer, arises and how it might best be prevented or cured, but also how depression and schizophrenia arise, why some people are more prone to risk-taking than others, and why some succeed in business whereas others are destined to remain unemployed. Just think of the rash of headlines, proclaiming that the "gene for" some trait or other has been discovered. Some recent examples:

"Study: Gene May Be Cause of Binge-Eating" (*New York Times*, March 20, 2003).
"Beer Gut Gene Discovered" (*Sydney Morning Herald*, January 9, 2003).
"Born to be Fat" (*Guardian*, January 11, 2003).
"'Fear-gene' found: scientists" (*Dawn*, December 24, 2002).

Though the details of these stories vary, they all have an underlying theme. They tell us that those elements of ourselves we regard as most individual, most personal, and perhaps most under our control, are actually encoded in our genome. We drink, we feel fear (or fail to), we put on weight, we are happy or sad in *just the same way* as we have red hair or brown eyes. We just are like that; there is nothing we can do about it (barring technological intervention). It's not a matter of will-power or choice ("A weak gene – not weak willpower – makes some binge-eaters stuff themselves, a study suggests," the *New York Times* article begins). We cannot alter our psychological traits, using the traditional means, involving choice and plans, therapy or lifestyle changes. Instead, we change them only by medical means, means which intervene directly at the level of the chemicals which are under the control of the genes concerned (the *New York Times* article tells us that the same study "also points to possible help: a future pill that might cool their appetites"). We might have thought we could "cure" depression by, say, improving the life of the depressed person. But we would be wrong: we ought to give her a pill.

The extent to which genes, allegedly, control our behavior and our minds is all too well known. It is repeated to us in almost every edition of every newspaper. Less well known, but perhaps more influential on scientists, natural and social, is the extent to which evolutionary biology provides the key to this control. We can discover the ways in which human beings are constrained in their behavior, not only by isolating the genes for a trait, but also by reconstructing their evolutionary history.

Of course, behaviors and psychological characteristics, especially prior to the development of recognizable cultures, leave few records. We cannot unearth the fossils of aggression or of generosity. But what we might call the rational reconstruction of evolutionary history, especially utilizing the tools of the mathematical discipline known as game theory, can tell us a great deal about what kinds of psychological dispositions can be expected to have evolved. Some kinds of behaviors are advantageous in the evolutionary struggle, and others disadvantageous, and as computer modeling of the process soon reveals, the disadvantageous ones are destined rapidly to disappear.

Since we are evolved beings, we ought to expect to discover the traces of this evolution in ourselves. We have opposable thumbs because our ancestors who possessed hands suited for grasping did better than those who lacked them. Similarly, we may find that we possess mental "organs" that are the result of our evolutionary history. It may be that just as we can (supposedly) read off the constraints upon our behavior from our genome, so we can deduce them from our evolutionary history. Given that some sorts of behaviors would have been selected against, in evolutionary history, we cannot possess the psychological dispositions that would enable us to act in these ways today. Because men and women play different roles in reproduction, we can expect different behaviors to have benefitted each sex in different ways in their evolutionary history. We ought to expect that these differences have become entrenched, so that like our opposable thumbs we are stuck with them (once again barring extraordinary technological interventions). Men are not from Mars, nor women from Venus. Both are from the Paleolithic, and they remain essentially Stone Age creatures.

It should be clear that these claims about the evolutionary and genetic sources of behavior have implications for morality, both broadly and narrowly conceived. If it is true that our genes and our evolved psychology incline us to act in certain ways, and make other ways of acting (variously) difficult to learn or to sustain, or downright impossible for us, then this has immediate implications for the kinds of societies we might hope to build. For instance, if our intelligence is a product of our genome, then certain kinds of inequality seem to be inevitable. Fundamental differences in the abilities and interests of men and women would appear to have similar implications. Thus, these evolutionary and genetic claims have important consequences for social policy and for our political aspirations.

Moreover, many philosophers and scientists have claimed that ethics itself can only be fully understood within the evolutionary context. If we are moral animals, then this must be the result of our evolutionary history. But evolution equates to the "survival of the fittest": it systematically rewards selfishness. If ethics evolved, then ethics must be a form of disguised selfishness, perhaps so well disguised that ethical people are not, and cannot be, aware of this. Of course, we believe, pretheoretically, that ethics is the opposite of selfishness. If this line of reasoning is correct, we must abandon our naive view of ethics, and reconcile ourselves to a world in which there is no true morality.

Oddly, many of the defenders of the more lurid genetic and evolutionary claims – that men and women differ fundamentally in their abilities, that rape is an adaptation, that intelligence is genetic – *deny* that their claims have moral and political implications. Odder still, they are very happy to draw moral and political lessons from their science, all the while denying that it has any such lessons to teach us. This book will examine their claims. Do the evolutionary and genetic hypotheses have ethical consequences, or are they somehow insulated from our moral life? If, as I suggest, they do have such consequences, what is their precise nature? And, most importantly, are these claims true?

I shall defend the view that the social, moral and political claims made on behalf of these sciences are wildly overblown. There is such a thing as human nature, and it really constrains what we can do, think and become. There are differences between individual human beings, but these differences are rarely the *direct* product of our evolved natures. Ironically, the failings of the Darwinian fundamentalists to understand the malleability of human beings stems from their failure to grasp an essential – *the* essential – fact about human nature. Human beings are, by nature, cultural beings. They are made to interface with an environment of artefacts, prostheses, and supplements. They come to be the intelligent creatures they are not on account of their native intelligence, but on account of their native ability to take advantage of an external scaffolding. *That's* the kind of beings we are. Neglect this fact, concentrate on the Stone Age mind alone, without the apparent distraction of the merely cultural setting in which it is embedded, and you miss the essence of the human. However, this implies that our differences are at least as much the product of social norms, of ways of life, as they are of our genes.

I am far from being the first to raise doubts about the adequacy of the Darwinian fundamentalist picture of human beings. This book is born almost as much out of frustration with the defenders of the importance of culture and the social to human nature as with the proponents of the cruder nativist views. Just as the nativists go wrong in denying the importance of history and culture, so the culturalists place themselves in an untenable position by asserting that human beings, at least insofar as they are rational and moral, are insulated from the forces of biology. Neither of these extreme views is true. Moreover, we need to move beyond the crude caricature and invective that has largely taken the place of reasoned argument on this ground. We do evolutionary psychologists a disservice, and we miss the point and power of their position, if we begin by assuming that they are a bunch of misogynists, or stooges of unrestrained capitalism. In fact, their personal views span the political spectrum. But their personal views are not under consideration: we are concerned only with their arguments, and with the implications of their scientific hypotheses. We must take these on their merits, not parody them, or, in the name of the inviolable dignity of humanity, reject them without further consideration.

It is only if we give their arguments fair consideration, assess their hypotheses and advance rival, ideally testable, hypotheses for the phenomena they seek to explain, that we earn the right to be heard. It is only then that their frequent charge, that we, their opponents, are obscurantists, deliberately closing our minds to the discoveries of science when these discoveries clash with our preconceived views of our powers and ourselves, will be false.

Many of the opponents of the evolutionary sciences, as these bear upon human nature and morality, accuse the evolutionists of being *too* scientific, of attempting to replace the irreducible human soul, the transcendent, with the material and the reductionist. But if by "science" we simply mean the best techniques we have available for gathering data, formulating hypotheses, and testing them, then it is impossible to be too scientific in the quest for knowledge. My complaint against crude sociobiology and evolutionary psychology is just the opposite: they are *not scientific enough*. They have not exposed their hypotheses to rigorous enough testing; they have ignored alternative explanations or given them short shrift. We ought to subject their hypotheses to rigorous testing because they have undesirable political and moral consequences. But we ought to reject them, when they are false, not because of these consequences, but because they are false.

Overview of the book

The moral implications of Darwinism have been hotly debated ever since *The Origin of Species* appeared in 1859. Chapter 1 explores these early debates, and traces the fate of the political movements that explicitly embraced one or another version of Darwinism. As we shall see, the political consequences were all-too-real, and helped to feed the currents of thought and action which led to the crimes of Nazism, as well as to the lesser crimes committed in the name of biological purity in the United States and in many European countries. All sides in the evolution debate condemn the crimes of eugenics and of Social Darwinism, but they differ on just what the mistakes made by these early bio-political movements were. I shall examine the claim, still commonly advanced today, that their mistake lay in seeing *any* political implications in what is just a value-free (and therefore politically neutral) science.

Chapter 2 turns to more contemporary debates, concerning the origin and status of an evolved morality. Here we are concerned with whether something answering to our everyday notion of morality could be the product of evolution, or whether we must reconcile ourselves to a radically reduced, thinned out, morality, a morality that is the expression of genetic selfishness. I defend the claim that morality, full-blown, could be the product of our evolutionary history: there is no *scientific* ground for moral skepticism.

Chapter 3 introduces the science of evolutionary psychology. As we shall see, this new discipline has a great deal to contribute to our understanding of ourselves. Unfortunately, many of its major figures have tied their standard to a set of dubious claims, especially about human gender differences. In this chapter, we set out these claims, in preparation for their detailed examination and assessment in chapter 4, where I argue that the rival, social, explanation for the data collected by evolutionary psychologists is (to say the least) more plausible than is their nativist hypothesis. Evolutionary psychologists miss the essential fact about human nature: that it is designed to be completed by human culture.

Chapter 5 turns to genetic explanations of human behavior. We often hear it said that, for instance, intelligence is sixty percent genetic. But what precisely does this mean? I show that it does not mean what many of the proponents of the importance of genes apparently take it to mean: that intelligence (for instance) is fixed and unalterable, that merely social interventions cannot change it. In fact, no matter what proportion of variation in intelligence (to continue with our example) is genetically caused – even if it were 100% – we would have no reason to think that, for example, alterations in educational policies could not have dramatic effects upon it. This sounds counter-intuitive, but only because we usually do not understand estimates of heritability, and what it is they measure. Once we understand these estimates, we see that the large claims made for them, for the importance of the genetic and the correlate uselessness of merely social interventions, do not follow from the evidence cited in support of them. What we know about genes and how they work gives us no reason to turn away from building a better society directly, through social programs, in favor of genetic or pharmaceutical interventions to the same end.

The book concludes with some brief examples of the ways in which the accretions of human culture transform our ways of living, of understanding ourselves, our psychological, and even our cognitive capacities. The ways in which we change ourselves and our environment, change ourselves *by* changing our environment, illustrate the extent to which our evolutionary past does not predict our future lives. We are evolved beings, moral animals, but we exhibit a degree of behavioral flexibility unknown elsewhere in the animal kingdom. Our biology constrains us, but these constraints are relatively few and broad. We can build our future, not *in spite of* our nature, but *because* of it: evolution has gifted us with the ability to create ever new, and ever changing, social worlds, to control our destinies and fight injustice. We are shortsighted and greedy, aggressive and xenophobic, but we are *also* rational and just, generous and hospitable. Which of our many, at once natural and social, conflicting dispositions shall have the last or the most significant say is not laid down in our biology.

Acknowledgments

A small portion of chapter 4 is reprinted from "Evolutionary Psychology, Human Universals and the Standard Social Science Model," *Biology and Philosophy* (forthcoming, 2004). I am grateful to the editor for permission to reuse this material. Various people helped at different stages during the writing process. In particular, I thank Tim Bayne, Steve Clarke, John Wilkins, and two anonymous readers for Oneworld, who all read part or whole of the manuscript and provided indispensable feedback. Ann Grand provided an excellent copy-editing service, which went well beyond the call of duty. No doubt there would be fewer errors remaining if I had heeded more of their advice.

1

The moral consequences of Darwinism

Man with all his noble qualities, with sympathy which feels for the most debased, with benevolence which extends not only to other men but to the humblest living creature, with his god-like intellect which has penetrated into the movements and constitution of the solar system – with all these exalted powers – man still bears in his bodily frame the indelible stamp of his lowly origin.

Darwin, *The Descent of Man*

In 1859, Charles Darwin published a book that sparked off a revolution. In that book, *The Origin of Species*, Darwin set out his theory of how the tremendous variety of plants and animals we observe around us came to be. Darwin's theories challenged many of our most fundamental views, our most cherished fantasies, not only about religion – though that was what captured many people's attention, and still continues to receive a disproportionate amount of space – but especially about humanity, its powers, and its place in the natural world. We have yet fully to come to terms with the Darwinian revolution, to gauge the extent of its implications for human life, and especially its implications for morality.

In *The Origin of Species*, Darwin carefully avoided much mention of humanity. Perhaps he felt that placing humanity at center stage of his story risked inflaming passions too much, or would prove too threatening to an audience among whom Biblical Creationism was still a widely held belief. But his audience did not miss the fact that Darwin's theories applied to human beings as much as to any other animal. Darwinism was widely rejected, then as now, because of its implications for the concerns which most of us hold dearest.

What was Darwin's theory, and why was – why *is* – it so widely regarded as threatening to our conception of humanity and to morality? We need, first of all, to have a clear picture of Darwinian natural selection before us, so that we can begin to grasp the extent to which it requires us to rethink our notions of ourselves as moral beings.

Descent with modification

Contrary to popular belief, Charles Darwin did not invent the notion of evolution. There had been theories of evolution before Darwin, including one propounded by his grandfather, Erasmus Darwin. Charles's innovation was not in proposing that life on earth was the product of natural selection, but in providing a convincing case for a particular mechanism of evolution.

Darwin began by noting, following the work of Thomas Malthus, that, all other things being equal, populations would increase exponentially. The average animal, of a given species, may give birth to dozens of offspring. If they all survive, and go on to have the same number of offspring themselves, generation after generation, the area will soon be swamped (if we begin with just two animals, and each of them have two offspring, and so on, we will have over two million animals in a mere twenty generations). Obviously, these kinds of numbers would soon become unsustainable. In fact, much lower numbers are usually unsustainable: an area can support only a small population of the animal in question. Typically, Darwin saw, most of the animals born must fail to survive long enough to reproduce. Whether they are aware of it or not, the animals are all in competition with each other for the resources they need to survive.

But which animals die and which live to have offspring of their own? Is it all just a matter of chance? Chance certainly plays a role, in the individual case, but averaged out over many organisms, its importance plummets. Animals which are better suited to their environment are more likely to survive than those that are less well suited (less "fit"). If all the offspring of a given pair are exactly the same, then they will all be equally fit. But they never are *exactly* the same. Instead, there are small differences between them. One is bigger, another is faster, a third brainier, and so on. Thus there are minute fitness differences between them. This gives some an (usually very slight) advantage over others.

This gives us two of the preconditions for evolution: competition between members of the same species, and (usually small) differences that give some of them an edge in the competition. We need to add one more: differences must be *heritable*. That is, offspring must tend to resemble their parents. If this is the case, then the initial small advantages can gradually accumulate. If, for instance, an animal has an advantage over its conspecifics (members of the same species) because it is faster, and therefore more likely to survive, its offspring will tend to inherit its speed. Indeed, given the small random variations we expect to find among offspring, some will probably be faster still. And their offspring will be faster again. If speed remains relevant to survival (perhaps because the animals are preyed upon by a speedy predator), we can expect the proportion of fast animals to increase. Eventually, only speedy animals will be born. In this case, however, since the competition is always continuing, there might be selection pressure for still faster animals.

If this process goes on long enough, and enough traits are altered through it, later generations of animals will come to be quite different from the first generation. Sometimes, one species of animal gives rise to different lineages, which diverge from one another so dramatically that they can no longer interbreed. If this happens, a new species has come into being. Darwin saw that, given enough time, all the resulting diversity of species we see could be the outcome of such *speciation* events. We are all – humans and clams, elephants and bacteria – descended from the same, very simple, ancestors.

Darwin's theory of descent with modification gradually displaced all previous evolutionary hypotheses. It is worth mentioning one of its competitors, if only because it is still frequently confused with the Darwinian account. According to *Lamarckism* (the theory proposed by the eighteenth-century naturalist, Jean-Baptiste Lamarck), the inheritance of acquired characteristics is the driving force of evolution.

During the course of their lifetime, animals acquire many abilities and physical features; Lamarck's theory was that such acquisitions might be passed on to their offspring. Thus (to give the classic example), each generation of giraffes acquires a slightly longer neck as a result of stretching to reach the leaves at the tops of trees. Darwin himself did not rule out some kind of Lamarckism altogether, but most Darwinians give it no credence at all. The problem is that there is no mechanism whereby acquired characteristics can be inherited. Inheritance is a function (largely) of genes, and my genes don't change when I do. There are non-genetic means of inheritance – most obviously, but not limited to, the cultural inheritance that is characteristic of human groups – but they are not the driving force of evolution. It is random variation, and not acquired characteristics, which accounts for the diversity of life.

We can no longer doubt that Darwin's theory was, in its broad outline, correct. Darwinian evolution, together with Mendelian genetics, which supplied the theory of heritability which Darwinism lacked (and which we shall consider further in chapter 5), provides the explanatory framework within which all of biology must be understood. As the influential biologist Theodosius Dobzhansky put it, "Nothing in biology makes sense except in the light of evolution." Yet evolution is still widely condemned, with a moral passion normally absent from debates over scientific hypotheses. What accounts for this resistance, stubbornly continuing from Darwin's day to our own?

Denying Darwin

One of Darwin's contemporaries (the wife of the Bishop of Worcester) is reputed to have said of his theory "Descended from monkeys? My gracious, let us hope it isn't true. But if true, let us hope it doesn't become more widely known."[3] Darwinism, as both its most passionate opponents and vigorous defenders agree, is *dangerous* (not for nothing did Daniel Dennett, an American philosopher, and enthusiastic Darwinian, call his recent book *Darwin's Dangerous Idea*). But whence the danger – or at least the perception of it?

It is common to suggest that opposition to the theory of natural selection is motivated by religious fundamentalism and nothing more.

Of course, blind allegiance to religious tradition is often an important factor in the still widespread rejection of Darwinism. If, as Darwin suggests, all life has evolved from a single common ancestor, then the biblical account, according to which God created each animal in its current form, must be false. In the face of this evidence, sophisticated believers have resorted to some now familiar means to reconcile their faith with evolution. They have, for instance, interpreted the creation story as an extended metaphor, rather than as literal truth. But the greater the plausibility of evolution, the less there seems to be for God to do: the more superfluous his very existence. Like the French mathematician and astronomer Laplace, responding to Napoleon's query about the place of God in his cosmology, we can say that we have no need for that hypothesis.

In any case, it is a mistake to think that opposition to evolution comes only from misinformed, or wishfully thinking, religious bigots. On the face of it, Darwinism is a threat not just to religious verities, but to our most fundamental conception of ourselves as autonomous beings, able to choose between alternatives guided by notions, not merely of the expedient, but also of the good and the right.

It might even be that much of the apparently religious opposition to evolution is motivated, at base, by concerns that are fundamentally moral, even humanistic. To suggest we are descended from monkeys seems to attack our cherished notion of humans as autonomous beings. If we are the products of evolution, then we too came to be simply as the result of billions of years of slow accumulation of tiny modifications.[4] There was nothing inevitable about our existence; evolution did not aim to produce us, and we are not, from its point of view, its flower or culmination. Moreover, we came to have the characteristics we possess because they are useful, (or were useful to our ancestors) not because they are ennobling. This is an unpromising mechanism from which to produce the godlike creatures we take ourselves to be. It seems more likely to produce modified apes than imperfect angels.

Hence the fact that evolution is widely seen as having deflationary implications. We think we're special, created in the image of the Deity, or possessed of transcendent powers (of free choice, for example). In fact, we are just one species among many. We think we are seekers after truth, engaged in the pursuit of the good, the right and the beautiful whereas our desires and cognitive powers are merely adaptations for survival. Above all, we think we're moral, the only truly moral animals, but nothing marks us out as special or different (or no more different than any other species) members of the animal kingdom. Our vaunted morality is itself the product of genetic selfishness, one more means whereby we propagate ourselves. It is the apparent deflationary power of Darwinism that, I believe, explains the vehemence of the opposition to it, as intense now as when it first appeared in nineteenth-century England.

In what ways, precisely, might Darwinism threaten to undermine morality? Firstly, it might be that Darwinism shows that morality isn't *real.* We believe that there are binding moral obligations upon us, but, in fact, there are not. We are merely "programmed" (by evolution) to think that there are. Religion might be an appropriate analogy. A number of scholars think that humans are innately religious: that we have a built-in tendency to believe in God.[5] But (many of them say) there is no God: God, and morality, is an illusion induced by evolution. Evolution thus undermines moral *realism.*

Secondly, evolution might show that it is unrealistic to expect people to obey moral injunctions. Perhaps there really is a morality; perhaps we really ought to take everyone's interests into consideration, turn the other cheek, and do unto others as we would be done by. But we might be too selfish to be able to live by this code. Evolution might have implanted self-seeking motives in us that are stronger than any moral motives we can range against them. On this view, evolution does not undermine moral realism; rather, it shows that humans are naturally too selfish to possess the requisite moral *motivation.*

Finally, it may be that evolutionary theory has some surprising lessons for us regarding the *content* of morality. It might teach us that there is a morality, which is binding upon us and which we can reasonably be expected to obey, but that that morality is quite diferent than we commonly believe. Proponents of this view hold that many of the actions we regard as moral are in fact *im*moral, and many of those that seem to be mere selfishness are in fact morally right.

The evolutionary attacks upon moral realism and moral motivation have captured most attention in recent years. In the early days of Darwinism, it was the third threat (as it was seen by opponents of evolutionary ethics) that took center stage. Some Darwinians took the theory to have important implications for the content of morality, while anti-Darwinians saw in the theory no more than an apology for selfishness and greed, under the guise of science. It is this third version of the evolutionary attack upon morality that we shall consider in this chapter. Examining this early critique of conventional morality will help set the stage for the contemporary debate, with which much of the rest of this book is concerned.

Darwin's defenders

Darwin had no taste for polemics. Fortunately for him, he had an able champion in Thomas Henry Huxley, who described himself as "Darwin's bulldog." It was Huxley who proselytized on behalf of evolution and who defended it against its many opponents. When, in 1860, Darwinism was discussed at a meeting of the British Association in Oxford, it fell to Huxley to put the case for evolution, against the skilful debating of Samuel Wilberforce, Bishop of Oxford. According to one, possibly apocryphal, account of what happened that night, Wilberforce mockingly inquired of Huxley whether it was on his mother's or his father's side that he was descended from a monkey. "I am not ashamed," Huxley replied, "to have a monkey for an ancestor, but I would be ashamed to claim descent from a man who used his great gifts to obscure the truth."[6] Whether this account is entirely false or merely embellished, from then on Huxley's name and fortune were irrevocably linked with Darwin's.

Darwin had another defender in Hebert Spencer. Spencer, a philosopher and sociologist, is today largely forgotten, but during his lifetime he enjoyed the rare combination of intellectual respectability and popular success. His books were best-sellers, and his ideas were taken very seriously. Spencer was as much an evolutionary theorist in his own right as a defender of Darwin (with whom he disagreed upon some points). His own theory of evolution predated the appearance of *The Origin of Species*, and placed greater emphasis on Lamarckian mechanisms than upon natural selection. After the publication of Darwin's work, however, the two theories intertwined, at least in popular consciousness. It was Spencer, not Darwin, who coined the famous phrase "the survival of the fittest," which still sums up natural selection in the minds of many people. Darwin endorsed the phrase by adopting it in later editions of *The Origin*.

Between them, Darwin's two eminent defenders were largely responsible for the triumph of evolution over its enemies. Thanks, in no small part, to their tireless work on its behalf, the fact of evolution was accepted by most biologists, and by an increasing number of people outside the sciences, within a couple of decades of the publication of the *The Origin* (ironically, however, the mechanisms Darwin proposed to explain evolution were almost as widely rejected until well into the twentieth century, when Mendelian genetics filled in the details of inheritance and vindicated natural selection). However, for all they had in common, Darwin's defenders had radically opposed views on the moral implications of evolution.

Despite the apparent glee he took in his defeat of Wilberforce, Huxley found evolution almost as troubling a doctrine as did the bishop. For many anti-Darwinists, natural selection is a doctrine of selfishness and cruelty, elevated to the status of a worldview. Darwinism, they believe, celebrates the survival of the fittest, and despises those who fall behind in their wake, and this alone is sufficient reason to reject it as an account of human history. Huxley agreed that if evolution were a complete explanation of human behavior, including our moral behavior, then it would have the immoral consequences the ant-Darwinists feared. Unlike Wilberforce, however, Huxley had no doubt that natural selection was true.

Huxley, like those today who agree with him regarding both the truth of natural selection, and its immoral implications, faced a dilemma. He could either give up on morality, at least as it had traditionally been conceived, or he could reject the sway of evolution over morality. Huxley emphatically chose the latter. It is probably true, Huxley admitted, that our moral sentiments are a product of natural selection. But, by the same token, so are the *immoral* sentiments, of which so many people give so much evidence. So far as natural selection itself is concerned, they are on a par: just two different kinds of survival strategies. We cannot decide which is better, higher, more worthy, by reference to natural selection itself:

The thief and the murderer follow nature just as much as the phil-
anthropist. Cosmic evolution may teach us how the good and the evil
tendencies of man may have come about; but, in itself, it is incompe-
tent to furnish any better reason why what we call good is preferable to
what we call evil than we had before. Some day, I doubt not, we shall
arrive at an understanding of the evolution of the aesthetic faculty; but
all the understanding in the world will neither increase nor diminish
the force of the intuition that this is beautiful and that is ugly.[7]

Morality, Huxley appears to be claiming, is a realm independent of evolution. The conclusions of biology may be true, but their truth has
no moral implications at all.

Huxley suggests that we make the mistake of thinking that evolution has moral implications due to a confusion concerning the meaning of "fitness." We have an unfortunate tendency to suppose that
"fittest" means "best." But this is an error. "Fittest" is a technical term in
evolutionary theory, and simply means "most likely to survive and
reproduce;" it has no other implications. The products of natural selection *might* be good, as well as fit, but their goodness, if any, is unrelated
to their fitness. More often, indeed, the products of evolution will be
just what the opponents of Darwin feared: bloody and cruel, truly
"nature, red in tooth and claw" (as Tennyson put it). Morality is far too
important either to abandon, or to remake in the image of natural
selection. Instead, Huxley argued, morality requires *opposing* natural
selection, not as a scientific theory, but as a social and moral doctrine:
"Let us understand, once for all, that the ethical progress of society
depends, not on imitating the cosmic process, still less in running away
from it, but in combating it."[8] Far from modeling morality on the
process of natural selection, Huxley argued that we ought to oppose
evolution in the name of morality.

Huxley's vision of the ethical implications of Darwinism, and the
consequent importance of combating it in the social realm, if not in the
scientific, lives on today in the work of several prominent biologists.
For George Williams, one of the most important evolutionary theorists
of the last few decades, Huxley was wrong only in that he did not go far
enough. He did not, Williams argues, realize just how thoroughly bad
nature is, and therefore did not emphasize sufficiently the need to
combat it in all its manifestations including the effects it has had on

our nature.[9] But it was not Huxley's view of the moral implications of Darwinism that was to win out in the minds of scientists, and of the broader population, it was Spencer's.

For Spencer, unlike Huxley, evolution had a moral message. For him, evolution was the story of progress. Evolution had within it an intrinsic drive toward complexity; a natural movement from simpler to more complex creatures. Thus, human beings, as arguably its most complex products, are the pinnacles of evolutionary achievement. Given that evolution is a progressive force, Spencer suggested, human beings ought to do everything possible to foster it, and we can best do that by ensuring that social conditions are suited to allowing it to do its work. If we attempt to interfere with its workings, it will be us, and our descendants, who will suffer.

For Spencer, evolution was best summed in his famous phrase, "the survival of the fittest." Those who prosper, those who win in the evolutionary competition, are those who are best equipped for life's struggles. Evolution is therefore a device for sorting out the best products of nature, and rewarding them for their abilities. In the process, a great many organisms – from unicellular bacteria to people – fall by the wayside. This is a regrettable, but inevitable, consequence of progress. It is not a side-effect that we can hope to avoid, because it is only by allowing the imposition of penalties on the unfit that we can hope to reap the rewards of evolutionary progress. If, for instance, we take steps to diminish the suffering of those who lose out in the evolutionary competition, we risk aiding the survival of the *un*fit. Those who, without assistance, would have died without progeny will instead survive and reproduce. The number of the unfit will increase; as a result, the burden upon the next generation will be that much the greater. To assist, out of misguided compassion, the weak, the foolish and the congenitally criminal, to cushion them from the worst consequences which flow from their behavior, is to interfere with the processes of nature, and to prepare for the next generation greater social ills, in the form of the degenerate progeny of these unfortunates: "To aid the bad in multiplying, is, in effect, the same as maliciously providing for our descendants a multitude of enemies. It may be doubted whether the maudlin philanthropy which, looking only at direct mitigations, ignores indirect mischiefs, does not inflict more misery than the extremest selfishness inflicts."[10] Since evolution has a direction, since its natural tendency is progressive, we have a duty to assist in its processes, or, at very least, to refrain from interfering in them. Nature is a well-ordered machine for sorting the worthy from the unworthy, and we impede its mechanism at the peril of ourselves and our children.

For Spencer, evolution was not merely a biological process that explained how we came to be the kind of creatures we are. It was also a political and a social model for us to follow. It contained within it the outlines of a good polity, and it produced all that was valuable. A good society was one in which each person was encouraged to pursue their own selfish ends, because as a result benefits accrue for the entire society.

Spencer's doctrine was one that was immensely attractive to those people who could see themselves as the winners in life's competitions. It flattered their egos, since it identified them with the fittest beings, and it provided a handy rationale for their activities. Wealthy industrialists like Andrew Carnegie fêted Spencer, and espoused his views, for they saw in them a justification for the capitalism that had enriched them. It was Spencer to whom Carnegie referred, in explaining why capitalism was inevitable and proper: "The law of competition, be it benign or not, is here; we cannot evade it; no substitutes for it have been found; and while the law may be sometimes hard for the individual, it is best for the race, because it ensures the survival of the fittest in every department."[11] In a similar vein, John D. Rockefeller invoked Spencer when he told a Sunday School class that "the growth of a large business is merely a survival of the fittest [...] This is not an evil tendency in business. It is merely the working out of a law of nature."[12] Darwinism, at least as seen through the eyes of Spencer, seemed to vindicate capitalism at its most ruthless.

To be sure, Spencer's view had its more benevolent side. If the evolutionary process is to do its work properly, if the truly deserving are to be rewarded, and only those who are truly unworthy to be punished, then it must operate upon a level playing field. Evolution teaches us that we must never interfere with the workings of natural processes, but, by the same token, it justifies interference when it is aimed solely at undoing the ill effects of previous meddling. Though organized charity was anathema to Spencer, individual philanthropy might have benign effects, if well targeted. The poor could be divided into two classes: the undeserving poor, who found themselves at the bottom rung of the social ladder due to their inferior inherited capacities; and the deserving poor, who had suffered misfortunes or injustices, and whose rank did not, therefore, reflect their capabilities. Charity aimed at improving the prospects of the latter enhanced the workings of the process of natural selection, by allowing those who were inherently capable of success in the struggle for survival a chance to compete on equal terms with everyone else.

Certain kinds of philanthropy, which aimed at providing equality of *opportunity* (though not of outcomes), were therefore mandated by Spencer. His wealthy enthusiasts embraced this kind of philanthropic work. Carnegie, for instance, specialized in endowing public libraries. Such libraries provided access to educational resources for the children of the impoverished, thus offering opportunities to those who had the innate qualities to take advantage of them.[13]

The political views founded upon the basis of (broadly) Darwinian principles came to be known as *Social Darwinism*. For the most part, Social Darwinism advocated *laissez-faire* capitalism as the best means to allow the process of natural selection to do its work. Social Darwinists were also frequently racists, arguing that the economic and political dominance of Western countries was the result of the biological superiority of the white race. There were, however, exceptions to both these generalizations. Prince Peter Kropotkin was a Russian anarchist who argued that natural selection favored organisms that cooperate, rather than those which compete selfishly. Charles Loring Brace, an American Social Darwinist, argued that evolution gave no support to racism. Some feminists invoked Darwin in arguing for political equality for women. But for the most part, Social Darwinism was politically conservative: its adherents supported the *status quo* and opposed government intervention to ameliorate the condition of the poor.[14] In what follows, we shall be concerned almost entirely with this dominant strand of Social Darwinism, and the term will be used to refer exclusively to it, unless otherwise specified.

These days, we tend to associate opposition to evolution with a certain strand of the political right. It comes, in the main, from religious fundamentalists, for example, from the groups which form such

a ... ty in the United
St ... nd in hand with
o ... ometimes, with
o

of other "constellations" of belief
CONSTELLATIONS

w ... evolution wars
te ... ogy teacher, for
st ... of a Tennessee
an ... ured headlines
Pu ... d the world. A
19 ... ed the events of
de ... *herit the Wind*
fo ... iliar script: the
gi ... power of reli-
ev ... Western world
he ... nt his heretical
... tural selection
that was on trial in Tennessee: it was the entire legacy of the Enlightenment, in fateful confrontation with the forces of superstition and obscurantism.

The victory of the representatives of Darwin at that trial – a victory in fact, though not in law, since Scopes was found guilty and fined $100 – is therefore widely regarded as a victory for science over prejudice. To some extent, that's just what it is: evolution is, after all, true. But there is ample evidence to suggest that the prosecution, led by the three times Democratic candidate for the Presidency, William Jennings Bryan, was motivated as much by justified concern over the pernicious political implications of Social Darwinism as by religious conservatism. Bryan saw in Darwinism a stick with which the poor would be beaten, and his tireless work to improve their lot undermined. Certainly, at least some of his opponents that day in Dayton, Tennessee, were not merely advocates of evolution as a scientific theory; they were also committed Social Darwinists. Clarence Darrow, one of the most famous lawyers of the day, defended Scopes. Darrow had volunteered his services at the urging of H. L. Mencken, who advised the defense during the trial, as well as covering it for the *Baltimore Sun*. Mencken, as the most famous journalist of the day, set the tone for the press coverage, ensuring that Bryan would be mocked. He told Darrow that the aim of the trial was not to defend Scopes, but "to make a fool out of Bryan," and thereby discredit fundamentalist opposition to Darwinism.[15] And Mencken was a fervent Social Darwinist.

For Mencken, the lesson of Darwin was fundamentally and explicitly Nietzschean. Evolution is a struggle for scarce resources: a struggle that necessarily has winners and losers. Through this struggle, and through it alone, are born the best products of civilization. The ruthless process of natural selection is not merely inevitable; it is the source of all value. Thus, for Mencken:

> There must be a complete surrender to the law of natural selection – that inevitable natural law which ordains that the fit shall survive and the unfit shall perish. All growth must occur at the top. The strong must grow stronger, and that they may do so, they must waste no strength in the vain task of trying to lift up the weak.[16]

Religion, for Mencken, was merely one means by which the weak attempt to impose shackles on the strong. "Christianity and brotherhood," Mencken wrote, are not fit "for the higher men, not for the supermen of tomorrow."[17]

The confrontation in Tennessee was not merely between religious fundamentalism and science. It was between two political ideologies: Bryan's populist leftism – his advocacy of a federal income tax and of women's suffrage, of a Department of Labor and opposition to capital punishment – and Mencken's libertarianism, anti-Semitism and misogyny. Mencken and Darrow won the public relations battle, but it was a victory not for, or not only for, free inquiry; it was a victory for the forces of conservatism. It helped to sweep away one powerful set of obstacles to the respectability of Social Darwinism, and to give to a political ideology the veneer of respectable science.

Eugenics

No matter how distasteful the views of some Social Darwinists were, they seem relatively benign when compared to the excesses of the eugenicists. Eugenicists were not prepared simply to allow the process of natural selection to do its work: they wanted to give it a helping hand. Eugenics came in two forms: *positive* eugenics aimed to encourage the best people to reproduce, and thereby ensure that future generations contained a higher proportion of the biologically fit; *negative* eugenics aimed to prevent the most undesirable from reproducing. In one or both forms, the eugenics movement flourished in the late nineteenth and the first half of the twentieth century.

Not all Social Darwinists were eugenicists, and not all eugenicists Darwinians.[18] Indeed, though evolution was widely accepted by the end of the nineteenth century, its Darwinian form did not gain ascendancy until the "new synthesis" of the 1920s and 30s, when a new generation of biologists demonstrated the genetic basis of inheritance using tools which were unavailable to Darwin. Nevertheless, it is generally accurate to see eugenics as the activist wing of Social Darwinism. Whereas the Social Darwinists advocated allowing natural selection to run its course, without interference (or, at most, with just that degree of interference which would establish a level playing field upon which it could act), the eugenicists advocated giving natural selection a helping hand. In between the two are figures like John Berry Haycraft, author of *Darwinism and Race Progress* (1895), who argued that diseases like smallpox and tuberculosis were friends of humanity, since they eliminated the weak, and that therefore they ought not to be treated by the methods of modern medicine.[19]

Eugenics was enormously (from the perspective of today unbelievably), successful. It had adherents across the political spectrum, including many in positions of power, and advocates among the best contemporary scientists. Figures as distinguished as Julian Huxley, one of the foremost biologists of his day, and a principal architect of the "modern synthesis" of Darwin and Mendelian genetics (as well as the grandson of T. H. Huxley) endorsed its themes. Huxley worried that improvements in public health in Britain would lead to an increase in the number of "defectives," and argued that measures should be taken to prevent them from reproducing.

Increasingly, measures *were* taken. Across northern Europe, where it was particularly influential, and in the United States, programs of involuntary sterilization of the allegedly unfit were enacted. In 1907, the state of Indiana passed a law permitting the sterilization of "defectives;" by 1933, twenty-nine other states had followed suit. Some scholars estimate that in the United States, between 1907 and 1974, hundreds of thousands of people were sterilized, many involuntarily.[20] In the United States, the measures were often explicitly racist. Scientists and politicians warned against the dangers of miscegenation, and pressed for laws banning interracial marriages. They were more successful in imposing limitations on the immigration of "inferior" peoples. No less a personage than Theodore Roosevelt warned that a "war of the cradle" was being fought, between the better classes of people and the degenerate members of society.[21]

But it was in Germany that eugenics was most enthusiastically received. After 1933, and the coming to power of the Nazi party, eugenics was a central plank of government policy. The Nazi emphasis upon the blood of the people, upon the need to purify it of foreign admixture and thereby ensure the greatness of the nation, was not aberrant in the political and scientific climate of the first third of the twentieth century. Nazi scientists and party officials admired and copied the similar views of American thinkers and policymakers.[22] But the Nazis went further, in their program of negative eugenics, than any other nation dared. They, too, enacted sterilization programs: by 1945, an estimated 360,000 Germans had been sterilized.[23] In addition, however, they began a program of "euthanasizing" the handicapped. Soon the program was extended: not only the handicapped, but members of supposedly inferior races, became its targets. Jews and the Romany people – gypsies – were its main victims, though Slavic peoples also suffered greatly at the hands of the Nazis. Massive factories of death, the concentration camps, were dedicated to the extermination of peoples whom Nazis saw as the parasites of Europe. Around six millions Jews were killed in these camps, as well as hundreds of thousands of other people.

It has been said that Hitler gave racism a bad name. He certainly did more than anyone else to make eugenics – and the milder Social Darwinism – disreputable. After the Second World War, eugenics went into a rapid decline. Its erstwhile intellectual leaders quickly distanced themselves from it or were marginalized; the legislation which had put its policies into practice was repealed. Eugenics did not suffer this fate, it seems, because it had been shown to be false, or because the theories that it had elaborated had been refuted. It lost favor because of its association with crimes of an unprecedented enormity. Racism lost intellectual credibility, as did the view that inferiority or undesirable traits were importantly heritable. Social reformers turned their attention to other ways of improving the welfare of nations: to educational policy, for example, and to other methods of intervening which did not aim to change the kinds of people who were born, but instead focused on the environmental determinants of behavior.

Assessing Social Darwinism and eugenics

Social Darwinism and the eugenics movement were among the casualties of the Second World War. They were discredited, not because scientists and policy makers recognized that the evidence was against them, but by association with one of history's most monstrous regimes. However, guilt by association shouldn't be sufficient to convince us that the ideas upon which Social Darwinism and eugenics were built were false. To be sure, it seems that these themes were *central* to Fascism, and we therefore have some reason to link Hitler's crimes quite directly to his Social Darwinist views. But it might be that Fascism caricatured ideas that were intrinsically sound, or misapplied them, or carried them far further then they ought to have gone. Perhaps, for instance, the central message of eugenics, apparently endorsed by Darwin himself, is true; perhaps we should take care to ensure that the best people reproduce in greater numbers than the less well endowed. If this is so, there are a number of steps we might be able to take to put eugenic policies into practice, without risking committing the crimes of Nazism. We could, for instance, provide financial assistance to encourage the brightest members of society to reproduce. We might place moral pressure on the less fit to remain childless, or restrict their access to reproductive services. In brief, there are many means we might employ in the pursuit of eugenic policies that stop well short of genocide, or even coercion. Perhaps Hitler misidentified the groups which ought to be discouraged from breeding, and perhaps he was wrong in thinking that only mass extermination could achieve eugenic goals, but maybe the basic idea – that we ought to be careful to breed the best members of society – is intrinsically sound.

However, we have very good reasons for rejecting the Social Darwinist package in its entirety. We can see this by critically examining the central arguments in favor of it. We might set out the Social Darwinist argument against the welfare state schematically:

1. Natural selection is a process that favors the fittest organisms;
2. The fittest organisms are the best and most valuable;
3. We therefore ought to follow the lead of natural selection, and aid it by promoting the survival and reproduction of the fit, and by limiting the access to reproductive opportunities of the less fit;
4. The welfare state interferes with the workings of natural selection, by allowing the unfit as much opportunity to reproduce as the fit;
5. We therefore have good reason to avoid implementing the social policies of the welfare state (or any other policies which would interfere with the process of natural selection).

This seems to be a plausible argument, if all the assumptions it makes are true. How reasonable are they? Firstly, is it true that natural selection favors the fittest organisms? So long as we recall that "fit," as it is used in evolutionary biology, is a technical term, we can conclude that it is indeed true that natural selection favors the fit. Indeed, it is true *by definition*: "fit" *means* "those who are statistically likely to be favored by natural selection." Of course, accidents sometimes happen, the fittest organisms fail to reproduce, and the less fit do well (in very small populations, this can have significant effects on the direction of evolution). But generally speaking, fitness translates into reproductive success.

When it comes to assessing the second proposition in the Social Darwinist argument, however, it is crucial to bear in mind the fact that "fitness," as used in evolutionary biology, is a *technical* notion. We cannot validly deduce from the fact that an organism is "fit" that it is somehow "better" or more valuable than its less fit conspecifics. Appearances to the contrary, "fit" does not mean "good," or even "better." It doesn't even mean something like "more likely than average to possess the characteristics which we value." We do not value the ability of a disease bacterium to reproduce successfully inside our bodies, especially if it kills or injures us in the process. More importantly, and less obviously, it is not the case that a fitter human being is more likely to have qualities we value.

In order to see this, we need to recognize that fitness does not refer to the possession by an organism of any determinate qualities whatsoever. Fitness is always relative to an environment. The organism that is fit in one environment may be quite unfit in another. Take the bacterium I just mentioned, for instance. We might intuitively think that the more virulent a bacterium, the fitter it is. Pretheoretically, we might have an image of "virulence" in bacteria as something like "strength," and imagine that the more virulent bacteria will therefore out-compete their less virulent conspecifics. Given the right conditions, however, there might be selection for *less* virulent strains of a disease bacterium. Consider the recent evolution of the myxoma virus, which causes the disease myxomatosis in rabbits. When this virus was deliberately released in Australia, the intention was to control the introduced rabbit population. Rabbits are not native to Australia, and cause a significant amount of damage to farming land. At first, the virus was very successful, killing close to 100% of infected rabbits. But researchers soon detected a fall in the death rates of infected rabbits. Part of the explanation is to be found in the process of natural selection as it worked on the rabbits: resistant rabbits were more likely to survive infection, and therefore more likely to have offspring which would inherit the resistance. But part of the explanation also lay in the selection pressures at work on the virus itself. The myxoma virus is spread from rabbit to rabbit by fleas and mosquitoes. Therefore, those strains of the virus that killed their hosts quickly gave themselves less opportunity to spread, since these parasites only bite living rabbits. The longer their host lived, the more opportunity less virulent strains had to spread. Thus, these strains gradually took over the population. Less virulent disease-causing organisms are fitter, at least under some sets of conditions.[24]

The lesson we should learn from the history of the myxoma virus is that the qualities which make an organism fit are not necessarily obvious. What characteristics will be favored depends, crucially, on the environment. We might think it possible to draw up a list of characteristics such that, no matter what the environment, an organism possessing them would be fitter than a conspecific lacking them. We might, for example, place physical strength and intelligence on such a list. But we would be wrong: though these are qualities that it is often useful to have, there are no such things as the absolute best qualities, regardless of the environment. In the right conditions – and we have no reason to think that these conditions are unusual – the weaker and less intelligent can outcompete the stronger and the smarter.

How might this happen? We must remember that phenotypic characteristics (the observable characteristics of organisms) have *costs*, as well as benefits. Most obviously, they have costs in terms of energy. It takes energy to run a big body, with a great deal of muscle mass. But energy is a scarce resource. Animals get their energy by consuming food, so the more energy they require, the more food they need. Having lots of strength can come in very handy, under the right conditions. But if you don't need the strength, then the effort and energy put into acquiring and maintaining it is wasted. Under these conditions, weaker organisms, which don't waste their energy, might well out-compete stronger. This should be obvious when we stop to think about it: if more strength were always better than less, then all species would be continually increasing in strength. But they're not: instead, the fittest animals are those that (other things being equal) have the *right* amount of strength to cope with the kinds of problems animals like them typically encounter, and no more.

Much the same kind of reasoning applies to brains. Brains are very energy expensive. Pound for pound, they use more energy than any other part of the body. We would expect brain size – and therefore intelligence – to be limited by this. And there are other forces working to keep brains smaller than they might otherwise be. Giving birth is much more difficult and dangerous for humans than for other animals, something for which the big brains, and therefore heads, of babies are largely responsible. But there are other, more direct, costs to having a large brain, at least in some environments. Big, intelligent, brains are advantageous in complex and shifting environments, where the kinds of problems that must be solved by the organism are unpredictable and varied. But if the environment is stable, and the range of fitness-relevant problems is predictable, it would be better to have the appropriate behaviors built in. Animals which have the right responses instinctually programmed into their behavior will perform these responses more often and more quickly than those who must reason their way to a response, or learn it from others. So, more intelligence is not necessarily better than less, even if more can be had within the limits of the available resources.

Thus, it is not true that fitter organisms necessarily have more of the kinds of qualities we tend to admire than do the less fit. Indeed, as we shall see in coming chapters, there might be good reason to think that arguably the most admirable qualities humans can possess, the qualities which make a person a moral being, frequently reduce fitness. Perhaps, however, we can rescue Spencer's view by arguing that, though it is not true that fitter organisms always have more admirable qualities than do the less fit, as a matter of fact, fitter human beings do have more admirable qualities than do less fit (setting moral qualities aside for the moment, since if Spencer is right most of us are in any case radically mistaken as to what constitutes morality). In typical human environments, for example, we might plausibly think that intelligence is a phenotypic quality which increases fitness. So long as natural selection favors those qualities that we independently identify as valuable, the Spencerian might therefore argue, we ought to refrain from interfering with it.

Let us accept, at least provisionally and for the sake of examining the rest of the Social Darwinist position, that this is correct: that in typical human environments intelligence is favored by natural selection. That is, in what evolutionary theorists call the *environment of evolutionary adaptation* (EEA), the environment in which human beings lived for most of our existence on this planet and for which it is plausible to maintain we are adapted, intelligence is a fit characteristic. But the EEA is very different from modern environments. In the EEA, we believe, human beings lived in small groups of several families, and survived by hunting and gathering. What was fit in that environment is not necessarily fit now, in modern cities (nor in the peasant societies of much of the Third World).

This fact makes the move from the view that natural selection favors qualities which are valuable in the EEA, to the conclusion that natural selection would continue to favor valuable qualities today, if only we refrained from interfering with it, a perilous one. It may very well be that many of the people who are most fit in modern environments – best able to accumulate resources, to attract desirable partners and, if they wish, to have many children – would be very unfit in the EEA, and vice versa. How well would Bill Gates do on the plains of the Serengeti? In all probability, not very well. How well would Andrew Carnegie, or John D. Rockefeller, or Herbert Spencer have done? We have little reason to believe that their fitness in the environment of twentieth century America and Britain would be any indication of fitness in the EEA (though it may be no indication against it, either). Recall that fitness is always relative to the environment, and that therefore we cannot describe any set of characteristics as *the* best, no matter what.

So far, we have been talking as though the environment is an independent variable in assessing fitness. But this is not merely a gross oversimplification: it is plain wrong. In fact, organisms do not merely adapt to a fixed environment: in doing so they reshape that environment. This is true at very many levels simultaneously. Not only do animals, alter their environment in obvious ways (for example by damming rivers and building nests) but also, simply by the fact of its existence, each organism modifies the environments of those around it. The environment of a bird consists not only of the trees that offer it nesting sites, but also of the insects that are its food, of its predators, and of other birds. Birds of the same species are crucial to its reproduction, and might offer mutual assistance, yet are also competitors for food, for mates, for nesting sites; birds of other species are potential competitors, but they might also aid it in some manner (perhaps by alerting it to the presence of predators).

Social Darwinists ignore all of this. They tell us that we interfere with our environment, for example by providing organized welfare, at our peril. If we aid the weak, they warn, we risk providing for our descendants a multitude of enemies: all those hungry mouths, unable to feed themselves, all those bad characters, unwilling to work and always on the look-out for an opportunity to take advantage of the vulnerable. We ought, they tell us, to leave the environment undisturbed (or perhaps restore it to its natural condition) so that natural selection can do its work of weeding out undesirables.

But we human beings have radically reshaped our environment. We live, those of us in the West at least, largely in built environments: a world of skyscrapers and houses, roads and shopping centers. For all of us, Chinese peasant or Australian office worker, the way we carry out the range of activities most central to our evolutionary fitness – the way we acquire the food and other goods which maintain our strength and that of our children, the way we ensure the viability of our offspring, the way we seek to attract and retain mates – is also very significantly shaped by our cultural environment. Fitness-relevant rewards accrue to individuals with abilities which seem, at first sight at least, to have nothing to do with the kinds of abilities which would have been valuable to our ancestors: ability to act in Hollywood blockbusters, to write pop songs, or to manipulate figures and choose stocks likely to yield a high rate of return, in the economies of the West; ability to write poetry in the Classical style (a prerequisite for joining the bureaucracy) in feudal China. What, we must ask the Social Darwinists, is special about these particular environments that we must regard them as sacrosanct? Why shouldn't we interfere with them? So far as I can see, there are two possible responses available to the Social Darwinist here: the *primitivist* and the *conservative*.

The *primitivist* Social Darwinists might concede the majority of our argument. That is, they might accept that there is no reason to believe that the characteristics of the environments in which most human beings presently live are such that the abilities that are most highly rewarded in them are really the abilities that are most valuable. The primitivist points out that the EEA for human beings is the African savannah, upon which our hunter-gatherer ancestors lived for perhaps one million years. Since this is our EEA, it is the abilities that would be rewarded in this environment which are truly valuable. And since most human beings do not now live a hunter-gatherer lifestyle, the abilities that are rewarded in most human societies are not truly valuable.

The primitivist might admit, therefore, that there is nothing to choose, from the point of view of Social Darwinism, between the world of unconstrained capitalism, which Rockefeller and Carnegie defended, and the Swedish welfare state (or a Communist Utopia). But this is only because both environments are utterly removed from our true EEA, in which the inference from "evolutionarily successful" to "valuable" – from "fit" to "good" – could reliably be made. The primitivist might go on to argue that, far from refraining from interfering with current social arrangements, we ought to be radically rearranging them, to bring them closer to the environments to which we are naturally adapted. To my knowledge, no one has actually argued that we ought to revert to the hunter-gatherer condition. But there are elements of primitivism surviving in the work of contemporary theorists who attempt to understand human behavior in a Darwinian framework: when, for instance, they say, as many of them do, that we are generally unhappy because we are not adapted to the social environments in which we now live.

More popular than the primitivist response to the argument I sketched is a *conservative* reply. Those who take this line reject the argument completely: it is not true, they allege, that the qualities that are most highly rewarded in contemporary societies are entirely divorced from the qualities which would have been favored in the EAA. After all, the conservatives point out, though it is true that organisms reshape the environment in which they live, the behaviors involved in that reshaping are as much a product of natural selection as are any other characteristics of the organism. It is, therefore, false to believe that, to the extent that we live in cultures, we escape the forces of evolution. Human beings just are a kind of animal which lives in characteristic kinds of social group, and which shapes and structures those groups according to their innate dispositions. Though it is true that the environments in which almost all of us live today are very different from the EAA, nevertheless, the environments we have made for ourselves will continue to reflect the central features of our ancestral social environment because we will shape them to reflect our inborn dispositions. In particular, they will be structured so that very much the same characteristics, qualities and activities are rewarded in the new environments as in the old.

This may seem very implausible, when we consider the differences in the daily activities of the hunter-gatherer and the stockbroker or computer programmer. But look deeper, the conservative urges, and the similarities become plain. What qualities were rewarded in the EAA? We cannot, at this stage, attempt to provide anything like an adequate catalog of the adaptive qualities of our ancestors, but we can easily pick out a few key characteristics. Our male ancestors who were reproductively successful faced three major sets of fitness-relevant challenges: they had to attract mates, compete with each other, and provide game for themselves and for their family. Physical strength would obviously have been an advantage in hunting and in competing with other males, as would speed and agility. The qualities needed to attract mates are more controversial, but there is good reason to believe that they would have included physical attractiveness and kindness. Women needed the abilities to gather food and to raise children. Of course, both sexes must have been fertile. For both sexes, intelligence would have been useful, both for its direct survival value (in enabling them to avoid predators, find food and devise the tools that would assist them), and as an enhancement to make them more attractive to potential mates.

Now all of these, the conservative claims, are qualities that are as much rewarded today as they were in the EEA. Or, more precisely, either these qualities are rewarded directly, or markers for these qualities are rewarded. It is easy to see how physical strength and agility are rewarded, as much today as ever. For some people, physical strength is rewarded through their employment. They are able to be more productive miners, farmers, or builders, because they are stronger than other people competing for the same jobs. For a lucky few, athletic prowess is rewarded beyond the dreams of a hunter-gatherer: by a contract with a major sports team, for instance. Notoriously, this kind of success is easily converted into reproductive currency.

It is also obvious how intelligence is still rewarded. It provides the abilities which enable many to secure employment, and, for a very few, it brings untold wealth. It is less obvious how capacities such as fertility are rewarded today, especially in Western societies that have undergone the so-called *demographic transition* to low rates of childbirth. In fact, fertility is not directly rewarded, but physical attractiveness is, and physical attractiveness is a marker for fertility. That is, men find certain women attractive because those women display the physical features (youth, unblemished skin, lithe bodies, and so on) that indicate they are healthy and likely to be able to bear healthy children. Thus it is her possession of markers for fertility that enables a Hollywood star or a supermodel to be so spectacularly successful.

We shall assess these suggestions in a later chapter. For the moment, let us assume that they are true, in order to discover what support for the Social Darwinist program might be drawn from them. The conservative argues that the same qualities that were rewarded in the EEA continue to be rewarded today, and that we can therefore conclude that these qualities are valuable. We ought not, therefore, to alter our environment in any way that might cause these qualities no longer to be rewarded. Too extensive a welfare state, for example, would sever the link between strength, intelligence, attractiveness, and reproductive success. It would allow those who are unable, through their own efforts, to provide food well enough to attract a mate, to avoid the reproductive consequences of this inability by ensuring that they – and any offspring they might have – receive it from other sources. In this way, the unfit will continue to pass on their genes, instead of falling by the wayside.

Is the conservative position tenable, assuming that its interpretation of the abilities rewarded in modern societies is accurate? It suffers from at least two weaknesses. Firstly, it makes the controversial assumption that people's (potential) abilities are fixed, and require only the right kinds of opportunities to be expressed. This is implicit in the kinds of charities the Social Darwinist rules as permissible or impermissible. Charities like Andrew Carnegie's endowment of libraries, which give people *opportunities* to take advantage of their innate capacities, are permissible, perhaps even obligatory. But charities that break the link between capacities and outcomes, such as the organized provision of the necessities of life, are impermissible. That this is a controversial assumption ought to be obvious: it is one of the fault lines which divide left from right in the politics of Western democracies. The right, like the Social Darwinists, believes that rewards generally reflect effort plus innate capacity, in such a manner that if people are provided with opportunities (in the form of elementary schooling, jobs open to talents, and so on), they will tend to rise to a level which reflects their ability. The left, on the other hand, typically claims that though there may well be such a thing as innate ability, very frequently people are deprived of the opportunity to express it, due to pervasive cultural factors. Thus, for instance, feminists often argue that we achieve sexual equality not simply by providing girls with equal access to the same resources as boys, nor just by having gender-blind employment practices, but also by altering the many features of our culture which implicitly convey to women the belief that they cannot succeed in some professions, and thus shape their self-image and self-esteem, and modify their aspirations.

So, the left argues, we need to do far more to identify and aid people with ability than simply provide everyone with opportunities, Carnegie-style. Instead, we need wide-ranging changes to our social structure and culture. We may even need to equalize incomes, if it turns out that people's expectations and aspirations are profoundly shaped by the conditions in which they were socialized. These are important and controversial questions, and we cannot hope here to settle the empirical and conceptual debates upon which they turn. For the moment, it is enough for us to see that the appeal, often made by Social Darwinists, to the facts of biology and inheritance as crucial evidence for conservative political views, is circular. These alleged facts support Social Darwinism only if its central assumptions are correct, and therefore cannot be invoked to justify those very assumptions.

Of course, this does not show that Social Darwinism is false. It might turn out that the central assumptions invoked by the conservatives are in fact true. But the second deficiency of the Social Darwinist position is more serious. Let us assume, for the sake of the argument, that Social Darwinists are right in saying that the qualities rewarded today are very much the same ones which were rewarded in the EEA, and that the actual distribution we see of expressed abilities around us is a good reflection of people's innate capacities. Does it follow from these premises that we ought to refrain from interfering with the workings of natural selection, so as to avoid bringing about a society in which rewards no longer reflect capacities? It is hard to see why. What would be *wrong* with bringing about such a society? Indeed, isn't it our moral *obligation* to alleviate poverty and misery: to feed the poor and house the homeless? Can we not, with Huxley, conclude that if natural selection is indeed a process by which the unfit are weeded out, morality requires us to fight against it?

There is a possible line of reply available to the Social Darwinists here. They might argue that, though it would indeed be a fine thing to improve the lot of the unfit, we cannot do so in a way that will not end up heaping even greater misery upon them and their descendants, and perhaps upon us and ours as well. We can aid the bad in multiplying, by providing them with resources, but this will only increase their number, and necessitate the provision of charity to an ever-growing multitude. Eventually, the numbers of unproductive people will exceed the numbers we can support, and we shall be forced to allow them to face the consequences that attend their lack of fitness. If we aid the unfit, we only put off the day of reckoning, and ensure that when it comes it will be the more terrible.

This line of thought is suggested by one of the rare passages in which Darwin himself seems to endorse the main lines of Social Darwinist thought:

> With savages, the weak in body or mind are soon eliminated; and those that survive commonly exhibit a vigorous state of health. We civilized men, on the other hand, do our utmost to check the process of elimination; we build asylums for the imbecile, the maimed, and the sick; we institute poor-laws; and our medical men exert their utmost skill to save the life of every one to the last moment. There is reason to believe that vaccination has preserved thousands, who from a weak constitution would formerly have succumbed to small-pox. Thus the weak members of civilized societies propagate their kind. No one who has attended to the breeding of domestic animals will doubt that this must be highly injurious to the race of man. It is surprising how soon a want of care, or care wrongly directed, leads to the degeneration of a domestic race; but excepting in the case of man himself, hardly any one is so ignorant as to allow his worst animals to breed.[25]

Darwin's thought seems to be along these lines: if we eliminate the diseases of poverty, we aid those who are innately weak, enabling them to survive and reproduce. But if we do so, we ensure that their weakness will be passed on, and therefore there will be more people who suffer from a weak constitution in the next generation. Hence the "race" will decline and the average quality of human beings will fall.

But we must remember the crucial lesson commonly and conveniently forgotten by the Social Darwinists: fitness is relative to an environment. The fact that I, or you, might have succumbed to smallpox, or bubonic plague, or any one of the other diseases that routinely carried off our ancestors does not make us any the less fit now, in our present environment, where such diseases are rare. Our ability, or lack of it, to survive in the EEA is irrelevant to our fitness here. It may well be true that the population's natural resistance to smallpox will fall if the virus is eliminated. So what? Unless we have good reason to believe that smallpox will return – and that if it does we shall not be able to deal with it – that should not worry us. As it happens, we possess effective vaccinations against smallpox, so we have no cause to worry. It is simply a confusion to think that altering the environment, so that what counts as fitness changes, necessarily *reduces* fitness. What would happen in a different environment is irrelevant to what happens in this one. To argue that those human beings who do well in this environment are not *really* fit because they flourish with the aid of medicine (or welfare) is akin to arguing that successful beavers are not really fit, because they wouldn't do very well without their dams. Human societies and beaver dams are both parts of what Richard Dawkins has described as the *extended phenotype* of those species; the things that they build around them are important parts of what makes them successful, not optional add-ons.[26]

Social Darwinism and the naturalistic fallacy

Ask most philosophers what was wrong with Social Darwinism, and they will have a ready answer – it committed the *naturalistic fallacy*. In fact, this supposed fallacy was the least of the Social Darwinist confusions. There are philosophical errors at the heart of the Social Darwinist program, but their exact nature is little appreciated.

The naturalistic fallacy is the alleged mistake of offering a naturalistic definition of moral terms. It was introduced by G. E. Moore, in his *Principia Ethica* (1903), and had Spencer as its explicit target. Spencer claims that more evolved conduct is, by definition, good conduct. Moore deploys his *open question argument* against this definition. Consider the following definition of "bachelor": a bachelor is an unmarried man. Moore asks us to notice the difference between the following two sentences:

1. John is an unmarried man, but is John a bachelor?
2. *Homo sapiens* is highly evolved, but is *Homo sapiens* good?

Sentence one is a *closed* question. If you understand the meaning of the word "bachelor" then you know the answer. It is true, as a matter of definition, that if John is an unmarried man then he is a bachelor. But sentence two is an *open* question. It is sensible to ask it, and to wonder what the answer to it is. For Moore, this showed that it could not be the case that "good" *means* "highly evolved," or anything like it.[27]

According to Moore, Social Darwinists like Spencer hold that "good" *means* "fit." This is certainly one way to interpret Spencer's contention that "the conduct to which we apply the name good, is the relatively more evolved conduct; and bad is the name we apply to conduct which is relatively less evolved."[28] But, Moore claims, the success of the open question argument shows that "good" cannot mean "fit." Indeed, the open question argument can successfully be deployed against any naturalistic definition of goodness. It will always be sensible to ask, of any entity that has the property with which goodness is allegedly synonymous, "But it is really good?"

This line of argument has convinced many philosophers. Yet, as it stands, it is Moore's argument that is fallacious, not Spencer's. If we take Spencer to be claiming that "good" is *coreferential* with "highly evolved" – that is, "good" refers to all and only "highly evolved" entities – then he is not committing any kind of logical error. Evolution is, after all, a science, and science often provides us with new and unexpected information about the reference of words. For example, Lavoisier, the famous eighteenth-century chemist, showed that water is a compound of oxygen and hydrogen. His contemporaries could not sensibly object to his discovery that "water" is "H_2O" on the grounds that it was an open question (to competent speakers of the language) whether or not water was H_2O. It *was* an open question, but Lavoisier closed it. Similarly, Spencer, or some other evolutionary theorist, might have closed the question of the reference of the word "good," showing that it refers to whatever is highly evolved.

Moore seemed to think that no naturalistic definition of "good" could succeed, because goodness just is a non-natural property. But his argument that goodness is a non-natural property was – the open question argument! This is completely circular. It amounts to saying that no naturalistic definition of goodness can succeed, because goodness is a non-natural property, and adding that we know that goodness is a non-natural property because no naturalistic definition of it can succeed.

If Moore's argument was patently fallacious, why were so many people convinced by it? I suggest that they were moved, not by Moore's argument, not by the contention that it is *fallacious* to identify "good" with "highly evolved," but by the obvious fact that is *wrong* to identify "good" with "highly evolved." It is wrong, not because it involves any kind of *logical* error (which is what committing a fallacy amounts to) but because it is simply, straightforwardly, false. If I claim that the moon is made of green cheese, I am not committing a fallacy. There is nothing logically invalid about the claim. I am just making a mistake. Similarly, the Social Darwinists were simply mistaken. We know that "good" just doesn't mean "highly evolved," and we know *that* because many things that are highly evolved are not good (and many good things are not highly evolved). Viruses and other pathogens might be as highly evolved as you like, but they are not good. God, if he exists, is (plausibly) good, but God is not highly evolved.

There is another reason why philosophers did not reject Moore's argument. They may have confused it with another, closely related, error, which is also sometimes called the naturalistic fallacy. To avoid confusion, we will call it by another of its names: *Hume's Law*, after the great eighteenth-century Scottish philosopher David Hume. Hume's Law states that we cannot validly derive a statement about what ought to be the case from premises that are purely descriptive: no deriving "ought" from "is." At first sight, this might seem quite counter-intuitive. Surely from the (purely descriptive) premise that "if we do not drink water, we will die," we can validly conclude that "we ought to drink water?" Hume does not deny that we ordinarily reason in this manner, but, he contends, when we do so we implicitly add a norma-tive premise to our argument. In this case, the premise might be some-thing like "dying is bad". The argument is valid, and we can use it to reach a normative conclusion, only because the premises are not, in fact, purely descriptive.

It is easy to see that Hume's Law and Moore's naturalistic fallacy are closely related. We have only to realize that if a naturalistic defin-ition of moral terms was ever to prove possible, Hume's law would be shown to be false. If we can define "good" in non-moral terms, then we could validly derive "oughts" from purely descriptive premises. If "good" meant "highly evolved," we might be able to conclude, from the fact that something was highly evolved, that it ought to be preserved. Hume's law therefore ought to be seen as provisional: it holds only so long as there is no plausible naturalistic definition of goodness in the offing.

It's not possible to commit the naturalistic fallacy, since there is no such fallacy. But people can and do commit the mistake of identifying goodness with the *wrong* natural property, and it's an error we ought to be on the look-out for. We often miss it, because we all share the tendency to make it. For example, we seem to have a powerful tendency to equate "natural" with "good." We tend to think that natural things are better than unnatural (indeed, the very word "unnatural" carries powerful pejorative overtones). Natural foods are better than artificial, natural childbirth is to be preferred to medically assisted, a natural manner is better than an affected one. It may be that many natural things are better than artificial substitutes (assuming for the moment that we can give a clear sense to the word "natural") but it is certainly a mistake to think that something is good, or even better, just because it is natural. Sickness and death are as natural as you like, but they are none the better for it. Most of us will gratefully accept "unnatural" antibiotics in order to fight off an otherwise life-threatening (but quite natural) infection.

Nevertheless, despite the fact that when we think clearly about the matter, it is easy to see that it is a mistake to equate "natural" with "good," so entrenched is this habit, so easily do we fall into it, that there is little doubt that the early success of Social Darwinism owed something to it. Rockefeller's justification of capitalist competition as the "working out of a law of nature" trades on this confusion. Another, closely related, confusion to which Social Darwinism was prey is implicit within the phrase "highly evolved." It involves equating the direction of evolution with progress.

Among Social Darwinists, Spencer was most explicit here. For him, evolution *is* the story of progress – though he had a somewhat idiosyncratic definition of progress. For him, progress, at every level – intellectual, social, political and biological – consisted of the transition from a less to a more complex and heterogeneous state; evolution was one more instance of the working out of this process.[29] But it is easy to see how evolution could be invoked in support of a less eccentric idea of progress. If evolution is equated with "survival of the fittest," or more accurately, the differential survival and *reproduction* of the fittest, then we should expect the proportion of fit organisms in the population to rise. Thus, if it weren't for our continual meddling with the forces of natural selection, we could expect the human beings of the early twenty-first century to be somewhat fitter, on average, than (say) the human beings of the seventeenth century. If they were, we could therefore conclude that humanity has progressed by means of evolution.

But this would be a mistake. For many reasons, natural selection cannot be equated with progress. If we focus on one species, in isolation from its environment, it is easy to sketch scenarios in which, through natural selection, average fitness actually *falls*. Imagine, for instance, that in a population of animals a random mutation crops up which makes its possessors stronger and more aggressive than average. This extra strength and aggression might translate into extra fitness: perhaps it enables the animal to compete more effectively for food resources, or for mates. If so, and if the mutation is heritable, we should expect the proportion of animals that possess it to rise. Indeed, it may go to *fixation*, which is to say that it will come to be possessed by all the organisms. Once this happens, however, it could well be that the very same characteristics that raised the fitness of the first organisms to possess them lower the average fitness of the group. Since all the animals are now stronger and more aggressive, damaging fights may be common. Average life spans might fall, as might the number of viable offspring born. Fitness has fallen, simply through the normal workings of natural selection. In just this way, according to Sober and Wilson, selecting the most productive (as measured by their egg production) chickens for breeding can lead to an overall decrease in egg output. The most productive layers may be the most aggressive birds; they may do well when surrounded by chickens less aggressive than them, which avoid confrontation, but they do badly when surrounded by chickens as aggressive as they are.[30] The solution, for farmers wishing to increase their egg production, is to select the most productive *groups* of chickens as breeding stock, rather than the most productive individuals: score a point for the idea of group selection, widely regarded as heretical by contemporary biologists (you'll find more on group selection in the next chapter).

When we widen our perspective to include other species, it is even easier to see why natural selection ought not to be equated with progress. Each member of each species competes, not only with its con-specifics, but also with members of the other species with which it shares its environment. Selection pressures operate upon all of them. Take a group of herbivores that is preyed on by big cats and suppose that their only method of defense is running away. In this environment, there is selection for running speed: the fastest animals tend to survive longer, and therefore have the chance to produce more offspring. Thus, the average speed of the population rises. This, we might think, is progress. However, just as the big cats exert selection pressure on the herbivores, so the herbivores exert selection pressure on the big cats. The cats compete amongst each other for prey, and the fastest ones tend to do better. So the average speed of the big cats rises as well. After many generations, both groups of animals are running significantly faster than their ancestors – but about the same number of big cats are killing about the same number of herbivores. Has progress really taken place? Or, with great expenditure of effort, has the evolutionary drama enabled each species to remain in exactly the same (relative) position as before? There is no naturalistic fallacy. "Good" might have turned out to mean "highly evolved," and evolution might have turned out to be progressive. But, so far as we can discover, neither of these is the case. We need to be on the lookout for arguments which, usually implicitly, make the mistake of assuming otherwise.

The return of eugenics?

In the eyes of many writers, eugenics is presently undergoing a renais-sance. The impetus for this revival has been the Human Genome Project, which seems to hold out the prospect of being able to genetically manipulate the characteristics of our children. We shall, many writers believe, soon be able to design our children: to specify their height, their intelligence, eliminate a propensity to depression, and build in the capacity for hard work. Should we fear the new eugenics?

Commentators are divided on the consequences of the new eugen-ics. For some, it offers the promise of taking our destiny into our own hands, and remaking ourselves in the image we desire. For others, it offers only the nightmare of division, inequality and the inevitable loss of our humanity. Interestingly, both sides invoke evolution in making their case. For Gregory Stock, the new genetic technologies will "transform the evolutionary process" allowing us to take conscious control over it.[31] We can now "fast-forward" the process, and guide it as we see fit. Lee Silver is even more enthusiastic in his support: "Why not seize this power? Why not control what has been left to chance in the past?"[32]

In contrast, for Francis Fukayama, the technologies which for Stock and Silver promise rational direction of what had formerly been left to the workings of blind chance threaten only inequality and division. At stake, according to Fukuyama, is nothing less than human nature itself. Our nature as a species, he argues, is a product of natural selection. If we take the process of evolution into our hands, then we give ourselves the power to choose our own nature. Fukuyama suggests that two calamities threaten if we begin to modify our natures. Our *commonality* comes under threat, and our *dignity* is undermined.

Fukuyama's argument for the threat posed to human commonality is far clearer than his views on human dignity, so let us examine this first. Today, Fukuyama claims, the genetic differences between people are significant, but they are not significantly *clustered*. That is, some people are born with enormous natural advantages – greater intelligence, health, good looks, and so on – but because we cannot control the process whereby traits are passed on from parents to offspring, the children of the better endowed are not necessarily better endowed themselves. However, once we have control over this process, the children of the rich will be doubly advantaged. Not only will they inherit their parent's wealth, and therefore have a far wider range of opportunities open to them but they will also inherit all their parents' natural talents, and more besides. Since the new genetic technologies will be costly, it will be the children of the wealthy who will benefit most: who will have their IQs raised, their personalities modified to be optimal, and their lives extended. In a very few generations, Fukuyama suggests, the human race will have split into two separate groups. The children of the rich will become "children of choice," and they:

> Will look, think, act, and perhaps even feel differently from those who were not similarly chosen, and may come in time to think of themselves as different kinds of creatures. They may, in short, feel

themselves to be aristocrats, and unlike aristocrats of old, their claim to better birth will be rooted in nature and not convention.[33]

This new class, he argues, will, quite literally, have been born to rule.

The second threat from the new eugenics to our common human nature that Fukuyama identifies, the threat to our human dignity, is far from clearly articulated in his work. In part, I suspect, this is because the underlying fear is amorphous and hard to pin down precisely. It is, nevertheless, very widely shared. The fear is that somehow, in tampering with our destinies, we risk losing something essential to our human nature. Acceptance of risk and contingency, it may be felt, is itself an ineradicable aspect of the human condition, an aspect, which, somehow, gives meaning to our lives and makes them what they are. If this is so, then in controlling our lives and our destinies, we risk emptying them of their essence, and creating a mode of existence that is radically impoverished. Perhaps a life emptied of its chance elements is a life without meaning. Or perhaps what is at stake is the risk of overreaching ourselves, of committing the sin the Greeks called hubris. We act hubristically when we attempt to usurp powers that are not appropriately exercised by us: when we, as the cliché has it, "play god." Many of the narratives we relate to each other to make sense of our new powers are centrally concerned with this risk. Mary Shelley's *Frankenstein* is paradigmatic of the story-telling tradition that reflects our anxiety at what we might do. In these tales, those who tamper with powers which were not meant for human beings bring destruction upon themselves and upon others, But the fear here is not just of bad consequences; instead, the disasters which follow are only a means of dramatizing the real damage, which is centered on the very act of abrogating to ourselves powers which are not on the human scale. To act hubristically is, once again, somehow to risk emptying human life of what is worthwhile in it, no matter what other consequences might flow.

It is easy to make sense of this accusation against a theistic background. If some powers properly belong only to God, if there are things which we are not "meant" – intended, where the intentions in question are those of the Creator – to do, then we can clearly see the source of the duties and obligations which we risk transgressing. But if there is no god, or if appeal to God is too controversial to serve as a source of obligations in a multi-ethnic, multi-faith society, then we need to make sense of the appeal for us to respect our limitations in some other way. Fukuyama appeals to our evolved human nature to make his argument. Evolution has its reasons, which we, its products, are not necessarily well equipped to comprehend. The very contingency and unplanned nature of natural selection is a strength: its products all the better designed for not having been designed at all "evolution may be a blind process, but it follows a ruthless adaptive logic that makes organisms fit for their environments."[34] The wisdom of natural processes, blind as they are, surpasses our foresight and cleverness.[35]

The new eugenics avoids the pitfalls of the old. It is not racist. It does not seek to eliminate the supposedly "unfit". It leaves decision-making in the hands of the people whose reproductive destiny is at stake, rather than imposing its will upon resistant or uncomprehending victims. It will not lead to Auschwitz, or even to the mass sterilization programs that characterized the less malevolent forms of the old eugenics. Instead, it merely opens up new choices, for those who wish to make them. In the eyes of some commentators, with these changes, from negative to positive eugenics, from state-imposed to individually chosen, the new eugenics shakes off all the elements which made the old immoral. It becomes one more consumer item, one more choice we can make from the menu that life in a technologically advanced and wealthy nation offers us. For others, as we have seen, the new eugenics is as threatening as the old, perhaps even more so because the risks are now so difficult to articulate, even to ourselves. For many, especially the scientists who work on the new technologies, genetic engineering promises to expand the sphere of human autonomy, while for others it threatens nothing less than the end of humanity, the end of what is most important about human nature. And both sides buttress their arguments by appeal to natural selection.

Can we settle this dispute, can we reinforce the borders we ought not to cross, or dissipate them altogether, by reference to evolution? Will a proper understanding of the process which gave rise to we large-brained social hominids, with our culture and our morality, allow us to understand our place in nature and (in apparent defiance of the naturalistic fallacy) thereby to settle not just what might lie within our power, but also what we ought to strive for, and what we should repudiate? This, ultimately, is what is at stake in understanding the evolution of morality. We shall see how morality might spontaneously emerge among groups of mutually dependent creatures. We shall examine the extent to which our evolved dispositions shape our current aspirations and our beliefs. And we shall investigate the extent to which our physical and mental characteristics lie in our genes, to which our biology is destiny. There is a great deal of intrinsic interest in these investigations. Moreover, much of it matters, or so I shall claim: on our biology and its evolutionary history turn questions which concern our fondest hopes and the extent to which they are achievable or to which they are mere delusions. Ultimately, however, what is at stake is our concept of humanity, and its proper place in the universe. Darwin once suggested that "he who understands baboons would do more towards metaphysics than Locke;" perhaps evolution can illuminate ethics and human nature just as clearly.

2

The evolution of morality

> Where it is in his own interest, every organism may reasonably be expected to aid his fellows. Where he has no alternative, he submits to the yoke of communal servitude. Yet given a full chance to act in his own interest, nothing but expediency will restrain him from brutalizing, from maiming, from murdering his brother, his mate, his parent, or his child. Scratch an "altruist" and watch a "hypocrite" bleed.
>
> Michael Ghiselin, *The Economy of Nature and the Evolution of Sex*

Could morality have evolved? Might the full suite of our ethical responses and judgments, our sentiment of right and wrong, itself be the product of natural selection? A lot of effort has been expended, by biologists and by philosophers, on this question; on attempted demonstrations that ethics might, or did, or could not, have come about by the process of natural selection. At first sight, this is a curious endeavor. After all, what does it matter where ethics comes from – whether it is the product of natural selection, a gift from God, or the reflection of values which are somehow eternally inscribed in the very fabric of the universe (to mention only some of the possibilities). What matters, we might think, is that ethics exists; that our conduct is and ought to be regulated by its demands, and that therefore we ought to get on with clarifying those demands without concerning ourselves with their source. However, there are multiple and intersecting reasons to think that the source of morality has a bearing on how we should behave.

It might be, for example, that a conclusive demonstration that morality could, or could not, be the result of natural selection would strengthen the case for one of the competing theories of the *justification* of our moral code. Some philosophers are skeptics, of one kind or another, about morality. Some are skeptical about its objectivity; for them, the demands and requirements of our morality represent merely one possible form a valid morality might take. Other philosophers are skeptical that its demands upon us are really binding. People who adopt this position might see morality as simply the reflection of class interests, as some Marxists have done, or as the attempt by the weak to ensnare the strong, as Nietzsche suggested. If it could be shown that, as a result of natural selection, we might be expected to share a common morality, certain of these views would seem much more plausible than others. Those philosophers who hold that other, equally valid, moralities are possible would appear to be vindicated. The path taken by evolution was not mapped out; the results of evolution are the contingent product of multiple forces, which might have led elsewhere (and which might yet lead us away from where we find ourselves today). Our moral system would not be uniquely rational, or uniquely moral, as many philosophers have thought. Instead, it would be just one of many, equally valid, possible systems.

To this extent, evolution lends support to philosophical skepticism, but in other ways it tends to undermine it. If morality is the product of evolution, then its demands upon us might be unavoidably binding, rather than the product of mere convention, as some skeptics have thought, and no amount of reflection on the fact (if it is a fact) that it could have been very different will enable us to shake them off. As an example, compare the demands of morality to our perception of color. This perception is also a contingent product of evolution: if evolution had taken a different course, our eyes might be sensitive to a different range of wavelengths of light; perhaps, like those of some insects, they might be attuned to ultraviolet light. If this were the case, then the range of colors we could distinguish would be very different from those with which we are actually familiar. But reflecting on this fact doesn't make our perception of color any less compelling. Similarly, reflecting on the fact that our morality is the contingent product of evolution might do nothing to shake the grip of the emotions that subserve it.

It might also be that debates over the *content* of morality could be settled by evidence about evolution. Those Marxists who see, in conventional morality, a rationalization of class interests will have to confront arguments which show that not merely morality in general, but even some of its fine details (including aspects which they see as expressions of class privilege), are the products of evolution.[36] More centrally, the debate between skeptics about morality (who believe that we are motivated simply by self-interest and we use morality as a convenient cover), and defenders of authentic altruism (who argue that humans are frequently motivated by a genuine desire for the welfare of others), has often been conducted with reference to the evidence from evolution. This debate will serve as a reference point as we explore the evidence that morality is the product of evolution.

What is morality?

Defining morality is no easy task. Fortunately, in everyday contexts, we can to some extent rely on our intuitive grasp of the concept: though we may not be able to articulate our intuitions very clearly, we know morality when we see it. However, if we are going to be able to answer difficult questions about its possible origins, and adjudicate debates between thinkers who argue for an evolutionary source for morality and those who contend that evolution could never give rise to anything more than a simulacrum of the notion, we need to be able to identify at least some of the central planks of morality. We shall need fixed points, to which we can refer and compare the kinds of proto or ersatz moral behaviors yielded by evolutionary models.

To a first approximation, we might describe morality as a system of *prescriptions* that are held to be *unconditionally* binding upon all rational agents. That is, morality is a set of rules, explicit or implicit, which, in so far as they are capable of assessing and controlling their actions, and regardless of their beliefs and desires, each person is required to obey. Morality is not something you can opt out of; it is incumbent upon all autonomous agents. Only those who cannot understand or obey its commands – members of other species, very young children, the insane, and, more controversially, those suffering from impulse control disorders and addictions – are excused from its demands, and then only because they cannot be expected to conform to it, not because it is not true for them. Morality, at least at its core, is objective. It is not open to being altered and its demands are inescapable.

Remember, we are concerned here only with the *concept* of morality. That is, we wish to analyze what we mean when we speak of a moral duty or prohibition. In saying that the concept of morality is of something objective and unconditionally binding, we are not committing ourselves to saying that anything answers to this concept. We are not, for example, taking sides between relativists and absolutists, or between moral realists and anti-realists. Just as we can analyze the concept of God (an eternal, omnipotent and omniscient being) without committing ourselves to being believers, so we can analyze morality without taking sides on moral questions, or even on whether there *are* any moral questions.

The concept of morality I have been expounding thus far, is, roughly, Kantian. That is, it is the notion of morality that received its first full elaboration in the work of the eighteenth century German philosopher, Immanuel Kant, whose work revolutionized all the central fields of philosophy. Kant argued that morality was encapsulated by what he called the *categorical imperative*, which is a rule that is unconditionally binding upon us, as rational agents, and which is delivered to us by our rationality. We are not concerned here with the details of Kant's view, but with its shape: for there can be little doubt that Kant's view of morality as an objective and unconditionally binding system of imperatives captures an important part of our shared concept.

However, it is plausible to think that Kant only gives us half the picture. As many philosophers have pointed out, Kant's morality is rather bloodless and abstract. He argued that an action had moral value only in so far as it was motivated by respect for the moral law alone. But most of us think that moral actions ought to be motivated by concern for other people, not for the moral law. We should, as Michael Stocker famously pointed out, think rather less of the friend who comes to visit us in the hospital because he feels it is a duty incumbent upon him, than of the friend who is motivated by concern for us and our welfare.[37]

Exactly what role desires and emotions ought to play in morality is controversial. But it is less controversial to maintain that they have *some* essential role. We can express the core of this intuition by saying that moral prescriptions are intrinsically *motivating*. There is something very odd about the idea of a person who sincerely assents to the proposition that we ought to give to charity, but isn't motivated actually to do it. To be sure, we are all too well aware that a moral proposition can fail to motivate us *sufficiently* to act upon it: we know, from experience, that we frequently find ourselves backsliding – being stingy with donations to worthy causes, finding excuses for not visiting sick relatives, and so on. Nevertheless, it seems that accepting a moral proposition has to connect up with our motivational system in *some* manner: if not by moving us to act on it, then at least by making us feel shame or guilt at our failure.

Indeed, some philosophers have gone so far as to suggest that there is nothing to morality beyond its subjective side, expressed in feelings, emotions, and dispositions to act. Kant's great rival, across many fields of philosophy, was the Scottish thinker David Hume, and it is with Hume that the idea of morality as, essentially, a set of feelings is most closely associated. By basing morality on feeling, Hume accounts for our conviction that there is an internal connection between accepting the truth of a moral proposition, and being motivated to act on that proposition. But if Kant's moral system seems rather bloodless, then Hume's seems unable to account for the apparent objectivity of morality. Our notion of morality appears to combine both Humean and Kantian ingredients, and any attempt to reduce one to the other captures only part of the concept.

Thus, the concept of morality is of a set of rather strange ("queer," as J. L. Mackie put it) facts: facts that are intrinsically motivating.[38] Most facts are not like that at all: we do not expect people to be moved to action simply by facts about the natural world (though it is common enough to be moved by such facts in conjunction with moral facts, or desires). Mackie thought that such queer facts were incoherent: nothing could answer to such a concept. We have a good grasp on what an objective fact is, a good grasp of what a motivating desire is, and no notion at all about how one and the same thing could be both at once.

The concept of morality, the standard against which we shall measure an evolutionary explanation, is a concept of a set of prescriptions that are objective, universally binding, and intrinsically motivating. Could we have come to possess such a strange concept as a result of evolution? Can the blind forces of natural selection really give rise to such an elaborate intellectual construction? More importantly, could evolution produce beings that can – indeed, are obliged to – *act* morally? Ought we to look elsewhere for the explanation of morality (or, more radically, disabuse ourselves of the notion that we ever do behave morally)?

So far, we have been concerned only with the *form* of morality: what can analysis of our concept of morality tell us about its structure? It is reasonable to believe that conceptual analysis can also tell us a great deal about the *content* of morality. If it does not have the right kind of content, we should be reluctant to call any system of prescriptions a morality, even if it has the formal features we have laid out. A moral system must be devoted, largely if not wholly, to concern for the welfare of other people. To that extent, it stands opposed to selfishness. We fall short of our concept of morality in so far as we act to benefit ourselves, directly or indirectly. Moreover, a morality must systematize norms of justice and fairness: it must prescribe equal treatment for everyone, unless there are relevant differences between them. We ought not to treat others badly unless they have done something to *deserve* such treatment. Morality must disregard arbitrary differences between people, and ignore, perhaps even compensate for, the effects of sheer luck.

If Mackie, with his argument that nothing can correspond to our idea of a moral obligation, presents us with a conceptual challenge to the concept of morality, evolution presents us with an empirical challenge to its content. If we are to explain how morality might have evolved, we not only need to show how we came to have this (allegedly incoherent) idea, but also why its content is precisely the opposite of what we should expect, given what we know about the process of natural selection. Since evolution is the result of a process that systematically favors selfishness, it is difficult to see how it could possibly yield beings who sincerely believe that they ought to be concerned with the welfare of others, or that norms of fairness and justice are binding upon them. Giving an evolutionary explanation of morality seems, at first sight, about as promising a task as giving a theistic explanation for the origins of atheism.

Evolutionary explanations of morality

The prospects for explaining morality as a product of natural selection do not appear to be very good. Think of the slogan often used to describe natural selection: survival of the fittest; this slogan seems to suggest that evolution is a process that rewards selfishness. Recall, briefly, the manner in which natural selection operates: imagine a population of antelopes that is subject to predation by lions. The antelopes have only one means of defense; at the first sign of danger, they flee. Now imagine that, by chance mutation, an antelope is born that is slightly faster than the others, and that the mutation responsible for its greater speed is heritable. On average, this antelope will survive for longer than its slower herdmates, and therefore will, on average, tend to have more offspring. The small statistical difference this advantage represents can, over many generations, be expected to prove decisive: the heritable mutation (let us call it a gene, for simplicity, though we shall have reason to question this common way of talking later) which is responsible for greater speed will gradually become more and more prevalent in the population. Eventually, every antelope in the population can be expected to have a copy of this gene; the gene has reached *fixation*.

Now imagine that a random mutation gives rise to a "helping" behavior. Various kinds of such behaviors can be imagined. Perhaps individuals with the helping gene lag behind, so that slower animals have a smaller chance of being eaten (the danger is now shared; the lion can choose which antelope to devour). Individuals who behave in this manner run a much greater risk than do those who flee. Possibly fatally for them, they will be out-performed, not only by those with the speed gene, but also by those who lack the gene for helping. Since more of them will fall victim to predation, they will have fewer offspring than other members of the group. The gene for helping will rapidly become extinct.

The lesson from this brief review of natural selection seems to be this: evolution rewards selfishness, and nice guys finish last. Even in the absence of predators, conspecifics are in competition with each other. Antelopes compete for the plants they graze; lions compete for prey. Both compete with members of their own species for mates. The competition between members of the same species is more direct and more intense than that between members of different species, since exactly the same set of scarce resources is required by each conspecific. In the struggle for life, it seems, there is no room for sentiment.

Darwin himself noticed this apparent implication of his theory:

> He who was ready to sacrifice his life, as many a savage has been, rather than betray his comrades, would often leave no offspring to inherit his noble nature. The bravest men, who were always willing to come to the front in war, and who freely risked their lives for others, would on an average perish in larger numbers than other men. Therefore it hardly seems probable, that the number of men gifted with such virtues, or that the standard of their excellence, could be increased through natural selection.[39]

Natural selection, it seems, cannot result in the evolution of behavior that is not fundamentally selfish.

Yet apparently altruistic behavior is actually quite common both in human beings and in other animals. One possible explanation of such behavior in humans is that we, and we alone, are able to transcend the limitations of our animal nature. Perhaps, it is suggested, our ancestors behaved selfishly, and therefore prospered (evolutionarily speaking), at the expense of their more altruistic kin. We owe our very existence to that selfishness, since the lineages founded by less selfish animals died out. Nevertheless, we do not have to obey the dictates of our genetic programming. We have suites of selfish instincts that are the result of evolutionary history, but we also have the ability to assess the behaviors these instincts urge upon us.

Though this is a possible explanation of why we have the capacity to act morally, it is not one that we can adopt with much enthusiasm. If this theory is true, at least in the manner in which its proponents have developed it, we should expect genuine morality to be relatively rare. Advocates of this view claim that our strongest emotions are keyed into behavior that benefits us and our genes, which implies that when we act morally, against the dictates of our programming, we do so only at the cost of great effort. The prospects for morality would not be very rosy on this view. Moreover, the proposal smacks of human chauvinism, which many people will find implausible. We are constituted very much like the other primates who are our close relatives; the differences between us are of degree, not of kind. Is it not arrogant to think that though, like them, we are programmed to behave in certain ways, we alone can transcend our program? How do we do this? Are we not biological machines like them? Is not our behavior the result of our evolved capacities? If we are naturally selfish, then perhaps we are deceiving ourselves when we claim that we act morally on *any* occasion.

Moreover, our acts of altruism appear very much like a variety of animal behaviors. If we are willing to defend our group at the cost of our own deaths, then so are bees. If we will selflessly share food with kin, then so will chimpanzees. Many social animals give alarm calls, apparently to warn the other members of the group of the presence of a predator. This looks like altruism: it benefits others while drawing the attention of the predator to the animal giving the call. We have no reason to think that these animals are capable of transcending their genetic programs. If they act altruistically, then altruism must be compatible with natural selection after all. Given these apparent similarities between ourselves and other animals, we should look, in the first place at least, for a unified explanation of our behavior.

What is altruism?

Before we examine this behavior, we need to clarify what we mean by altruism. A behavior is technically altruistic if it benefits others at some cost to the animal whose behavior it is. To express the concepts we need here, it's useful to adopt the so-called "gene's eye view" of evolution. According to this view, the gene, and not the organism or the species, is the unit of selection. That is, evolution is ultimately for the benefit of the genes. As Richard Dawkins, one of the great proponents of this view, puts it, genes build *survival machines* the better to propagate themselves.[40] We tend systematically to overemphasize the importance of these survival machines, the bodies (including the brains) of animals and the morphological characteristics of plants, because they are the kind of entity we are programmed, by our genes, to deal with. But it is the genes which matter, which control the process, and for whose benefit the entire show is run.

This view – let's call it the *Selfish Gene* picture, after Dawkins' famous book – is much misunderstood. How can genes be selfish? After all, they are not conscious entities; they don't have desires or even instincts. Lacking these properties, genes can't literally be selfish, but it is still helpful to think of them *as if* they were. If Dawkins is right, genes are the unit of inheritance, that is, they are the only aspect of our physical constitution that is passed on (in the form of copies) from parents to children (in fact, even Dawkins would admit that this is a simplification, but it is a useful one for our purpose). Genes, unlike bodies or minds, are potentially immortal, in the sense that identical copies can persist for as long as life goes on. Because genes get copied, and bodies don't, bodies are "invisible" to natural selection. Thus, any improvements – or, more likely, impairments – undergone by an organism's body during its lifetime will not be passed on, unless they have a genetic basis. Since genes, and genes alone, get copied and reproduced indefinitely, evolution automatically selects for whatever is in the interests of genes. If a particular genetic mutation arises which causes, in one way or another, that gene to become more numerous in the population, then it will be selected for. It might rapidly go to fixation. Everything happens *as if* genes are selfish, as if evolution is for their benefit, and as if they are pulling our strings.

With this as our background, we are now in a position to define altruism. In the technical sense in which we shall be using it, a behavior is altruistic if, and only if, it increases the *fitness* of other organisms, at some cost to the fitness of the organism whose behavior it is. Fitness is measured in terms of the ability of the organism to propagate its genes (that is, in terms of its ability to reproduce). This allows us to state the problem of altruism quite neatly: why does natural selection not eliminate genes that lead to such altruistic actions? By definition, it seems, such a gene would decrease in frequency in a population, since fewer copies of it would be passed on to the next generation, while copies of the genes contained in other organisms – organisms whose fitness it had enhanced – would increase in frequency. We should expect the altruistic genes to disappear rapidly.

One possible answer to this question I mention only to dismiss. Mightn't it be the case that altruistic genes remain prevalent in the population for the simple reason that there are no alternatives available? If every organism in a population possessed copies of the altruistic gene, then so long as the species survived, so would the gene. Though genes could survive in this manner over the short term, the evolutionary time span with which we are concerned is immensely long – at least three *billion* years. This allows plenty of time for altruistic genes to be eliminated. In every generation there are a number of random genetic mutations, many of which will not code for the observable characteristics of the organism – its *phenotype* – at all. Of those that do influence the phenotype, the majority will be harmful, and will quickly be eliminated. But some will influence the phenotype in such a manner as to cause it to produce copies of itself at an increased rate; these genes will rapidly propagate. Given the frequency of mutations, and the immensity of the evolutionary time span, genes just cannot survive for no other reason than that there is no alternative. Alternatives crop up all the time.

So, how are we to explain the puzzle of altruism? One popular approach is to *explain it away*. According to the biologists who take this view, altruism does not need to be explained, because it does not exist. What they undertake to explain is the *appearance* of altruism. To assess this claim, it will be helpful to have before us some examples of apparently altruistic behavior. Altruistic behavior in animals ranges from the risky to the reckless to the (literally) suicidal:

- Risky behaviors might include the alarm calls given by many animals and birds. When vervet monkeys see a predator, they sound a warning to the rest of the troop, emitting different sounds for different kinds of predators. The troop responds appropriately to these calls: on hearing the "leopard bark," they run up trees; when they hear the "snake call," they stand up on their hind legs and look around them, and so on. This appears to be altruistic behavior on the part of the monkey giving the call because it risks attracting the attention of the predator to itself. It therefore seems likely that monkeys that engage in this behavior will tend, on average, to leave fewer offspring than those that don't. The *troop* benefits from the behavior, but the individual monkey loses.
- Reckless behaviors are those that are apparently *unnecessarily* risky. The monkey that gives a warning call takes a risk, but might make an effort to minimize it. But the animal who engages in reckless behavior seems to run a risk greater than seems to be necessary to

achieve its aims. For instance, the *stotting* of some animals – repeatedly jumping in the air with all four legs straight – seems to be reckless in this sense. Gazelles who spot a wild dog might stott, rather than run away. The stotting serves as an alarm call, but it is a curious one. Not only does it attract the attention of the predator, it also gives it a head start on the chase. It is as though the gazelle is deliberately drawing the fire of the predator: risking its life for the good of the group.

- Suicidal behaviors are those that benefit other members of a group, at the ultimate cost to the organism of its life. A well-known example of such suicidal behavior is the stinging action of the honey bee. A bee which stings an animal threatening its hive dies soon afterwards, because the barbed sting sticks in the animal, and when the bee pulls away its abdomen is ruptured. It seems as though the bee sacrifices its life for the good of the hive.

Darwin suggested *group selection* explained the persistence of such apparent acts of altruism in the animal kingdom. Though individuals who behave altruistically suffer for it, the groups to which they belong do better than those that are not blessed with such unselfish members. Thus, truly altruistic behavior could evolve. Darwin saw in this process the origin of morality:

> It must not be forgotten that although a high standard of morality gives but a slight or no advantage to each individual man and his children over the other men of the same tribe, yet that an increase in the number of well-endowed men and an advancement in the standard of morality will certainly give an immense advantage to one tribe over another. A tribe including many members who, from possessing in a high degree the spirit of patriotism, fidelity, obedience, courage, and sympathy, were always ready to aid one another, and to sacrifice themselves for the common good, would be victorious over most other tribes; and this would be natural selection.[41]

For most of the twentieth century, biologists frequently invoked a hypothesis something like this to explain acts of apparent altruism. However, the group selection hypothesis faces a major problem. Imagine two groups, one of which has a high proportion of altruists, while the other has none. The altruists engage in risky behavior, with the result that, on average, they leave behind fewer offspring than do selfish individuals. We can measure the fitness of each kind of behavior, and represent it numerically. We'll use "number of offspring" as our measure of fitness. These numbers are for illustration only, but let's suppose that selfish individuals in the group consisting only of selfish individuals have two offspring each, whilst selfish individuals in the group with a high proportion of altruists have, on average, three off-spring each, since they are benefitting from the altruistic behavior of their fellows. The altruists, we'll suppose, have 2.5 offspring each: more than the selfish members of the other group, because they, like their selfish fellows, benefit from the altruism of others, but less than the selfish members of their group, due to the risks they run.

Each group has 100 members. Group 1 is 70% altruistic; Group 2 is 100% selfish. Let's examine what happens to each for two generations.

	Group 1	Group 2
First generation:	70A	100S
	30S	
Total:	100	100
Second Generation:	175A (70 x 2.5)	200S (100 x 2)
	90S (30 x 3)	
Total:	265	200
Third Generation:	438A	400S
	270S	
Total:	708	400

Just as Darwin predicted, groups with altruists in them grow more quickly than groups composed exclusively of selfish individuals. Succeeding generations will do even better; if reproduction continued at this rate, in the next generation the altruistic group would contain 1095 altruists, and 810 selfish individuals, while the selfish group would contain only 800 individuals. It was this kind of trend which impressed Darwin and other group selectionists. Though the altruists do less well than the selfish individuals in their group, their group will outperform a wholly selfish group. It looks, therefore, as though altruistic genes could be selected for.

Notice, however, that the *proportion* of altruists in each generation declines. In the first generation, altruists were 70% of the total population. In the second, the proportion has declined to 66%, and by the third it is 61%. In a few generations, the proportion of altruists will drop below 50%, and it will keep declining. One consequence of this fall is that we can expect the benefits of altruism to the group to fall as well. If, for example, the altruistic act is the giving of alarm calls, then the lower the proportion of altruists in the population, the higher the proportion of attacks by predators which are not preceded by a warning (other things being equal). But the smaller the percentage of warnings, the greater the damage inflicted by predators, on altruists and the selfish alike.

Thus, as altruists begin to be outnumbered by selfish individuals, they tend increasingly to pay the costs of their risky behavior without receiving much benefit in turn from other altruists. Their fitness will fall; which translates directly into a fall in their rate of increase. Of course, the rate of increase of selfish individuals will fall too. The mixed group will continue to reproduce more quickly than the wholly selfish group – indeed, it may well supplant it entirely. But as the proportion of altruists falls, the mixed group begins more and more to resemble the selfish group. Eventually, the proportion of altruists will dwindle to zero. Altruism will have allowed the group to out-compete its rivals; on this point the group selectionists are correct. But so long as the process continues unchecked, altruism is destined to disappear. Ultimately, the formerly altruistic group will be just as selfish as the group it has supplanted.

Richard Dawkins puts the point in this way: altruistic groups might out-compete selfish groups, but they are vulnerable to *subversion from within*. Because, within any group, altruists are outperformed by the selfish, they will eventually be driven to extinction. Ever since George Williams drew this melancholy conclusion to the attention of biologists, group selection has been widely regarded as a dead letter.

However, those who drew the conclusion that altruism could not evolve by group selection did so too hastily. Group selection is not *impossible*; it just requires a very special set of circumstances. We saw that so long as the group continues in existence, the proportion of altruists in it declines, and as a consequence the benefits they bring, to each other and to selfish individuals, fall as well. Altruism can evolve by group selection just so long as groups do *not* stay together. Instead, the group must establish colonies, and the proportion of altruists in the "daughter" colonies must be higher than the proportion of altruists in the mother group.[42] It is certainly possible that both these conditions can be satisfied. Our figures showed that the absolute number of altruists in the group could be expected to increase, at least initially. We also noted that the altruistic group could out-compete selfish groups. If the altruistic group were to take advantage of the demise of the selfish group by colonizing its territory, and if the colonizing populations themselves consist disproportionately of altruists, then the new group can reap the benefits of altruism. Of course, the proportion of altruists in the colony is destined to decline, eventually necessitating a new round of colonization. So long as altruistic groups produce offshoots at a great enough rate, and a high enough proportion of the members of the new colonies are altruistic, altruism can prosper via group selection. Interestingly, if this occurs, then some of the groups that are out-competed by altruistic colonies might themselves be formerly altruistic mother populations.

How frequently is this special set of circumstances encountered in nature? Some biologists believe that it is common enough to be the source of at least some of the altruism we observe in other species, and perhaps of human altruism as well. However, it is clear that group selection can only be part of the story. Though many animal groups splinter in various ways, often as a result of young adult males leaving, or being driven out of, the group, there is little evidence that new populations differ in any significant way from their parent group, so far as the proportion of altruists is concerned. Nor is there any evidence of such selective colonization by early humans in the EEA, the environment in which, most evolutionary psychologists believe, our predispositions to behavior were laid down. The likelihood is that if group selection, as we have outlined it so far, is the only source of altruism, then altruism will be a rare commodity.

As we saw, Darwin, and after him many evolutionary biologists, believed that group selection accounted for altruism. But it is the apparent failure of group selectionist hypotheses, which, more than anything else, explains the current fashion among biologists for dismissing altruism. Faced with instances of apparent altruism, they seek to explain them away, to show that what seems to be altruism is really disguised selfishness. Darwin was right, these biologists believe: only group selection could explain the existence of altruism. But group selection is rare or non-existent, and therefore altruism is absent from the natural world.

I divided apparent acts of altruism into three categories, each one apparently harder to interpret as disguised selfishness than the last. Can merely risky behavior really be selfish? Biologists have expended a great deal of ingenuity on explaining these phenomena. As we saw, giving an alarm call is a risky behavior, which is to say that it is, apparently, at least minimally altruistic. It seems that animals that give such calls lower their own fitness while raising the fitness of others. Biologists who seek to explain away apparent altruism therefore owe us an explanation which demonstrates that this behavior does not lower the fitness of those who practice it.

In fact, there are a number of credible explanations. I'll briefly sketch two, both due to Richard Dawkins. He calls the first the *cave* theory, from the Latin word used by English schoolboys to warn of an approaching teacher. Dawkins' idea is that these schoolboys do not act for the sake of others, but for their own sake. They warn one another of the teacher's approach because they know that they are more likely to avoid strife *themselves* if their peers also refrain from further misbehavior. Similarly, Dawkins conjectures, animals that give alarm calls do so not to help each other, or their group, but to ensure their own safety.

It is easy to see how this might work. A flock of birds is rooting in the undergrowth for food. One of them happens to glance up and notices an eagle circling. The predator has not yet spotted the group, but it is only a matter of time. How should this particular animal act – what kind of behavior will evolution select for? The creature might freeze, hoping that another member of the group might catch the eagle's attention. This would be straightforwardly selfish behavior. But, if it adopts this course of action, it has not done everything it can to minimize its own risk. The longer its fellows continue to move about openly and noisily, the greater the chance the eagle will see the group, and, once its attention is drawn, it just might spot the selfish animal first. Wouldn't the bird do better to hiss a warning, directing the whole group to freeze into immobility, and thus reduce the chances of the eagle spotting any member of the group? Mightn't this course of action be the best, measured in the selfish terms of reproductive fitness?

Dawkins' second explanation is also an attempt to show that giving the alarm is selfish. He calls it the "never break ranks" theory. Imagine a flock of birds, one of which spots an eagle as before. In this case, however, freezing is not as a good an option as fleeing into the branches of a nearby tree, where the foliage is too thick for an eagle to follow. A selfish bird might take to the wing immediately, attempting to get to safety before any of its flock-mates have even noticed the predator. However, as soon as it takes to the air it risks drawing attention to itself; it will be a lone target horribly exposed to the swooping eagle. Far better to give a loud call, causing the entire flock to rise and make for the trees at once. If it follows this course, it will be one bird among hundreds, perhaps even thousands, and its personal risk of falling victim to the eagle will be very small. Thus, the apparently altruistic act of giving an alarm call is shown to be an entirely selfish action after all; an action adopted because it minimizes the risk to the caller.[43]

We might find this strategy plausible when it is applied to risky behavior, but surely reckless actions cannot be explained in the same way? Surely the stotting gazelle's actions cannot be shown to be selfish? In fact, most biologists believe that stotting is not altruistic. Indeed, it is not directed at the gazelle's fellow herd members at all; any benefit they receive from it, such as being alerted to the presence of a predator, is incidental to its function. Rather, stotting is directed at the predator, and its function is to demonstrate the stotting animal's health and vigor. Gazelles who leap athletically thereby advertise that they would be difficult to hunt down. Their display therefore encourages predators to look elsewhere for their next meal: to other members of the herd. Far from being an altruistic act, stotting is selfish. It evolved because gazelles that stott survive at the expense of those who don't.

Kin selection

We might find these reinterpretations of apparently altruistic risky and reckless behaviors reasonable, but find it hard to apply such a strategy to suicidal actions. How can these actions be in the best interests of the organisms who engage in them? Bees that sting animals that threaten the hive do not simply *seem* to endanger their own lives; they (almost always) *actually* die. It seems as though these bees sacrifice their lives for a greater good, for the hive as a whole. Surely this, at least, is a genuinely altruistic act?

It is in explaining this kind of action that the "gene's eye view" really comes into its own. From this perspective, you will recall, everything happens as if evolution is for the benefit of the genes. Genes which, in whatever manner, contribute to behaviors that lead to an increase in their numbers in the next generation will be selected for by evolution. Dawkins and other gene-selectionists often say that genes, unlike the bodies they help make and which carry them, are potentially immortal. Strictly speaking, this is false, for a reason that is important here. Genes do not usually *themselves* outlive the bodies that are their vehicles. Instead, it is *copies* of genes that live on in the next generation. Reproductively successful organisms leave a greater representation of their genes in the next generation, in the form of such copies, than do the less successful.

Once we realize that it is copies that count, we see that organisms have a range of strategies available to maximize reproductive success. The most obvious is the most direct: have offspring. Genes are arranged on chromosomes, long strands of DNA. There are forty-six such strands in humans, arranged in twenty-three pairs. Organisms that have this pairing arrangement are known as *diploid*. Each of our cells is diploid, which is to say that they have two sets of twenty-three chromosomes. There is one exception to this rule, however: sex cells (sperm in males and ova in females). These cells are *haploid*; they contain only a single set of twenty-three chromosomes. In sexual reproduction, the haploid cells of males combine with those of females to create a new organism which, like its parents, is diploid: it receives a single set of chromosomes from each parent.

Each of our sex cells has a (more or less) random selection of our genes within it. Since we are diploid animals, and our sex cells are haploid, each gene has a 50% chance of finding its way into each sex cell (though, as we might expect, natural selection favors genes which are able to distort this process in their favor).[44] The upshot of all this is that for any particular gene, the chances that a single offspring of an animal will possess a copy of it by descent are 50%. In other words, the degree of relatedness between parents and offspring in a sexually reproducing species is 50%.

This "coefficient of relatedness" (to use the jargon of biology), is exactly the same as that which holds between full siblings in sexually reproducing diploid species. For each gene you receive from your mother, there is a 50% chance that you share it with your sister or brother (since you each got a random selection of 50% of her genes); that is, your degree of relatedness on your mother's side is 25% (50/2) or 0.25. But if you also share the same father, then you have precisely the same degree of relatedness on his side, giving a total degree of relatedness of 50% or 0.5. We can use the same logic to show that grandparents and grandchildren have a coefficient of relatedness of 0.25, as do half-siblings, and uncles and aunts with their nieces and nephews. First cousins have a coefficient of relatedness of 0.125, as do great-grandparents and their great-grandchildren. And so on.

Since reproductive success, measured from the gene's eye view, concerns the extent to which we are able to get *copies* of our genes into the next generation, we can increase our fitness in one of two ways: either by having offspring of our own or by taking steps to ensure the reproductive success of our close relatives. Frequently, of course, we can do both, but sometimes we have to choose; when we are faced with such a choice, the best course of action (again, from the gene's eye view) will depend on the circumstances. If my circumstances are such that I cannot afford to raise offspring of my own – my resources are limited in some way, or my chances of securing a mate are low – I might do best by assisting others. Even if I am able to have offspring of my own, it might be that I do better by refraining. Imagine a case in which a diploid, sexually reproducing animal is faced with a choice between bearing one offspring itself, and assisting a full sibling to raise three. Since the coefficient of relatedness between such an animal and its own offspring is 0.5, it does better by raising three nephews and nieces. Each such relative has a degree of relatedness to it of 0.25, and 0.25 multiplied by three is greater than 0.5.

Biologists use the term *inclusive fitness* to refer to reproductive success in this extended sense. The inclusive fitness of an organism is a measure of its success in increasing the proportion of copies of its genes in the next generation, by whatever means. From the perspective of inclusive fitness, many apparently altruistic acts can be seen to be instances of genetic selfishness. We can, for example, see why it might be sensible, from a genetic point of view, for an organism to forgo having offspring of its own, in order to assist its kin with raising theirs. We can even see how, under the right circumstances, it might make sense for an organism to sacrifice its life for its relatives. J. B. S. Haldane, the great evolutionary biologist, was reportedly asked if he would lay down his life for a brother. "No," he replied, "not for fewer than two brothers, or eight first cousins."

Biologists call the process of natural selection through enhancement of the reproductive fitness of close relatives *kin selection*. Kin selection allows us to explain the existence of many kinds of behavior which otherwise seem quite mysterious. A puzzle remains, however. Though it is apparent that reckless behavior, and even, in the right circumstance, suicidal behavior, can be selected for through kin selection, how do we account for the fact that bees (and other social insects) so willingly and frequently lay down their lives for the community? Though it may be understandable that diploid, sexually reproducing beings, like ourselves, would sacrifice their lives for their kin *in extremis*, how do we explain that bees' very first line of defense involves the ultimate sacrifice?

The clue lies in the unique system of reproduction of most of the social insects. To take bees as an example: almost all the bees in a hive are sterile; their reproductive systems shut down by the pheromones released by the queen, who is the mother of the entire hive. Her female offspring, who become the workers and guards of the hive, are all full sisters. But, due to an oddity of their reproductive system, they are more closely related to one another than are human siblings. The Hymenoptera – ants, bees, and wasps – are haplo-diploid. Female bees are diploid: they hatch from fertilized eggs and so possess two sets of chromosomes, one from each parent. But male bees hatch out of unfertilized eggs, and so have only one parent: their mother. Thus, no male has a father, or any sons. As a result, male bees are haploid, possessing only a single set of chromosomes. In consequence, every female bee has a 50% chance of sharing any one of her mother's genes, but, since her father had only one set of chromosomes to pass on, she has all her father's genes, as do all her female siblings. Full sisters therefore have a coefficient of relatedness of 0.75, rather than 0.5. So, they are more closely related to their sisters than they would be to offspring of their own, should they have any! This fact explains why bees are better off sterile, assisting their queen to produce more near-clones of themselves, than they would be rebelling and going in for reproducing themselves. It also explains why a propensity to lay down their lives for one another has been selected for. Such "sacrifices" are simply one more way in which a bee acts – selfishly – to ensure that copies of its genes will be represented in the next generation.[45]

Reciprocal altruism and game theory

I have sketched a variety of mechanisms whereby altruism is shown to be disguised selfishness. Apparently altruistic acts may be aimed quite directly at the good of the organism, as in the case of alarm calls and stotting, or they might be instances of kin selection, in which an individual sacrifices his or her own reproductive interests for the sake of their investment in the reproduction of close kin. It is unlikely, however, that all apparently altruistic acts can be explained through these mechanisms. Not all altruistic acts are aimed at close kin, and not all are amenable to interpretation as direct (though disguised) selfishness. Sometimes, animals simply seem to help one another. Indeed, sometimes this helping behavior crosses species boundaries.

Over the last twenty years, evolutionary biologists have turned to the mathematical discipline of *game theory* to aid them in understanding these phenomena. Game theory provides us with a set of tools with which to model *strategic* interaction. A "game" – here the term is used to refer to any kind of interaction between two or more players in which there is a question of winning and losing, profit and loss – is strategic if the best "move" depends not merely on the state of the game, but also upon what the other players do. Most ordinary games are strategic in this sense: the best spot to place a lob in tennis depends crucially on where one's opponent is moving. Thus cricket, football, chess and poker are all strategic games, whereas golf, in which the player competes against the course as much as opponents, is not importantly strategic.

Most of the games we are familiar with are *zero-sum* games. In a zero sum game, the gains of one player automatically translate into the losses of another. In these games, cooperation between opponents is out of the question: only one player or team can win. But the games which interest us most here are *non-zero-sum* games, in which it is at least possible for separate players to do well without their gains coming at the expense of others' losses. Game theorists are especially interested in games which may appear to their players to be zero-sum games, but which, from the appropriate viewpoint, can be seen to be non-zero-sum. Many economic interactions are like this: participants see themselves as competing with one another for scarce resources, but if they cooperate with one another, they might increase their returns.

The most famous game of all is known as the *prisoner's dilemma*:

Two prisoners are being interrogated separately by the police. They are accused of committing a crime together, but the police do not have sufficient evidence to convict them. Each is offered the same deal: if they will confess their guilt, but agree to testify against their codefendant, they will be released on a good behavior bond. If they stay silent, however, and their codefendant accepts the deal, it will be she (or he) who is released, while they go to jail for ten years. If both the accused confess, each will go to jail for five years. And if neither confesses, the police will be unable to secure a conviction. However, they will be charged with and convicted of with some lesser crime – perhaps resisting arrest – and each will receive a six month jail sentence.

Game theorists construct a *pay-off matrix* to model this kind of situation. Let's call staying silent *cooperate*, and confessing *defect*. In this matrix, the options for player one are displayed to the left of the boxes, while those for player two are above the boxes. The top set of numbers in each box represents the pay-off to each player, in years, with the pay-off to the first player separated from that to the second by a comma. The second set of numbers, in brackets, represents each player's ranking of the options, from most preferred (1) to least preferred (4).

	Cooperate	Defect
Cooperate	1/2, 1/2 (2,2)	10, 0 (4,1)
Defect	0,10 (1,4)	5,5 (3,3)

Thus, player one would most prefer to defect while player two cooperates. If she were able to secure this result, she would go free, while player two would go to jail for ten years (we assume that each player is concerned with only their own welfare, which is to say minimizing their jail-time, and does not care one way or the other what happens to the other player). If player one cannot secure this result, then she would most like her second-ranked preference, in which both players cooperate, to be the outcome, since in this scenario she will go to jail for just six months. The situation in which both players defect is ranked third by her (five years' jail each), while the outcome she most wants to avoid is that in which she cooperates while her co-accused confesses, since in this situation she would end up serving ten years in jail.

We can see immediately that this is a non-zero-sum game. Though it is possible for one player to "win" at the expense of the other – if one cooperates while the other defects – it is also possible, if both cooperate, for both to secure a good result. And since it is extremely unlikely that either would be able to convince the other to cooperate while they defect – remember, we are assuming self-interest here – it seems obvious that the outcome they should strive to bring about is mutual cooperation. However, while they might both prefer this result to any other (with the exception of the unobtainable situation in which they defect on a cooperator), and it would be a mutually satisfying arrangement, it is not clear that it is available to the players.

To see this, we need to realize that each player is better off defecting, no matter what the other player does. If Jack cooperates, then Jill is better off defecting – she gets off scot-free, rather than going to prison for six months. But if Jack defects, then Jill had better defect as well, since if she cooperates with a defector, she goes to jail for five years. In the jargon of game-theory, "defect" is the *dominant* strategy, which is to say that it ought to be chosen no matter what strategy is employed by the other player. However, the prisoner's dilemma is a symmetrical game: whatever holds for one of the players is automatically true for the other. If "defect" is dominant for Jill, then we may be sure that it is dominant for Jack (we can easily confirm this by noticing that no matter what Jill does, Jack is better off defecting). Since "defect" is dominant for both players, that is just what they will do, if they are rational. As a result, each will go to prison for five years.

But if mutual defection guarantees the players a worse result than mutual cooperation, than cooperation is in both players' interests. If this is the case, surely, it is rational for them to cooperate, not defect. There must, we cannot help but think, be some way in which the players can come to an agreement, and secure a better outcome for each. But how? An obvious way to proceed is via explicit bargaining between the players. Perhaps the unsatisfactory outcome of the prisoner's dilemma is the result of the isolation of the players. The police, we might think, separate them in order to prevent them from coming to an agreement. If we allow them to discuss the situation, we might hope to secure mutual cooperation.

Very well then, let's try it. Having been interrogated separately and informed of their choices, Jack and Jill are sent back to adjoining cells to think things over. There, they discuss their predicament. Each sees that mutual cooperation is preferable to mutual defection, so they come to an agreement. They promise each other that when they are interrogated again, they will cooperate; in other words, they will not testify against each other. Now, if each keeps his or her side of the bargain, they will avoid five years in prison each. But what ensures that they will stick to their agreement? As Jill is taken back to the interview room, she might reason thus:

Suppose Jack sticks to the agreement. Then he will cooperate. In that case, if I cooperate I will go to prison for only six months. But if I defect then I won't go to prison at all. If Jack cooperates, then I'm better off defecting. But if I'm better off defecting, then so is Jack. Surely he'll see this, and defect. And if he defects, I had better do the same, to avoid ten years in prison. So whatever Jack does, I ought to defect.

Of course, Jack will defect as well. So both players will go to jail for five years each. It is difficult to see how this result can be avoided. Though mutual cooperation is in each player's best interests, mutual defection seems the inevitable result.

What has all this to do with evolution? At first sight, very little. One way to express the paradoxical implications of prisoner's dilemma-type situations is to say that when its conditions apply, rational agents do less well than irrational. Whereas two irrational agents might cooperate because they fail to see that "defect" is the dominant strategy, rational individuals will recognize that whatever the other player does, they are better off defecting, will act accordingly, and end up worse off than irrational agents. Though this is certainly a fascinating discovery, it seems quite irrelevant to our question. We are concerned, here, with whether morality might have evolved. To approach this question, I have focused mainly on non-rational animals, from bees to birds. I have taken this approach because I am concerned with discovering what kinds of dispositions and motivations our evolutionary history might have bequeathed to us, on the assumption that our fundamental desires will, to some extent, reflect that history. Now we discover that in certain kinds of situation it is difficult or impossible to bring rational agents to cooperate with one another, even though doing so is in their interest. This might be bad news to some, but, we might think, neutral or even good news for us. Since we are concerned with what kinds of dispositions we might have developed *before* (or perhaps at the same time as) we evolved rationality, the fact that rationality can be a barrier to cooperation is irrelevant.

Unfortunately, the apparently tragic implications of the prisoner's dilemma for human cooperation cannot be so easily evaded by the evolutionist. It is certainly true that our distant ancestors did not and could not reason as to what strategy to utilize when they found themselves confronted with a choice between cooperation and defection. We, like every other living thing on this planet, are descended from the one-celled organisms that were the first living creatures; such organisms had no capacity for any kind of thought at all. But even single-celled organisms like bacteria can find themselves in prisoner's dilemma-type situations, and the reasoning which shows that humans will engage in mutual defection in such circumstances seems also to apply to bacteria.

Imagine, for instance, a group of bacteria, of a single species, occupying a small rock pool. The number of bacteria that the pool can maintain is strictly limited, because each individual produces waste products, which break down only slowly. These waste products pollute the bacteria's environment; if the pollution exceeds a certain level, a mass die-off will occur. It might even be that death on that scale will cause further pollution of the water, leading to the extinction of the entire population. So, it is clearly in the interests of the bacteria as a group to limit their population. If they can maintain their numbers below a critical threshold, which I shall call n, then the population will thrive, but if they exceed it, then the entire group faces extinction.

This scenario can easily be modeled using game theory. Here, "cooperate" translates as "limit your rate of reproduction, so as to cause no net increase in numbers," and "defect" as "reproduce at some (unspecified) faster rate". Imagine, further, that all bacteria currently follow the strategy of cooperating. What does it mean for a bacterium to implement a strategy? Clearly, it cannot mean that it weighs up the consequences of various alternative actions, and selects that action which has the best outcome. A bacterium is not capable of sophisticated mental processing; indeed, it is not capable of mental processing at all. All we mean by saying that it follows a strategy is that it tends to act in some manner that is in accordance with one of the alternatives in our model. In this sense, bees, when they lay down their lives for the hive, are following a strategy that we might usefully label "cooperate." Bees do not deliberate about how to act; they follow a program that has been laid down for them by natural selection. Bees which behaved in this manner in the past had more descendants (better, possessed genes which increased in number in future generations) than did those which did not, and therefore the genes which encode this manner of behaving gradually went to fixation in the population, which is to say that all bees now behave in this manner when faced with those circumstances.

If bees follow a program, this is even truer of bacteria. We assume, therefore, that all the bacteria in our population follow the programmed strategy of cooperating, and the population in the rock pool remains below n. But now suppose that a mutation occurs among the bacteria, so that individuals with that mutation will defect (that is, reproduce at a faster rate). How likely is such a mutation? Given the length of evolutionary time, the rate at which mutations occur, and the short generation time of bacteria, it is extremely likely, as long as the behavior for which it codes is not very different from those in which the bacteria already engages, and it has no special costs in terms of the resources required to sustain it. (It is extremely unlikely, for example, that a mutation will suddenly occur amongst our bacteria which enables those who inherit it to fly, since flying is an ability that requires a great many evolutionary steps.) Since the mutation in question seems to meet these conditions, it is likely that it will occur, sooner or later.

Bacteria with the "defect" mutation will, by definition, tend to leave more offspring than those without. For this reason alone, they are fitter than bacteria that cooperate. We can therefore expect the "defect" mutation rapidly to go to fixation. Of course, when this occurs the number of bacteria in the population rapidly exceeds n, with the result that the whole population goes extinct! Even so, the result might be inevitable, for this reason: each individual bacterium is better off defecting than it is cooperating. If all the other bacteria cooperate, then a single defector increases its fitness at no cost, because it is unlikely that the defection of any one bacterium will causes the population to exceed n. But if the other bacteria defect, then it will inevitably pay the cost that results from increasing pollution, and therefore must seek to produce as many copies of its genes as possible, in the hope that one will manage to survive the coming cataclysm. In other words, "defect" is dominant for the bacteria, just as it was for the rational players of the prisoner's dilemma.

This is bad news for us, for it seems to indicate that cooperation cannot evolve by natural selection. Since cooperation is an important part of morality – especially when the alternative is selfishly doing someone else down to get some benefit – the apparent failure to demonstrate its compatibility with natural selection seems to reinforce the case of those people who hold that evolution is fundamentally unethical (which presents us with a further dilemma: either we accept the truth of evolution, and give up on ethics, or we attempt to find grounds for rejecting, or at least limiting the power of, evolution in the name of ethics).

The prisoner's dilemma iterated

Our failure to "solve" the prisoner's dilemma seems, in one important sense, to be bad news for those who wish to vindicate morality. It apparently suggests that skeptics or cynics about morality are right; morality might be no more than disguised self-interest. We have reason to sacrifice our own narrow interests for those of our close genetic relatives, but these reasons are ultimately self-serving; they represent the victory of genetic selfishness, rather than of moral selflessness. We sacrifice ourselves for others, but only because we (rightly, from a genetic point of view) regard them as, in some sense, extensions of ourselves. If we are right in thinking that morality requires us to give at least some weight to everyone's interests, regardless of the degree to which they are related to us, then it seems it cannot evolve.

We are forced to this melancholy conclusion on the condition that the kind of model for strategic interaction we have just constructed captures the real-world interaction of organisms accurately. However, we have good reason to think that a great deal of the interaction between potential game players is significantly different from the prisoner's dilemma model in one important respect: we deliberately structured our game so that each player chose only once. Though there are many such one round (in game theory, *one shot*) games, many others are *iterated*. Iterate the prisoner's dilemma, and the incentives for cooperation are greatly increased.

Of course, a genuine prisoner's dilemma – in which the pay-offs are jail sentences – cannot be an iterated game. In any possible outcome of a single round of such a game, at least one player is in prison, and therefore no longer available as a strategic partner. So, let us change the scenario to make the iterated game a possibility. For the moment, we won't attempt to model a real-life situation, but will be content with an abstract model. Imagine a version of prisoner's dilemma, then, in which two players compete for money. Obviously, this kind of game can be repeated indefinitely. To fix our ideas, we can assign the following values to the pay-offs: the *temptation*, the amount of money a player receives if they defect while the other player cooperates, will be $8; the *reward*, the money each player receives for cooperating with a cooperator will be $5; the *punishment* for mutual defection $2 and the *sucker's pay-off*, received by the unfortunate player who cooperates with a defector, will be zero. Once again, "defect" is the dominant strategy: in any particular round each player is better of defecting, no matter what the other player does. In a one shot game with this structure, rational players will defect. But what is true of one shot games is not necessarily true of iterated games.

Robert Axelrod, an American political scientist, set out to discover the best strategy to follow in an iterated prisoner's dilemma. He utilized a novel method to test various strategies: he ran a tournament, and invited game theorists, political scientists and psychologists to submit strategies. Axelrod then ran the strategies against each other on a computer. Each strategy competed against every other strategy, and itself, in iterated games of prisoner's dilemma. A variety of strategies were submitted, some of them very complex and subtle. But the winner of the tournament was one of the simplest strategies: a strategy now known as tit-for-tat (TFT). TFT began each game against a new player by cooperating; thereafter, it simply copied whatever move the other player made last time. Thus, if the second player cooperated, TFT cooperated as well, and did not defect unless the other player defected first. In the technical vocabulary of game theory, this makes TFT a *nice* strategy. It is also a *forgiving* strategy, in that it only punishes defectors once. If the other player returns to cooperating, TFT responds in kind.

Why does TFT out-perform other, less nice, strategies, when "defect" is the dominant strategy? Though each player will do better, in any *particular* round, by defecting rather than cooperating, when their scores are tallied over many rounds, players who always defect do badly. We can see this by considering the iterated prisoner's dilemma in an evolutionary context. Earlier, we saw how a population of organisms

which adopted the strategy "always cooperate" was vulnerable to invasion and eventual displacement by mutants playing "always defect"
(subversion from within). But now let's examine what happens when
we introduce a third strategy into the mix: TFT.

Richard Dawkins has provided a thought experiment to model
such a situation. He asks us to imagine a population of birds, who are
parasitized by a tick. The tick must be removed, because it carries a fatal
disease, which the birds will contract if the tick is left too long. Each
bird can remove ticks from its own body, but it cannot reach the back
of its own head, and so requires the cooperation of another bird to
remove ticks from there. Dawkins supposes that the population is initially composed of cooperators. But, he points out, such a population is
vulnerable to invasion by defectors, who accept grooming from any
other bird, but never groom others in return. Since grooming other
birds has a cost (in terms of time which could have been used for for-
aging), birds that never groom will do better than those that do. Thus,
defectors will be slightly fitter than cooperators, with the result that this
strategy will spread. Eventually, "defect" will go to fixation.

But now imagine that, by chance mutation a third strategy arises.
These birds play TFT: they willingly groom any bird once, but if that
bird fails to reciprocate, they refuse it further grooming. How would
such a mutant fare in a population of defectors? A lone TFTer would do
very badly: it would spend a lot of time grooming other birds – since it
will groom any bird once – and will never be groomed in return. Its sad
fate will simply be to contribute slightly to the fitness of the defectors,
perhaps before dying of the tick-borne disease. But if TFT can get a
foothold, however small, in the population, everything changes. Two
TFTers, who associate preferentially with one another, can do better
than the population average, since they are assured of having their
ticks removed, whereas defectors can only have their ticks removed
once each. So long as the benefit they receive from being groomed by
each other exceeds the cost of grooming, they will be fitter than
the defectors. If this is the case, then TFT may very well increase in the
population.

Thus, a population of cooperators is susceptible to invasion by
defectors, and TFTers can invade a population of defectors. But TFT
will not go to fixation. As the proportion of TFTers increases in the

population, the probability that any given defector will meet a TFTer with which it has not previously interacted increases. Thus, its chances of being groomed rise, and a small number of defectors may be able to hold on. In addition, a large number of TFTers provide a hospitable environment for cooperators. Indeed, when cooperators interact with TFTers, they are indistinguishable from each other. As a result, the number of cooperators in the population may rise, which in turn provides opportunities for defectors.

Because no one strategy has a decisive advantage over the others, none will go to fixation. What actually happens will depend on the details of the situation – exactly how much it costs to groom other birds, or the penalty incurred by failure to be groomed – but the upshot will be a *polymorphism* of strategies, in which each strategy is represented in some proportion. Any departures from this polymorphism increase the pay-offs to other strategies, which leads to an increase in these strategies, which reduces the pay-offs to the first strategy. For example, if the number of cooperators increases, defection becomes more profitable, as defectors are able to take advantage of cooperators. As a result, cooperation becomes a less profitable strategy, and the number of cooperators falls, leading to a decrease in the number of defectors who prey on them. So a polymorphism of this kind is not static, but it is quite stable over time. Unless conditions change, so that the pay-offs alter, departures from such a polymorphism are usually small and brief.

There are three ways such a polymorphism could be realized. One is in the manner we have assumed in the foregoing, in which different individuals reliably play different strategies. Or a polymorphism could be realized by individuals playing all of the strategies with a certain probability: that is, the same individual sometimes behaves like a cooperator, sometimes like a TFTer, and sometimes like a defector. Or, finally, a population might consist of a combination of all kinds of individuals, in which some always cooperate, some always defect, some always play TFT, and some switch between strategies.

Perhaps the world we live in and share with others is just such a stable polymorphism, in which most people cooperate, or play tit-for-tat, most of the time, but where some people always cooperate (we call them saints), some always defect (we call them evil), and others switch between strategies depending on their costs and benefits. None of us will be surprised to learn that usually reliable cooperators become defectors when the risk of detection is low. But, though it is easy to use game theory to model the behavior of rational actors, and the results may be quite plausible as a description of actual human society, can it be applied to the behavior of other organisms, which do not possess our ability to predict the consequences of behavior? We have seen that, when we limit ourselves to simple strategies such as "always cooperate" and "always defect," rationality is not required for organisms to pursue strategies, nor for processes to occur which can be described using the tools of game theory. But tit-for-tat, surely, is beyond the cognitive grasp of all but the most complex animals – to say nothing of the complex accounting required when individuals switch between strategies. Since behavior in the "lower" animals is programmed by their genes, we can predict that the strategies they pursue will be simple. But that is bad news. As we are concerned with whether morality might have evolved, if conditional strategies such as TFT are beyond the capability of most or all non-human animals, and we must therefore limit ourselves to "cooperate" and "defect," then we can predict that morality cannot have evolved. Populations of cooperators are vulnerable to invasion, which implies that morality must be a recent innovation, if indeed it exists at all.

Fortunately for us, there is evidence that strategies like TFT do not require rational minds to implement them. Cooperation based on upon reciprocity is a genuine feature of the animal world. The most famous example here is a slightly macabre one: the behavior of vampire bats. Vampire bats, as their name suggests, live on the blood of other animals. Each night they seek a large mammal, and try to inflict a painless bite upon it. They then drink blood for around thirty minutes before flying back to their roost. The bats need to feed almost every night: if the hunt fails two nights in a row, they risk starvation. On any given night, from seven to thirty per cent of the bats in a colony will fail in their search for blood. However, those that are successful are able to store blood in their stomachs, and regurgitate it. They can therefore donate this blood to other bats. Gerald Wilkinson studied the bats for five years, and discovered that the benefits of such donations to starving recipients exceeded the cost to donors.[46] A blood donation was worth about eighteen extra hours of life to a starving vampire bat: sufficient time to hunt again. But the donation cost only about six hours of the time a satiated bat had until starvation. In this situation, all the ingredients for a prisoner's dilemma are in place. We have the following pay-off matrix:

	Cooperate (Feed)	Defect (Don't Feed)
Cooperate	12,12 (2,2)	−6,18 (4,1)
Defect	18,−6 (1,4)	0,0 (3,3)

The benefit of cooperation is measured at twelve hours of life, which is the eighteen hours gained by a starving bat that is fed, minus the six hours' worth of life the feeding bat expends in cooperating. We can see that the preference ordering for each bat (once again represented by the numbers in brackets) is identical to that in the classic prisoner's dilemma. This means that "defect" is dominant: no matter what the other bat does, each bat is better off if it defects. Yet bats do frequently feed one another. Given that this is the case, we can predict that the three conditions necessary for the evolution of TFT must be fulfilled in vampire bat colonies: the game is iterated, the bats interact with one another repeatedly, and they are able to recognize one another.

It is easy enough to see why the game is iterated. Night after night the bats fly out of their cave or hollow tree in search of blood. The bat that is successful on one night might fail the next; thus each bat will frequently find itself in a position to play one or other of the roles in the game. Wilkinson found, moreover, that bats tend to roost together. Vampire bats live in groups that share a roosting spot; though one will occasionally leave for another group, in general the groups are very stable. Thus, the same bats interact with one another repeatedly. Finally, Wilkinson found that bats could recognize each other. In these circumstances, it is not surprising that bats do not follow the strategy that is dominant in the one shot game. Instead, they play TFT. Wilkinson tested this hypothesis by removing bats from different colonies, and starving one at random for a single night. He found that the bats were much more likely to regurgitate blood to the hungry bat when it was returned to their cage if it was a bat that had previously fed them. Thus, it seems that bats keep some kind of rough score, good enough to be able to play TFT. TFT does not, it seems, require the sophisticated cognitive equipment of a primate.

Indeed, there is evidence that much simpler animals than even vampire bats can play TFT. Robert Trivers, one of the most important figures in the development of models to study reciprocal altruism in non-human animals, suggests that TFT explains the relationship between predatory fish and the much smaller fish that clean them. These fish are often the right size to make a good meal for the predators. Yet they do not attempt to eat the cleaners; instead, they seek them out, and when they locate them, go into a kind of trance while the smaller fish removes parasites from their bodies. The small fish sometimes actually swim into the mouth of the larger, and out of their gills, in the search for the parasites.

It is obvious that each player in this game stands to benefit from the interaction. The large fish have their parasites, which otherwise might cause serious problems, removed. The small fish gain a meal. But why don't the bigger fish defect? Why don't these fish accept the cleaning services of the smaller, and then round off the experience by eating them? The answer seems to lie in the fact that cleaner fish are relatively easily recognizable – they have distinctive markings and ways of moving – and offer their services from a fixed location. Since the cleaners can be located again and again, the game is iterated. Hence, the mutual defection which characterizes one shot games is avoided. Instead, the fish play TFT.

The moral emotions

Contrary to what some discussions of evolutionary game theory suggest, TFT is no panacea. For one thing, if two players engage in it, it is vulnerable to mistakes: one defects by accident, and sets off a chain of mutual defections. ("Tit-for-tat killings" is, after all, how we often describe cycles of violence in the Middle East and elsewhere.) Moreover, it is a viable strategy only under the right conditions: nothing guarantees that the pay-offs of iterated interactions will be such as to make mutual cooperation in the interests of all players.

And even when the pay-offs are appropriate, TFT can break down. Psychologists who conducted experiments in which subjects played prisoner's dilemma against each other soon noticed that if the number of rounds was fixed in advance, cooperation tended to evaporate. The reason for this phenomenon is easy to see. Imagine a ten round game of prisoner's dilemma. We should expect the players to cooperate with one another in rounds one through nine, simply because they know that defection would set off a chain of mutual defections, and would lower each player's overall gain. But round ten is, effectively, a one shot game. There is no longer any point in cooperating, since the other player cannot retaliate on the next round. In a one shot game, as we know, defect is the dominant strategy; we can therefore expect each player to defect in the last round. But rational players soon learn that the last round is effectively removed from the iterated game. They therefore turn their attention to round nine, the next to last round. They quickly see that there is no point cooperating in this round: since they know the other player will defect in the next, they do not need to establish their goodwill. Hence, this round is effectively a one shot game as well. But with round nine removed from the iterated game, round eight becomes the last round, and the same reasoning applies. And so on. By making the game a fixed number of rounds, the incentive to cooperate is effectively removed.

Nevertheless, the conditions under which TFT is a viable strategy are sometimes met with in nature: interactions occur in which the pay-offs are appropriate, and the number of rounds is not fixed. In these circumstances, TFT turns out to be a powerful strategy, which can yield something like morality. Indeed, it may even explain the evolution of our sense of justice. In order for TFT to evolve, it must be possible for the players to be able, and be motivated, to detect cheats. As we have seen, vampire bats that refuse to feed other bats are refused food in turn, and therefore are less fit than those who cooperate. But it is not sufficient for bats to *behave* appropriately. This behavior does them no good unless it is recognized by others, that will one day be in a position to reciprocate. Thus bats will be motivated not only to be cooperative, but also to be *seen* to be cooperative. Indeed, this very fact provides them with an incentive to *appear* to be more cooperative than they really are. The better their reputation, the more likely it is that they will be fed, but if there is a cheaper way of raising their reputation than actually feeding other bats (which costs them a not insignificant six hours of time in which to find their next meal), they can be expected to take it. Thus, Trivers predicted, we should expect to find that sophisticated methods of cheating evolve: methods that do not involve the blatant refusal to cooperate but instead give the appearance of cooperating, without the substance. Once such mechanisms of cheating emerge, however, natural selection will place a premium on methods of detecting the cheats. We can expect to see an evolutionary "arms race," in which there is competition between ever more sophisticated methods of cheating, and ever better methods of detecting cheats.

One product of such an arms race might be our distinctive moral emotions. The moral emotions are comprised of two sets of partially overlapping feelings: the feelings we get in response to violations of moral norms, and the feelings which motivate us to live up to our moral obligations. For example, we feel certain types of anger in response to perceived injustices, while we feel guilt and shame in response to actual or projected wrongs on our own part. How can the evolutionary arms race between cheats and detectors give rise to these emotions? Trivers suggests that the selection pressures on both sides – both the pressures that favor more efficient means of cheating and those that favor more efficient methods of detecting cheats – might encourage the development of such feelings. One reason the moral emotions might be needed is to fill in the inevitable gaps in cheater detection systems. No matter how vigilant the members of a group are, opportunities for *free riding* will inevitably arise. A free rider, in the ter-minology of economists, is someone who enjoys the benefits which come from the provision of a public good – navigating her ship with reference to a lighthouse, driving on the roads paid for by taxes, or, least metaphorically, riding on public transport – without paying the cost. Free riding is rational, in a narrow sense of that word, when we have good reason to believe that we can get away with it. In the absence of the moral emotions, it might be rational more often.

Imagine a group of hominids in which there is a notion of moral obligation, but in which the moral emotions have not evolved. One member of the group free rides; perhaps he finds a food source which he ought to share with the others, but which, he believes, he can get away with saving for himself. He eats some, and hides the rest in a tree for later. All goes well at first, but on his last journey to the tree, he is followed by someone whose suspicion has been aroused by the free rider's unexplained absences. How should the members of the group react to this act of treachery? If they are – narrowly – rational, they will weigh the costs of punishing him against the benefits. On the one hand, allowing incidents of free riding to go unpunished sets a bad example, perhaps tending to increase the frequency with which it occurs. On the other hand, there may be significant costs to punishing the free rider. Sanctions will, presumably, have some element of coercion; they must involve, or at least be backed up by the threat of, physical force. But such force carries risks; even if the free rider is no stronger than average, in any physical confrontation both sides risk damage. And the free rider has just feasted; he is likely to be fitter and stronger than his would-be punishers! In addition, he might be a valuable member of the group, whose cooperation is needed in hunting or trading. Perhaps the appropriate sanction for his crime is banishment, but the group cannot afford to lose one of its members. All in all, though it might be rational to draw up lists of crimes and their appropriate punishments, when the time comes to punish those who transgress, it might be rational to do nothing.

If this is the case, then our little group has a problem. If it becomes known that free riding will not be punished, then the system of reciprocal altruism is in danger of breaking down. Without some kind of punishment, in effect, the group is no longer playing TFT but has reverted to "always cooperate." But we know that groups of cooperators are vulnerable to invasion by defectors. That is what we might expect to happen here: those members of the group who can avoid sanctions will free ride, whenever possible. As a result, they will be fitter than average, and their behavior will go to fixation. The dilemma facing our group is this: it is rational to promise to behave in certain ways, if certain conditions are realized, but it is not rational actually to behave in these ways in those conditions. It is rational to have systems of punishment in place to punish free riders, in order to discourage free riding, but very often when it comes right down to it, it is not rational to punish them! But if that is the case, then free riders will see through the threats of punishment, and behave as they like. A system of sanctions that will never be enforced is entirely superfluous.

The ordinary prisoner's dilemma presented us with a similar problem. There we saw that under the right conditions, being rational is not all that rational. If only the players in a one shot prisoner's dilemma were less rational, they might do better for themselves. Similarly, our group might be able to secure better outcomes for themselves if they were less rational. If they were so irrational as to carry out their threats of punishment *even if in doing so they hurt themselves*, then potential free riders would have a powerful incentive to refrain from transgressions. Emotions might plug this gap, allowing us to be less than fully rational on those occasions when it is rational not to be rational.[47] People – and perhaps some other animals – get angry, for example. Angry people are notorious for their inability to assess situations rationally; they often act to punish those who have made them angry without thinking of the costs to themselves. Imagine, now, our potential free rider, considering whether he should share his find with his tribe or hide it for his own consumption. He knows that his conspecifics are likely to get angry if they find him cheating, and that angry people do irrational things. The costs of cheating rise in this scenario, and our free rider might instead decide to share his find. Thus, the propensity to act irrationally in certain circumstances might be rational, in the sense that it is evolutionarily fitter.[48]

Other emotions might also be explicable in terms of their contribution to reciprocal altruism. Affection for certain group members, and antipathy to others, encourages us to play preferentially with those who reciprocate. This is especially the case if we know that these people will feel gratitude for our aid, which will motivate them to return it, and would feel guilt if they refused to reciprocate. Shame motivates wrongdoers to recompense those they have wronged, and thus tends to restore them to full status as members of the group, and therefore as potential partners in mutually beneficial exchanges. Sympathy motivates aid for others, and so on.[49]

This is good news for us: it seems to show that the emotions that underlie morality might be the product of natural selection. But the picture is not entirely rosy. If it is rational to possess the moral emotions, it is even more rational to *seem* sympathetic, and therefore trustworthy, than to actually *be* it. That way, you get the advantages which come from participation in exchanges, while remaining open to the possibility of defecting – without costly feelings of guilt or shame – if the opportunity presents itself. We might expect the ability to seem more "moral" than one really is to be strongly selected. Thus, we can expect animals who play TFT to be more strongly motivated to reciprocate when so doing is public, and therefore reputation-building, then when its pay-off is smaller. We can expect them to evolve methods of advertising that they are reciprocators, and that sometimes these adverts will be deceptive. But we can also expect that methods of detecting cheats will keep pace with these innovations. Trivers suggest that here we might have the origins of self-deception. There are characteristic cues which give us away when we are lying – sweaty palms, a quaver in the voice, and so on. These cues can be hidden, but as we all know from experience are hard to disguise. Far better, Trivers argues, if we are able to hide our own deceit from ourselves. If we believe that we are more moral, more prone to altruism than we really are, then we will be far more convincing in our attempts to deceive others. Self-deception might be an inevitable spin off of the profitable ability to deceive others.[50]

"Altruism" or altruism?

The concept of altruism with which we have been working is a technical one, drawn from the work of biologists. On this usage, a behavior counts as altruistic if it boosts the fitness of other organisms at a cost to the inclusive fitness of the agent. We have seen that biologists have powerful tools with which to demonstrate that much of what seems, in this technical sense, to be genuine altruism, is actually disguised genetic selfishness. When organisms aid their kin, they may boost their inclusive fitness. When they give help to other animals, even to members of other species, they may be engaged in reciprocal altruism; in helping others in expectation of a return that outweighs their costs. Even our moral emotions might be the product of genetic selfishness.

If that is all there is to morality, it seems that we shall be left with a bare simulacrum of it, shorn of its substantive content. Is morality no more than genetic selfishness? When people help one another, are they playing tit-for-tat: only assisting in the expectation of a return? This, we want to say, isn't morality at all. Strictly speaking, I do not act morally if I act only in my long-term interests, or even worse, in the interests of my genes. Altruism, genuine altruism, requires that we help others *for their sakes*, and not for our own.

We can easily convince ourselves that whatever else it is, reciprocal altruism is not genuine morality, by looking at the kind of downright *immoral* results to which it can give rise. If we act only in the interests of our genes, then we have little reason to aid those who will never be in a position to reciprocate. To be sure, we can think of some reasons to aid such people. Most obviously, aiding the indigent might be a good reputation-building strategy, if the aid is given publicly. By giving help when there is no possibility of reciprocation, we advertise our "altruism," thereby encouraging others to play TFT with us to our mutual benefit. Perhaps those who never give – or, more accurately, are never *seen* to give – to the indigent are regarded as potential defectors, and avoided by prospective partners in exchange.[51] Even secret giving can be explained using the resources biologists have available: if it is true that self-deception is an evolved adaptation, which disguises our selfishness from ourselves the better to hide it from others, then perhaps such apparently disinterested acts of charity are engaged in the better to convince ourselves of our own morality. In either case, the ultimate explanation is genetic selfishness. Altruism is revealed to be mere "altruism." The very fact that we need to disguise our true motivations even from ourselves shows how wide the gap is between our concept of morality, and the poor copy the biologists offer us.

Many philosophers and biologists have come to just such a melancholy conclusion. Once we realize that our moral emotions, supposedly our finest feelings, are the products of an evolutionary history in which long-term selfishness was systematically rewarded, we see that there really is no such thing as morality. Morality is – was *supposed* to be – about helping others for their sake, fairness and equity, equal consideration and justice. But it has its roots in selfishness and it bears the stamp of its origins.

In the light of these conclusions, some thinkers have gone so far as to argue that there really is no such thing as morality. It is a myth, as Richard Joyce puts it; and our belief that there is such a thing is unjustified.[52] He compares our situation to that of a paranoid person, John, who believes that Sally is persecuting him. Sally *might* be persecuting him, but given that we know that John is paranoid, we have little reason to rely upon John's testimony. He would believe that Sally was persecuting him, whether she was or not. Similarly, we would believe that there were moral facts and obligations whether there were or not: the dispositions to believe these things are built into our brains by evolution. Just as John's belief is unreliable because of his mental biases, so ours are unreliable because of ours.

Michael Ruse, a very prominent philosopher of biology, comes to similar conclusions.[53] Because the (alleged) existence of morality doesn't explain why we believe in morality, it is redundant. It plays no role in explaining our beliefs, nor our actions. Evolution explains both, not morality. This seems to me a mistake. The error lies in measuring morality against an inappropriate standard. It might be useful here to compare evolutionary explanations of morality with evolutionary explanations of belief in God. Several biologists have suggested that belief in God might be biologically adaptive.[54] Neuroscientists have even managed to locate the region of the brain that seems to play an important role in religious experience: the temporal lobe, which, when stimulated with powerful magnets, causes most people to have "God experiences."[55] Now, if this is true, it seems to me to be very bad news for theists. If belief in God is a product of evolution, and can be produced with the simplest brain manipulations, then we have little reason to place much faith in religious experience, whether our own or others. Given that most people would believe in God whether or not he existed, and would continue to have religious experiences in the absence of the divine, the actual existence of God seems redundant to an explanation of religious experience. As Michael Persinger, whose work on the temporal lobe opened up this line of enquiry, put it, neuroscience seems to show that "religion is a property of the brain, only the brain and has little to do with what's out there."[56]

This is exactly the claim made by Joyce and Ruse. Morality, they say, is a product of our minds, and has little to do with what is out there. But they miss a crucial difference between religion and morality. Religion is, precisely, concerned with what is "out there." If there is a God, his existence is entirely independent of our belief in him. If his existence is explanatorily inert, then this is very bad news for theists. But it is very plausible to think that morality is not like this. It is not independent of us and our beliefs, in the way in which God (and neutrons and giraffes and Italy) is. Instead, it is at least partially constituted of our beliefs and moral emotions. If pretty much all rational beings share a moral reaction (for example the strongly held belief that torture is wrong), and that reaction is a response to actual facts in the world (in this case, the suffering of victims of torture) then the fact that there is nothing *beyond* the feelings of observers and victims to refer to is neither here nor there. We have all we need to constitute moral facts.

The temptation to measure entities against inappropriate standards is a perennial one. It's the kind of temptation that led some philosophers to think that colors aren't *really* real. They realized that the colors we see are partially the product of our perceptual systems. For eyes like ours, (some) roses are red. For insects, they might be another color, or no color at all; under the sun of a different world, they might be brown or blue. So these philosophers concluded that colors weren't real: not *fully* real; as real as shapes and hardness and so on. In fact, the problem lay not with the colors, but with the tests they were required to pass before they counted as part of the furniture of the universe (as philosophers like to put it). If we all agree that roses are red – that they appear red to almost all of us, under conditions almost all of us agree count as normal – then they *are* red. We are mistaken if we think that colors are real in *the same way* as squares are, if we think that redness is simply "out there" like atoms and giraffes. But this is no reason to think that colors aren't real at all. So long as we can all agree upon them, and we have much the same experience of them, there is no reason to think that their ontological status is somehow lesser than those objects that exist regardless of our responses to them. The fact that we can use colors for such important tasks as controlling traffic demonstrates that we have no qualms about their existence.

Colors are a kind of thing that owe their existence to our perceptual equipment, as well as the physical features of colored objects. This does not make them illusory. We are not making a mistake when we say that roses are red. It is nothing like saying that moon is made of green cheese, or mistaking, from a distance, a gnarled tree for a person. Nor is it a merely subjective assertion (it is not like the statement "vanilla ice cream is the nicest," the truth of which varies from person to person). If we can count as mistaken in applying a predicate like "red," as we clearly can (I will usually be mistaken if I say that grass is red), and if we have clear and generally agreed upon conditions for the application of our color terms, there seems to be little reason to think that there is anything "iffy" about them.

But if we can say this for colors, then it seems that we can say it for morality as well. We have (relatively) clear criteria for the application of moral predicates. There are clear examples of moral mistakes ("torturing babies for fun is good") and generally agreed upon moral paradigms (it is not just Christians who recognize that Mother Theresa or Saint Francis of Assisi were good; not just Buddhists who recognize the goodness in Siddhartha Gautama). So what if our evolved capacities, dispositions and emotions play an ineliminable role in constituting moral goodness and badness? Our perceptual system, which is just as certainly the product of evolution, plays an equally significant role in constituting color. Since almost all of us – all except those who we rightly regard as suffering from an abnormality, whether it be psychopathy or blindness – share the same reactions, and since we have agreed-upon conditions for the application of our color (moral) terms, we have no reason to regard them as illusions.[57]

Moreover, just like our color perception, our moral reactions track real properties of events and people. Color perception reliably tracks the surface reflectant properties (roughly, the wavelengths of light reflected by the surface) of objects, so that objects appear different colors if their surface reflectant properties alter. It is harder to say what our moral reactions track, but it is clear enough that, at least to some extent, they track physical features of the world. They certainly are keyed quite closely into perception of suffering in others. The extent to which this is so – the extent to which we could describe all moral properties and events in purely physical terms – is a contentious issue among philosophers. But all sides agree on this much: the moral reflects physical features sufficiently so that the moral is *supervenient* on the physical, which is to say, whether or not we can adequately capture moral properties in physical terms alone, there are no moral differences between two situations unless there are physical differences. To this extent, we can be sure that our moral emotions are reliable guides to physical features of the world.

The philosophers who think that the evolutionary history of morality somehow undermines our usual conception of it are not yet done, however. They might claim that even if my argument shows that morality is not exactly an illusion, nevertheless, the picture of morality that emerges from it is very different from the picture I sketched at the beginning of this chapter, where we found that morality was a system of prescriptions, essentially concerned with the welfare of others, which were objective, unconditionally binding, and intrinsically motivating. Morality has a Kantian side, concerned with true beliefs, and a Humean side, concerned with motivations to action. But the defense of morality just outlined vindicates only part of the analysis. If morality is real in so far as, and because, the emotions that underlie it are real and generally shared, then only its Humean side is vindicated. Hume argued that morality was entirely to be explained in *subjectivist* terms; in terms, that is, of the emotions aroused in us by the contemplation of actions and states of affairs that we judge to be morally good or bad. We, like most evolutionary ethicists, have followed Hume in focusing upon the feelings that motivate actions, both ours and those of other animals, and in asking whether they are likely to include dispositions to care for the welfare of others. We have been concerned with morality as a *subjective* phenomenon, manifested in the feelings to which evolution might give rise. But this is not the whole of morality, as we have analyzed it. Morality, we said, was as much about belief as feeling. If we are forced, in the light of evolution, to give up on the cognitive side of morality, then the picture of the moral that will emerge will be radically altered. Evolution will have undermined not morality *per se*, but at least our commonsense concept of it.

Some philosophers have argued that this is just the route we should take. Michael Ruse is a case in point. Like us, Ruse locates the basis of the moral emotions in reciprocal and kin altruism (indeed, I have mined his work in developing the account of the origins of morality presented here). But Ruse is, explicitly, a Humean; for him, therefore, there is nothing more to morality than the kinds of emotions and dispositions which natural selection has implanted within us. He grants, as he must, that we cannot help but think that morality is objective, that it somehow transcends mere feelings. But the apparent objectivity of morality is, he claims, an illusion, foisted upon us by the same evolutionary process that gave us the moral emotions. We shall be more strongly motivated to act upon our desires if we believe that they reflect something beyond them, so the illusion of objectivity is functional, and has an evolutionary source. It remains, nevertheless, an illusion.[58]

But if we are forced to revise our concept of morality in the light of evolution, rejecting its cognitive side and the illusion of objectivity, we shall be left with a problem and a mystery. The problem is that, just as evolutionary theory might predict, people's moral emotions are much stronger and much more reliably triggered by close kin and members of one's community than by the more distant. People are often much more upset by a small slight to their parents or siblings than by a great injustice a thousand miles away. This is a problem, because many of us think that everyone ought to be given equal consideration, no matter where they are. In some of our moods, almost all of us think that the significant interests of the distant needy should outweigh the trivial interests of ourselves, our community and our close kin. Yet we continue to behave as if we didn't believe this: we spend money on extravagant presents for ourselves and for our family, and ignore (or donate little to) famines in Africa. If morality is just a matter of shared feeling, then perhaps it extends no further than the range of our reliably triggered moral emotions. Perhaps we are just wrong in thinking we have significant obligations to the distant needy. So Ruse, for one, concludes.[59] This is a problem, because it seems to involve the sacrifice of a very significant part of the content of our morality. If it is possible to retain this part, so that we can criticize others (and ourselves) when we neglect the distant needy and hope thereby to enlarge the scope of moral concern, this would be greatly preferable to following Ruse down the road of restricting the range of morality.

The subjectivist picture of morality, at least as developed by Ruse, has costs, both moral and conceptual. It also leaves us confronting a mystery: why is it that some of us almost all of the time, and most of us at least some of the time, have succeeded in expanding the scope of our moral concern beyond the targets which evolution predicts? Why is it that many people feel guilty when we remind them how many Ethiopian lives could be saved by the money they spend on chocolate bars or new shoes? Why is it that the circle of moral concern has grown over the past two hundred years, so that many people formerly excluded from it, or given little moral weight, have been included as full members of the moral community: people of all races, homosexuals, women, increasingly even animals? These changes have been too swift and too widespread to reflect genetic mutations. Instead, they are much more plausibly seen to be the upshot of moral *argument*. Sentiment *follows* conviction; it does not always lead it. It seems that there must therefore be a role for the cognitive elements of morality.

We can only make sense of moral argumentation, especially, but not only, as it is involved in the process of our expanding the sphere of moral concern, if we suppose that we engage in debate using our concept of morality as a constant reference point, *and* that our moral emotions are flexible enough to be shaped by the outcomes of our debates. We began to include blacks as full members of the sphere of moral concern, for instance, when rational arguments showed that there were no morally relevant differences between them and members of other races already in the sphere. It may well be that many people were intellectually convinced of this long before they responded appropriately, because intellectual conviction did not automatically engender emotional response. Eventually, however, most of us came to care (almost) as much about injustices to members of other races as to members of our own. The concept of morality had forced a revision in our moral responses.

But how did we come to have this concept? How did we go from having certain emotional responses to a range of acts and threats, to having a concept that we could then turn upon the very emotions which (presumably) engendered it? Here I get speculative. I suggest that the concept of morality is itself the product of evolution, and that we have come by it from an unexpected source: as an inevitable by-product of the development of that *im*moral phenomenon, self-deception.

Trivers's argument, you will recall, was that self-deception evolved because it was in our genetic interest to be taken in by our own claims of morality. Most of the time, it is in our interests to behave in accordance with the demands of morality upon us, but it is also in our interests to keep an eye out for occasions on which defection is profitable and we can get away with it without damage to our reputations. We want to *seem* moral without always *being* moral. But we'll be able to evade the increasingly sophisticated cheater detection mechanisms of our conspecifics only if we can fool *ourselves* into believing that we really are altruistic, that we sometimes act *for the sake of others*, and not merely because we expect a return. It seems to me that this hypothesis has an interesting implication. If we are to deceive ourselves, if we are to believe our protestations of selflessness, we must necessarily believe that morality is possible. Our acceptance of our own, perhaps false, claim to be a moral being requires that we possess the concept of morality. The notion we need here cannot be of morality as merely an adaptation, in any narrow sense, of a morality founded on reciprocal altruism, because our aim is precisely to convince potential reciprocators that we do not limit our concern to those who can benefit us. Trivers-style self-deception requires us to possess the *full* notion of morality, not its ersatz copy. It is altruism we must believe in, not "altruism." Thus, the idea of morality, the idea we have appealed to to criticize the copy foisted upon us by biology, might itself be the product of natural selection. We are evolved to believe in morality, the better to promote our own, narrower, concerns.

Once we have the concept, however, we are able to use it. We are able to judge our own and others' behavior against its standards, and not merely against those of genetic selfishness. We are able to begin the process of elucidation of the content of morality, the exploration of what it requires of us, in the Socratic manner: by examining our concepts. In this sense, moral philosophy might rest on an evolutionary basis. It is evolution that gives us our concept of morality, the very concept that we might utilize to criticize the genetic selfishness of evolution.

Stephen Jay Gould introduced the term *exaptation* in evolutionary biology. An exaptation is a characteristic of an organism which has been selected for because it fulfils one function, but which is then utilized for a quite different purpose. For example it has been suggested that feathers initially evolved due to their qualities as effective insulation: they enabled their possessors to regulate their body temperature more effectively. However, the animals that possessed them later found they could be put to different uses: they enabled gliding, and eventually flight. I am suggesting that morality might be an exaptation. We evolved a set of moral emotions, and, as a consequence, a conception of morality as objective and unconditionally binding. We then *exapted* this concept: using it is an independent measure of behavior. We turned it back against its origins. Morality, I suggest, might have had its source in the very self-deception we now condemn in its name.

Morality on other planets

I shall briefly consider one final evolutionary argument against moral objectivity. This one is inspired by reflecting on the fact that we humans may very well not be the only moral beings in the universe. Morality, full-blown, may have emerged on other planets. But what would alien morality look like? Some evolutionary ethicists argue that the kinds of actions that we regard as obligatory might be held to be immoral by some aliens. If their genetic constitution were different to ours or if their evolution took a different path, then the illusion of objectivity under which they labor might attach to actions we regard as immoral. Surely this is sufficient to show that objective morality is an illusion? If there were an objective morality, then it would be binding upon all rational creatures (as Kant pointed out). But there is no such morality.

What are we to make of this argument? The contention that the contents of our morality is sensitive to the details of evolutionary history is plausible. What counts as harming and benefitting someone, most obviously, is in important part a function of their biology, which makes them vulnerable to certain dangers and in need of certain resources and opportunities. But this fact is surely not sufficient to establish the species-relativism of morality. The fact that Australians are required to drive on the left hand side of the road, while Americans are required to drive on the right, does not establish any kind of interesting moral relativism. Similarly, the fact – if it is a fact – that, if evolution had taken a different path, we might have been required to eat one another's feces (to use Michael Ruse's rather off-putting example) is not sufficient to establish the species relativism of morality. It still might be the case that, considered at a high enough level of abstraction, all beings would evolve the same morality. It would differ in its specific injunctions ("eat up all your brother's feces!") but its most general principles would be just the same ("treat others as you would have them treat you").

What if evolution had taken a *radically* different path, so that not only might different kinds of actions harm and benefit different kinds of creatures, but there might even be different *kinds* of creatures? Would this be sufficient to establish a species-relativism strong enough to refute moral objectivity? At least one philosopher has argued that it would (and that reflection on this fact should be sufficient to undermine the illusion of objectivity, even in the absence of evidence that evolution actually has unfolded differently elsewhere in the universe). Waller asks us to consider a kind of creature something like the Borg in *Star Trek*: as intelligent as *Homo sapiens*, but with no notion of individuality, perhaps because of a haplo-diploid chromosomal arrangement like ants and bees. These creatures would have fundamental moral obligations quite different from ours, and would find our emphasis on the individual and her rights "not merely absurd, but morally odious".[60]

I am not sure that the discovery that our morality is merely local should cause us to question its objectivity; it might be that local objectivity is objectivity enough. Be that as it may, I am in any case unconvinced that Waller's thought experiment succeeds in showing that our morality is local. Who is the subject of moral obligations, in Waller's thought experiment? He seems implicitly to assume that each ant-like entity is comparable to each one of us. But this seems to me a mistake. It might be better to think of the entire community of ant-like entities as an individual being, so that the community would be the appropriate subject of rights and obligations. If this is correct, then the fact that each ant-like entity has no rights against the community is no more interesting than the fact that my skin cells have no rights against me: they are part of me, and are appropriately sacrificed for the greater good. If, on the other hand, each ant-like entity should be conceived of as an individual in its own right, then we can insist they are making a mistake in rejecting our notion of individual rights.

Evolved morality is real morality

Ruse, Waller, and the other evolutionary deflationists are half right. They are right in thinking that morality must have its origins in (genetic) self-interest; it could not have been selected for otherwise. They are also right in thinking that evolution alone could give us the Humean side of morality, its subjective and motivational side. However, they are wrong in thinking that unless we reject philosophical naturalism altogether, and accept a supernatural source for morality, we need to conclude that that is all there is to morality. Instead, evolution is capable of endowing us with the notion of morality as an objective system, and providing us with the means of acting in accordance with it. That is to say, evolution can account for the origins of a morality which meets all the conditions of our analysis: both its Humean, motivational, side, and also its broadly Kantian, objective side.

Morality comes to us as a product of our evolutionary history. This history systematically favored (genetic) selfish behavior and eliminated genetic altruism. Yet it gives us the very concept that leads us to condemn selfishness and approve of selflessness. Evolution provided us with a concept we can turn back against evolution. From the mindless and mindlessly selfish rose beings capable of rationality and morality.

Throughout this book, I shall be concerned with steering a middle course between those thinkers who deny the significance of evolution (and more generally our biology), for thought and morality, and those who claim that we can capture everything that is significant about human beings in essentially biological terms. As we can already begin to see, both sides capture part, but only part, of the truth. We have morality only as a consequence of our evolutionary past. Moreover, our morality continues to bear the clear traces of that past in it, and it is reasonable to think that it always will, no matter how long we human beings survive. However, the morality we have, today, is very different from the core of proto-morality we share with vampire bats and cleaner fish. It is more extensive and more demanding, as a result of millennia of rational elaboration of its content. Children today inherit this morality from their parents and from their culture. They are *taught* an ethic of equal concern. Our inheritance from past generations is not only via our genes, but also through our socialization and our education. As a result, the intellectual and moral development of each child follows a quite different route, to a quite different destination, from that of its hunter-gatherer ancestors. Our evolutionary past constrains what we can think and believe and hope for; equally, it opens us up to unexpected, and ever-changing, vistas of transformation and (we can hope) progress.

3

The Stone Age mind

Just as one can now flip open Gray's Anatomy to any page and find an intricately detailed depiction of some part of our evolved species-typical morphology, we anticipate that in 50 or 100 years one will be able to pick up an equi-valent reference work for psychology and find in it detailed information-processing descriptions of the multitude of evolved species-typical adaptations of the human mind, including how they are mapped onto the corresponding neuro-anatomy and how they are constructed by developmental programs.

John Tooby and Leda Cosmides, *The Psychological Foundations of Culture*

The vogue for finding moral lessons in evolutionary theory has now largely passed. Though philosophers, biologists and game theorists continue to expend a great deal of effort on trying to uncover the biological sources of morality, they now, on the whole, think their work has few implications for our understanding of how we ought to behave. In this chapter, we turn to another area of intellectual inquiry which tries to understand the human mind within its evolutionary context, and which hopes thereby to illuminate *contemporary* ways of thought, both normal and pathological.

There have been two waves of evolutionary theorizing about human mind and behavior in the past quarter of a century. The first was sociobiology, which attracted a storm of controversy. The second, more recent, and as yet less well known, is evolutionary psychology.

Both claim that the application of Darwinian ideas to human beings yields new insights into our behavior, and into what kinds of societies we might hope to achieve. Moreover, as I shall argue, their claims are directly relevant to our morality and our politics.

Sociobiology's best-known proponent is E. O. Wilson; indeed, the movement takes its title from his magnificent volume of that name, published in 1975. *Sociobiology: The New Synthesis* was devoted to the study of the social behavior of various species of animals (Wilson's primary area of expertise is the study of ants), and made many important contributions to the field. But it was his attempt to apply these ideas to human beings that attracted the most attention. Critics eviscerated Wilson for his claims that human behavior should be seen as biologically driven, and aimed at enhancing the genetic fitness of the actors. Sociobiology did not attempt to draw moral lessons from the large-scale process of evolution. It was careful to avoid the mistake of identifying what has evolved with what is good, or to see in the (supposed) direction of evolution a model for human societies. But it did claim that human behavior, preferences, desires, and abilities were the product of natural selection, and that we *therefore* were constrained in what we might achieve. To this extent, claimed its critics, sociobiology was continuous with Social Darwinism: yet another apology for the status quo – for capitalism, male dominance, racism, and war – based upon its supposed inevitability.[61]

I shall not discuss sociobiology here; at least, not directly. Few people today continue to describe themselves as sociobiologists. The debate has moved on, and is now centered on evolutionary psychology. Evolutionary psychology builds upon the work of sociobiologists, to such an extent that some people regard it simply as "rebranded sociobiology."[62] However, it is plausible to maintain that evolutionary psychology has contributed a distinctive approach to sociobiological questions – a focus upon the mind, and upon the empirical testing of hypotheses – which was largely absent from sociobiological speculations. In any case, I shall focus on the work of people who describe themselves as evolutionary psychologists.

The central claim of evolutionary psychology is simple. Most features – and almost all complex features – of the physiological structures of organisms are adaptations that enabled their ancestors to flourish in their ancestral environments. So (for example) we have kidneys because they remove waste from our bloodstream. That our physiology can be broken down into component adaptations is something we could predict from natural selection. An inspection of the morphology of organisms confirms this prediction: indeed, their organs are very frequently superb adaptations to their local environment.

This is as true for human beings as for any other animals. Our bodies, too, are so well adapted to the environments in which our ancestors lived that we can be sure that a great many of our features are the product of natural selection. But we have no reason to think that natural selection applies only to bodies. After all, it is not only the physiology of other animals that has been shaped by natural selection, but also their behavior. Natural selection did not produce sterile castes of workers in the eusocial insects (that is, those insects which live in colonies with extensive division of labor and a high degree of cooperation, such as bees and ants) and then leave them to work out for themselves that they ought to aid the queen in producing as many of their sisters as possible. Rather, it selected the appropriate kinds of behavior, at the same time as it selected the kinds of physiology best suited to the life of a eusocial insect. Indeed, it had to: in the absence of the appropriate kinds of behavior, having the right kinds of morphological characteristics would not have constituted an advantage to the social insects. If this is true of other organisms, shouldn't we expect it to be true of ourselves? Shouldn't we expect our behavior, and therefore the minds that are very often proximate (that is, immediate) causes of that behavior, to be adapted to the environments in which our ancestors lived?

The foundational claim of evolutionary psychology is, therefore, that human minds are adapted for the environments in which our ancestors had to make their way. But this is not the controversial claim. Stated in this general and abstract form, the claim is *obviously* true. Of course human beings are cognitively, as well as physiologically, adapted to ancestral environments. Only human beings, for example, have the brain structures that underlie fully-fledged natural languages, as well as the morphological features (such as vocal cords), which permit us to speak. Decades of intensive effort to teach other animals to understand human languages have yielded few positive results, yet almost every human child picks up their native language (plus any others which are regularly spoken around them) with apparent ease. There can be no doubt that this capacity is innate, in the sense that humans are born with brain structures (or, perhaps better, the propensity to develop brain structures) which, in the right environment, will enable them to learn a natural language. Nor can there be any doubt that this ability is heritable, or that it is an adaptation, selected for because it increased the fitness of our ancestors. Indeed, studies of patients who have suffered neurological trauma, or developmental disorders, have enabled us to locate the parts of the brain dedicated to processing language with a fair degree of precision. Just as evolutionary psychology claims, we have mental organs that are adaptations, which enable the kinds of behavior characteristic of human beings.

Since all sides recognize (or ought to recognize) that our minds are the product of evolution, and are very likely to bear traces of our evolutionary past, the debate between proponents of evolutionary psychology and their critics does not turn on the question of whether human beings possess cognitive adaptations. Instead, it focuses on the number and specificity of these adaptations. Evolutionary psychologists claim that the human mind consists of a large number of mental "organs," each dedicated to a specific task, each relatively isolated from the others and therefore acting relatively autonomously, whereas their critics typically maintain that the mind is best thought of as a general purpose learning tool, which enables human beings to adapt to a very wide range of environments, and which gives to their behavior a degree of plasticity unknown among other species.[63] As we shall see, a great deal turns on this apparently esoteric question, not just for abstruse debates in the philosophy of mind and cognitive science, but for morality as well.

In the middle part of the twentieth century, *behaviorism* dominated psychology. Behaviorists, led by B. F. Skinner, argued for a radical version of the position I have attributed to the opponents of evolutionary psychology. For Skinner and his disciples, the mind was no more than a general purpose learning device. Of course, no one can coherently deny that *something* is innate in the brains of animals. If the mind was entirely a blank slate, we would be unable to account for learning itself. The mind must be capable of noticing resemblances between stimuli, for instance, or it could not recognize the reoccurrence of similar inputs and learn from their association. Skinner's claim was that the mind contained *little more* than the machinery required for learning. Apart from a few simple devices to recognize similarity and difference, the most important piece of machinery was a reward and punishment center. All animals are naturally attracted by pleasure and repelled by pain. Skinner's suggestion is that it is on the basis of these facts about ourselves, and our learning mechanisms, that all behavior is shaped.

Specifically, Skinner claimed that, in the course of development, animals would learn to associate certain stimuli with feelings of pleasure and pain. These feelings would act as *reinforcers* of its behavior, causing it to be more likely to repeat behavior associated with positive reinforcers, and more likely to avoid behavior associated with negative. Skinner's inspiration here was the work of the Russian scientist, Ivan Pavlov. Pavlov had noticed that if he rang a bell every time he fed the dogs in his laboratory, the dogs came to associate the sound of the bell with food. They would soon begin to salivate at the sound of a bell, even in the absence of food. For Skinner, the ringing of the bell was a conditioned association, and the conditioning was successful because it was reinforced by the food, which is a stimulus that dogs naturally find pleasurable (note that it is a very simple matter to give an evolutionary explanation of why dogs – in fact, all animals – find food naturally rewarding, since those of their ancestors who didn't like food would have been unlikely to have many descendants). Skinner's more radical claim was that all behavior, human and other animal alike, was conditioned in just this way. Everything we do, we do because we have been rewarded for acting in similar ways in the past. Accordingly, merely by altering the nature of the reinforcers, human behavior could be remade, in any image we pleased: if we would only put aside our fantasies about human free will and worth (get *Beyond Freedom and Dignity*, as the title of Skinner's didactic novel dramatizing the Utopian power of his work had it), we could solve all the problems which plague human life.

The behaviorist vogue has passed, and for good reason. The evidence, from many different regions of psychology and neurobiology, that the minds of animals are not the all-purpose learning machines envisaged by Skinner, is now overwhelming. One piece of data that behaviorism finds it difficult to account for is the compartmentalization of the brain. Brain imaging studies, and evidence from people who

suffer strokes which damage a region of their brain, have shown convincingly that the same functions are handled in the same areas of the
brain in almost all people. People who suffer a stroke that predominantly affects the right hemisphere of their brain often become very
impulsive. If the damage occurs in certain regions, they might develop
a range of bizarre symptoms, such as anosognosia, in which the
(apparently otherwise rational) patient denies that there is anything
wrong with a paralyzed limb, or even somatoparaphrenia, in which the
patient denies that the limb is theirs at all. It is worth reproducing a
short dialogue, reported by Eduardo Bisiach, to get a sense of just how
specific and strange the effects of local brain damage can be. Bisiach
held his patient's paralyzed hand between his own hands, and asked the
patient to look at them:

> Examiner: Whose hands are these?
> Patient: Your hands.
> Examiner: How many of them?
> Patient: Three.
> Examiner: Ever seen a man with *three* hands?
> Patient: A hand is the extremity of an arm. Since you have three
> arms it follows that you have three hands.[64]

Though the brain is sometimes able to adapt to deficits and damage,
especially if they occur while the person is young, when functions usually served by one brain region can relocate to another, the evidence
that many functions are normally localized is now overwhelming.
Damage to specific brain regions causes quite specific impairments:
patients may lose just the ability to recognize faces, just the use of
language (aphasia), or even just experience difficulty with certain parts
of speech, such as pronouns and articles.[65]

A thoroughgoing behaviorist might come up with some way to
accommodate these findings. It's odd, from a behaviorist point of view,
that the brain is so compartmentalized, but it's not decisive proof that
the brain doesn't *function* as an all-purpose learning device. It just
turns out, the behaviorist might argue, that for some reason the
learned associations are stored in different regions of the brain. But
there are other data, drawn from just the kinds of experiments the
behaviorists loved, which show that the evidence against behaviorism

cannot be so easily dismissed. If we investigate conditioned learning in different animal species, we find that there are limitations, constraints, and dispositions that directly contradict the claims of behaviorism.

According to behaviorism, animals are just as capable of learning one set of associations as another. However, when this assumption is tested, it proves to be false. Instead, there are differences in the kinds of stimuli that are salient for different animals. For example, rhesus monkeys reared in captivity, which never encounter the snakes common in their natural environment, can easily be taught to be afraid of them. In one experiment, captive-born rhesus monkeys were shown a film of wild monkeys reacting fearfully to a snake. Though the captive monkeys had exhibited no fear of snakes before seeing the film, afterwards they were terrified of even a toy snake. But all attempts to make them fearful of a toy rabbit or a flower, using film which had been cut to make it seem as if the wild monkeys were reacting with terror to these objects, failed miserably.[66] Similarly, male white-crowned sparrows reared in isolation from other birds of their species fail to learn their characteristic song. If a white-crowned sparrow is reared with older males of a different species of sparrow, it may come to learn their song. But if it is reared with at least one other adult male white-crowned sparrow, it learns only its song.[67]

Behaviorism finds it hard to account for these results. Both examples show that a lot of behavior is learned, just as Skinner argued. Without the appropriate stimulation, neither the sparrows nor the monkeys come to behave in species-typical ways. But certain sorts of stimuli are much more salient for different species, and certain associations much easier. The brains of these animals are learning machines (among other things), but they are not *all-purpose* learning machines, as behaviorists supposed. Instead, they come pre-structured, in such a way that some kinds of learning are relatively easy (requiring only brief exposure to relevant stimuli), some more difficult, and some downright impossible. Moreover, the kinds of stimuli that are particularly salient are precisely those that are evolutionarily relevant. Rhesus monkeys find snake-fear relevant, because snakes represented a constant threat in their environment of adaptation, and white-crowned sparrows' brains are especially well set up to learn their song because their ancestors used it to attract mates and defend territory.

There is evidence that some stimuli are especially salient for humans. Think of the typical stimuli of phobic responses, where people find themselves reacting with inappropriate and intense fear in situations in which (as they acknowledge) they are perfectly safe. The objects of this fear are frequently just the kinds of things our ancestors would have good reason to be fearful of: snakes, spiders, heights, open spaces (which would make them visible to predators), and so on. There is also some experimental evidence that human beings form some associations much more readily than others: associating mild electric shocks with images of snakes more easily than with images of frayed electric cords.[68]

Noam Chomsky's work in linguistics provides further support for the claim that the human brain is not an all-purpose learning machine, but is instead pre-structured in significant ways. Chomsky claims that, beneath the evident differences between the six thousand or so human languages, there is a shared, deep, structure. This structure, he argues, is innate: it is preprogrammed into the human brain, in the same way that the song of the white-crowned sparrow is programmed into its brain. Like the sparrow, the human child will not learn any language at all, unless she is exposed to one: it is the structure of language that is innate, not the language itself. But she possesses a language-acquisition device, which (if she is presented with the relevant stimulus at the right time) will enable her to pick up any human language with an ease belying the enormous complexity of the task. For many evolutionary psychologists, this very ease clinches the case against behaviorism. They invoke the *poverty of the stimulus* argument, noting that the range of language to which a child needs to be exposed is really quite small, in comparison to the variety of the utterances of which she is then capable, and the sheer complexity of the language learned.

Further evidence for the hypothesis that language is somehow innate comes from the birth of new languages. Sometimes, people find themselves in a situation in which they lack a common language, as, for example, did the slaves on board the ships that took them from Africa to the Americas. In these circumstances, people often devise a *pidgin*: a skeletal language with which to communicate. A true pidgin has little grammatical structure, and is very limited in expressive power, but an interesting thing occurs when a new generation is born to people who speak a pidgin. Apparently spontaneously, the children elaborate an entire grammatical structure, forming a new, fully-fledged, language on the basis of the pidgin. These new languages are called *creoles*, and possess the full expressive powers of any natural language. The persuasive suggestion of Chomsky and his followers is that, when children are exposed to a language, even a pidgin, their language acquisition device goes to work, and provides it with a full-blown grammar. Thus, they endow the new language with the deep structure common to all natural languages, spontaneously giving birth to one of humankind's most complex products.

We could continue to pile up the evidence, but it is surely not necessary. The conclusion is inescapable: radical behaviorism is false, because human minds – like those possessed by other animals – are not blank slates or even all-purpose learning devices. Instead, they come pre-structured in important ways, and these structures constrain how we, as a species, are capable of behaving and thinking. So much ought to be uncontroversial. Though there are still people who reject this view, they are misinformed, and their position is untenable. But how far should we go down the nativist road? Just how much, and just what, is innate in the human mind? Are the constraints many or few; are the limits they set broad or narrow?

The parties to this debate typically assume that there is but one answer to this question. Either nothing is significantly innate in the human mind, or we come into the world with a set of in-built dispositions that strongly structure our preferences and capabilities. My hunch is that this is a mistake: the degree to which the mind is pre-structured varies across different parts of life. We have strong in-built likes and dislikes in food, for example; it is very difficult to get human beings to prefer rotting meat to sweet fruit. But there is no reason to think that just because our food preferences are significantly innate, so are our political preferences and the kinds of social lives to which we can adapt.

In this and the next chapter, I shall examine evolutionary psychology at its most controversial: as it argues for significant constraints on our social life and gender relations. Before we get to these claims, however, it is worth examining the kinds of arguments advanced by evolutionary psychologists, setting out the different kinds of constraints upon the human mind that its practitioners identify, and isolating the ways in which their claims might be significant for our morality and politics. The thesis that I have been examining up until now, that the brain is strongly compartmentalized, has attracted the most philosophical debate. But there is a second important thesis characteristic of evolutionary psychology, which is, I suspect, more important for human morality, and which attracts more popular attention: the claim that our desires and preferences are to be understood as evolved adaptations.

Modularity

Followers of Chomsky postulate that the normal human mind possesses a language acquisition device. According to many psychologists, cognitive scientists, and philosophers, such a device is a mental *module*; a component of the mind that is dedicated to one task (or a small number of tasks) and which it performs in relative isolation. Evolutionary psychologists claim that we possess many such modules: a module for face recognition, a module for estimating distances in visual perception, and so on. Each module is *informationally encapsulated*, that is to say, its internal workings are isolated from the information available to the rest of the mind. The Müller-Lyer illusion is a classic example of informational encapsulation:

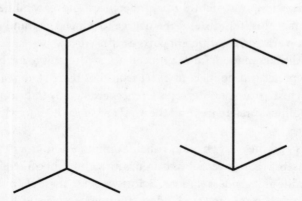

Figure 1: The Müller-Lyer illusion

Both vertical lines are precisely the same length, yet we cannot help see-ing the one on the right as longer. The information that the lines are the same length does nothing to dissipate the illusion; hence, the module concerned with estimating length must be informationally encapsu-lated.[69] The information that the lines are the same length is not available to it. Similarly, the knowledge that a particular spider is harmless is not available to the module responsible for the fear reactions of the phobic.[70]

Psychologists have long known about phenomena such as the Müller-Lyer illusion. They study them for what they might reveal about the workings of the perceptual system, and the manner in which the brain processes information. These studies take their place in a long tradition of studying instances where judgments go wrong, in order to see what light they cast on more normal cases. But the actual phenomena have traditionally not been regarded as important. Psychologists did not con-clude, from the existence of optical illusions, that people generally make mistakes in their judgments. However, recent work by evolutionary psychologists elevates the importance to cognition of illusions and other (alleged) biases. For these psychologists, the biases and bents that careful study reveals to be inherent in the human brain give important clues to the manner in which we negotiate and interpret the world. They suggest that we see it through lenses made for us by natural selection.

Some of the modules allegedly discovered by evolutionary psych-ologists are directly concerned with our moral life. For example, Leda Cosmides and John Tooby argue that human beings possess mental modules that enable their possessors to solve problems that would fre-quently have been encountered in the EEA, including problems of direct relevance to morality, such as the fair sharing of scarce resources. Cosmides and Tooby adapted a pre-existing tool, the *Wason selection task*, to argue for the existence of these mental modules. They com-pared the performance of subjects on two Wason selection tasks.

Wason selection task 1

You are employed by the city of Cambridge to study the use of public transportation in the area. According to a previously published report on this topic, the following statement is true:

If a person goes into Boston, then that person takes the subway.

You are interested in discovering whether this is still true. You are presented with a number of cards, which record the transportation habits of Cambridge residents. On one side of the card is printed their destination, and on the other their means of transport. Here are four such cards:

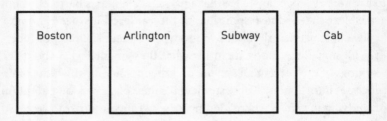

Figure 2: The Wason selection task, version 1

Is the rule true for the people whose transportation habits are recorded here? Which cards *must* you turn over to test the rule?

Wason selection task 2

You are an anthropologist studying a Polynesian people called the Kaluame, a tribe ruled over by the dictatorial chieftain, Big Kiku. He makes all those who swear loyalty to him tattoo their faces as a sign of their allegiance. Thus, all, and only, Big Kiku supporters have tattooed faces. Since Big Kiku is very unpopular with members of other tribes, being caught in another village with a tattooed face is certain to get the unfortunate Kiku supporter killed.

One day, four men who have been kicked out of their own villages come to Big Kiku starving and exhausted. They beg him for food. Big Kiku agrees to feed them, so long as each has his face tattooed. They must get their tattoos that night, and in the morning they will be fed. Each man agrees to the deal.

However, an informant tells you that Big Kiku hates some of these men, who have previously betrayed him. You therefore suspect that he might cheat on this occasion. The cards below record information about the fate of each man. On one side is recorded whether or not the man had his face tattooed, and on the other whether or not Big Kiku fed him the next day.

Figure 3: The Wason selection task, version 2

Which cards *must* you turn over to discover whether Big Kiku cheated any of these men?[71]

These two tasks are structurally identical. In both cases, the rule to be tested is of the form *modus ponens*: if *p* then *q*. Thus:

If you travel to Boston, then you take the subway.
If you have your face tattooed, Big Kiku will feed you.

To discover whether this rule is violated, we can ignore cases in which *p* is not the case. If you travel anywhere *other than* Boston, it does not matter how. The rule does not apply to your action, and you cannot violate it. Similarly, if you did not have your face tattooed, the second rule does not apply. We can also ignore cases in which all we know is that *q* was the case. The rule does not state "everyone who travels by subway goes to Boston." We can therefore ignore cards which tell us that the person travelled by subway. Turning them over cannot falsify the rule, no matter what they say on the other side. Similarly, we can ignore cards that tell us that Big Kiku fed the man concerned. Plainly Big Kiku did not cheat this man, whether he fed him either as a result of having his face tattooed, or for some other reason.

Therefore, we need only to turn over cards which tell us that *p* is the case, in order to test whether *q* indeed follows, and cards which tell us that not-*q* is the case, in order to see whether, in violation of the rule, *p* was the case. When we think of the selection task in this manner, the solution is obvious. In the first task, we need turn over only the card that tells us that the person traveled to Boston (in order to see whether they indeed traveled by subway) and the card that tells us that the person traveled by cab (in order to see whether, in violation of the rule, they went to Boston). In the second task, we need turn over only the card that tells us that the man got the tattoo (in order to see if Big Kiku fed him, true to his word) and the card that tells us that Big Kiku gave him nothing (in order to see if the man got the tattoo). We can ignore the others.

Logically, the two tasks are identical. However, if you are like most people, you probably found the second much easier to perform than the first. Cosmides and Tooby found that between 65% and 80% of subjects gave the correct answer in Wason selection tasks like the second, whereas only about 25% of subjects were able to give the right answer in selection tasks like the first. Why is this? Cosmides and Tooby argue that an important difference between those selection tasks we find difficult and those we find relatively easy is that the second kind are all concerned with free-riding, or other types of cheating, in social situations. We are much better at solving logical problems where cheating is at issue than those that turn upon more abstract questions. Yet the logical structure of the problems remains the same.

The fact that the substance of the problem makes an important difference to our ability to solve it constitutes, for Cosmides and Tooby, further evidence that the brain is not an all-purpose learning device. Just as studies of perception and illusion show that we have informationally encapsulated modules for judging distance and depth, so the study of the ease with which we comprehend social situations reveals that we have modules in the brain dedicated to the tasks of social life. In particular, the Wason Selection Task reveals that we possess a cheater-detection module, dedicated to enabling us to navigate the difficult waters of life in social groups. The explanation of the origin of this module, like that of the module or modules involved in perception, is evolutionary. Our ancestors faced recurrent problems to do with depth and distance perception in the EEA, the solution of which was, literally, a matter of life and death. So important was it to get quick and accurate answers to these questions that people with a dedicated brain module had an advantage over their conspecifics, and therefore had more numerous descendants. Similarly, and as we have seen in the previous chapter, they faced recurrent and important questions to do with social interaction and the detection of cheats. A brain module dedicated to this task therefore evolved alongside those involved in perception.

Cosmides and Tooby hope that further research will increase the number of modules discovered. Eventually, they believe, we will learn that most or all our important decisions are delegated to different parts of the brain, not undertaken by an all-purpose central processor. For the moment, little further evidence for the existence of morally relevant modules has been forthcoming, and even their most convincing example is vulnerable to challenge. Some philosophers and psychologists reject the claim that the apparent ease with which we negotiate Wason selection tasks dealing with social situations is evidence for a cheater-detection module. These challengers hold that it is the *familiarity* of the information and its *relevance* to everyday life that is most important, not its subject matter, and subsequent studies have been dedicated to testing this hypothesis.[72] A second significant challenge to the modularity explanation for performance on the Wason task comes from the traditional opponent of evolutionary psychology: social explanations. Whatever the EEA may have been like, it is obvious that we today must negotiate a complex social world, in which behavior is structured, in important ways, by norms and expectations. In this environment, we are constantly preoccupied with the moral or immoral behavior of others. From childhood, we are taught the importance of norms of fairness, and the need for constant vigilance in seeing these norms adhered to. So, it is not surprising that we acquire the ability to detect violations of those norms quickly and efficiently.[73]

Whatever the intrinsic interest of the subject, we needn't spend a great deal of time on the claim that the brain is massively modular. No doubt, if true, it will have interesting implications for morality, but until we know just what modules we might have, we are unable to see what the implications might be. Moreover, they may be far from earth-shattering. The fact that we have modules for this or that is an obstacle to the plasticity of human behavior, but it may not be a particularly significant one. What follows from the claim that we have a cheater-detector mechanism? Very little, so long as we can shape the content of the norms upon which that mechanism can go to work. If evolutionary psychology proves to have truly momentous consequences for human morality, it is likely that this will be not because it reveals the existence of modularity in the mind but because of what it shows about the fixity of human desire.

The evolution of desire

Evolutionary psychologists claim that our desires and preferences are the legacy of our evolutionary history. Since certain desires and preferences proved to be adaptive, they went into fixation, and the genetic basis for them became a permanent part of the human genome. A simple example should make the general form of this claim clear. There are remarkably robust, cross-cultural, commonalities in the taste preferences of normal human beings. For example, we tend to like sweet tasting and fatty foods. As any parent will tell you, it is difficult to get children to eat, never mind to enjoy, the subtle flavors of vegetables. What explains this preference? Perhaps our sweet tooth is an adaptation. In the EEA, our ancestors were engaged in a constant struggle to find sufficient calories to sustain life. In this environment, people who preferred energy-rich foods – that is, foods containing sugar and fat – had a decisive advantage over those with what today might seem more refined taste-buds. As a result, we come into the world with an in-built preference for high-calorie foods. Today, of course, for many of us in wealthy countries, this taste is dysfunctional. We find it all too easy to consume sufficient calories for our needs; for some, the challenge lies in resisting our evolved preferences, not in giving them full reign. In a new environment, a formerly adaptive preference wreaks havoc, in the form of obesity, strokes and heart attacks. Nevertheless, we have the preference because it was once valuable.

I believe it will help, at this point, to introduce some terminology. Biologists call evolutionary explanations *ultimate* explanations. To give an ultimate explanation of a characteristic is to explain it in terms of its selection history, of what it is ultimately *for*. The explanation of our preference for sugar in terms of its adaptive function in the EEA is an ultimate explanation: it explains the phenomenon in terms of its function, and it was this function that was the target of natural selection. But an ultimate explanation of a behavior tells us nothing about how it is implemented in the life of organisms. Evolutionary psychology aims to fill this gap, with its stories about modularity and about preferences. These are *proximate* mechanisms, the mechanisms that are actually at work in individual organisms. A taste for sugar was selected for because of the fitness advantages that accrued to organisms with this taste in the EEA, but neither today nor in that environment did people eat sweet things because doing so gave them an advantage in terms of fitness. Rather, they acted upon the proximate mechanism, the desire for sweet tasting foods, which evolution had given them, as a reliable means of motivating them to do what was in their (genetic) interest.

According to evolutionary psychology, this story is generalizable. For every typical human desire and aversion, there is an evolutionary explanation. We have these desires because acting upon them increased the fitness of our ancestors. We do not, typically, act to increase our inclusive fitness. But when we act as we want to – when we pursue sexual opportunities, career ambitions, loving relationships, and esthetic satisfactions – we nevertheless act, unknowingly or not, to enhance our fitness. As Daly and Wilson, two of the most eminent evolutionary psychologists, put it, "Apprehensions of self-interest – such as the absence of pain and hunger, or the positive satisfactions derived from social and sexual success and from the well-being of one's children – evolve as tokens of expected genetic posterity."[74] Evolutionary psychology provides an evolutionary (ultimate) explanation for the existence of the desires (proximate mechanisms) upon which we all act. We like sugar because it is sweet, but it is sweet (for us) because eating it was, in the EEA, adaptive.

The claims of evolutionary psychology

The simple example of our evolved taste for sugar hints at the kind of challenge to morality presented by evolutionary psychology. If many of our desires and aversions are adaptations, in the manner in which our tastes seem to be, then we shall find that we have a hard time constraining, channeling, or altering them, if and when they prove to be obstacles in the way of constructing better norms and a more just world. If, as evolutionary psychology claims, a great many of our desires are adaptations, they will be difficult to control, and the limits they impose upon human behavior might be significant.

The significance of these constraints will greatly depend upon what desires we prove to have. It is only if these desires are importantly concerned with central aspects of our social and moral life that they will represent real obstacles in the way of shaping our social world. As we shall see, evolutionary psychology claims that it is indeed some of our morally central desires and preferences that must be understood as adaptations.

Sexuality

Perhaps the most interesting set of results here – certainly the one that has caught the public's attention – concerns the evolution of sexual desire. A great deal of ingenuity, and ink, has been devoted to the claim that our sexual preferences are adaptations. After all (other things being equal), sexual success translates quite directly into reproductive success, so any strategy that enhances it will give organisms a decisive fitness advantage. Successful sexual strategies will rapidly go to fixation. On *a priori* grounds alone, we might expect that human sexual behavior will show the effects of millennia of evolution.

Evidence from animal studies buttresses the claim that sexual strategies have been shaped by natural selection. Robert Trivers, with his concept of *parental investment*, provided a key to understanding central aspects of sexual behavior. In sexually reproducing organisms, the minimum level of resources that the members of each sex are required to contribute to their offspring diverges widely. Typically, though not invariably, the female is the more heavily investing parent, while the male is able to get away with investing much less. This is especially the case in mammals, in which females lactate to feed their offspring.

In a situation in which there is this kind of disparity, Trivers predicts, the more heavily investing sex will be very picky in its choice of sexual partners, for they will be left, literally, holding the baby. However, if the minimum investment on the part of the other sex is small enough, we can expect them to be very eager to mate with as many partners as possible, thereby improving reproductive success and fitness. Natural selection should reward those organisms that are able to maximize the number of their offspring (other things being equal), and this strategy promises a direct route to such success. So, we should expect members of the lightly-investing sex to be motivated by proximate mechanisms that drive them to seek out multiple sexual partners.

As Trivers put it, the members of the heavily investing sex become a "limiting resource" for the other. That is, their reproductive success is limited only by their sexual access to fertile members of the other sex. Trivers, and the sociobiologists and evolutionary psychologists who have built upon his work, have been able to explain a great deal of sexual behavior by looking at it through the lens of parental investment. They can explain, for instance, why males are frequently much more willing to mate with a large number of partners than females are, why males frequently compete with one another for mates, and why females usually do the choosing.

Consider, for example, the behavior of elephant seals. In this species, females invest heavily in offspring: while nursing a pup, she loses between 200 and 450 kilograms, while the pup increases from its birth weight of fifty kilograms (which already represents a significant investment) to about 200 kilograms. On the other hand, the minimum investment needed by a male to have a reasonable chance of producing offspring is low – merely the energy required for a few seconds' mating, and a teaspoonful of sperm. Given this disparity, we can expect male elephant seals to be highly motivated to compete for access to females. And this is precisely what happens. Male elephant seals compete ferociously for access to "harems" of females, so ferociously that though deaths directly resulting from their battles are rare, dominant males often die after only a year or two of controlling a harem. However, the pay-off, in terms of reproductive success, is worth the cost. Fewer than ten percent of all male elephant seals ever succeed in mating with a female, but the lucky few who succeed in controlling a harem might easily end up inseminating over one hundred females.

This great variation in reproductive success is essential to understanding the sexual strategies pursued by different sexes. Males play a high-stake, high-risk game, in which the jackpot is having their genes well represented in the next generation, but in which there are few winners. Females, on the other hand, play a low-risk strategy. Almost all females succeed in having one pup a year, and very few have more than one. Since females can easily find a mate, but can have only a relatively small number of offspring, they can be expected to be choosy, if they are able to be. Since males find it relatively difficult to secure a mate, but are able, under the right conditions, to father hundreds of offspring, they have little reason to be choosy, and will mate with any accessible female.

Elephant seals also exhibit a notable degree of *sexual dimorphism* as a result of this intense competition between males. Sexual dimorphism is the extent to which, on average, the members of each sex differ. In some species, the degree of sexual dimorphism is slight; in elephant seals, it is quite dramatic. Since reproductively successful male elephant seals must compete, there is strong selection pressure on them for the characteristics that will enable them to succeed. Body size is strongly correlated with success; accordingly, males weigh about four times as much as females.

This brief excursion into the sociobiology of elephant seals has provided us with many of the tools and perspectives we shall need to understand and evaluate the claims of evolutionary psychology relating to human sexual behavior. Before we turn to our main subject, however, let us briefly consider two other animal models, in order to illustrate the power of the parental investment viewpoint, and to provide further insight into the nature of sexual selection. Elephant seals are unusual among mammals in one way: the degree to which females exercise mate choice is relatively low (though not non-existent). In some other species, the sex that invests relatively little in the offspring puts all its effort into turning the heads of members of the other. Take bowerbirds, for example. Male bowerbirds certainly compete, but this competition does not take the violent form it does in elephant seals. Instead, they compete for the attention of females. Each adult male constructs a "bower" – a nest of twigs and grass, constructed on the ground, which comes in a variety of forms, depending on the species. At the entrance to the bower, he places an assortment of colored objects, ranging from flowers and mosses to bits of plastic. These have no apparent purpose, other than to attract females. Females mate with the builders of the most impressive bowers, then fly off to construct the nest in which the young will be reared.

The bowerbird combines male competition with female selection. These features, in one form or another, are very common across animal species. In general, males compete with one another to be chosen by females. The bowerbird, like many other birds, also exhibits a marked degree of sexual dimorphism. The kinds of characteristics that vary according to sex reflect the ways in which members of a species compete with one another. Accordingly, in male bowerbirds, it is not large body size that is favored by natural selection. Since females choose, and are apparently attracted to bright colors, male bowerbirds have much brighter plumage than do females.[75]

Trivers predicts that, other things being equal, males will compete, while females choose. This prediction is a consequence of another, more fundamental, forecast: that females will tend to invest more heavily in offspring than will males. Why will females be the more heavily investing sex? There are biological factors that incline natural selection to work to this end. At a very fundamental level, females are inevitably the more heavily investing sex. Female gametes (sex cells) are generally very much larger than male gametes; in some birds, the egg weighs as much as fifteen percent of the female's body weight. In addition, the egg is relatively expensive to produce, since it contains the nutrients required by the growing embryo. Females produce a small number of eggs, each of which represents a great deal of investment, whereas males produce an enormous number of sperm, which are easily replaced. This disparity in initial investment is intensified in those animals in which fertilization is internal to the female, since she is then committed to carrying the fetus, channeling resources to it, and giving birth to it. In mammals, lactation ensures that female investment (of time, energy, and resources) must continue after birth, if the infant is to survive. Thus, while it is not inevitable, across all sexually reproducing species, that females invest more heavily than males in their offspring, there are biological factors which ensure that females are rarely able to escape with low levels of investment, and that when investment is unequal, it will rarely be the male who invests more heavily.

The power of any theory is best demonstrated by its ability to explain apparent exceptions to its predictions. How, then, does the parental investment perspective account for cases which are, apparently, exceptions to its rule? Some species exhibit reversed sex-roles. In these species, females compete for access to picky males. Mormon cricket males are very choosy about the females they will mate with, rejecting lighter in favor of heavier females. In these, and other reversed role species, it turns out that the male invests more heavily in the offspring than the female. Male Mormon crickets produce a mass of nutritious substance for their mates, called a *spermatophore*, which contains both the male sex gametes and the energy the female needs to produce eggs. The spermatophore represents up to twenty-seven percent of the weight of the adult male Mormon cricket, and therefore is a sizable investment. Indeed, he is likely to produce only one spermatophore in his life. Since he makes a larger investment in reproduction, he can be expected to play the role of choosing, while the females compete to be chosen.

Can we transfer these kinds of findings from non-human animals to human beings? Can we, on the basis of the extent of parental invest-ment of human males and females, predict what roles each will play in sexual behavior? This was precisely the aim of many sociobiologists. They made predictions about human behavior, based on the patterns they observed in other animals. Human beings, they claimed, were more or less typical representatives of sexually reproducing species. They pointed out that human beings are mammals, and that as a result human females are committed to investing heavily in their offspring, if they are to reproduce at all. They will have to bear the costs of produ-cing large and relatively scarce eggs, gestating the fetus, and breast-feeding the baby. Males, in contrast, can get away with very low levels of parental investment. Thus, we can expect that females will be very choosy about their sexual partners, while males will seek to maximize their number of sexual encounters. Males will compete for access to females, who will choose among them. We can expect to find evidence of sexual dimorphism in human beings, particularly along the dimen-sions relevant to male competition. And this is exactly what we do find: males are, on average, larger and stronger than females. To be sure, the degree of sexual dimorphism is modest, when compared to other pri-mates. Male gorillas, for instance, are very much larger than females. But gorilla sexual behavior is more similar to that of elephant seals than to humans, in that the males pursue the same high-risk, high-gain strategy of attempting to control a harem of females and exclude other males from access to reproductive opportunities. Since sexual dimorphism is closely correlated with polygyny, and its absence with monogamy, we can infer that human beings are mildly polygynous.

Indeed, in human cultures polygyny is relatively common, whereas polyandry (one woman marrying more than one husband simultaneously) is very rare.

Thus, sociobiology advanced its claims about human behavior largely on the basis of observed similarities in morphology and social organization between human beings and other animals. The behaviors upon which it focused are, supposedly, adaptations; we can therefore expect them to have been selected for by evolution. Evolutionary psychology takes over a great deal from sociobiology, with regard both to the content of its claims, and to the kinds of backing it provides for them. What it adds are the methods of experimental psychology, particularly the rigorous testing of hypotheses under controlled conditions, in order to refine and confirm its predictions. The most comprehensive work on human sexuality by an evolutionary psychologist is that undertaken by David Buss.[76] Buss frames predictions using the resources of sociobiology, then tests them using those of psychology. That is, he first asks himself what recurrent problems our ancestors would have needed to solve in the EEA, and then proceeds to test whether the genetic basis for solutions to such problems has been laid down in the human genome.

The reproductive problems faced by each sex are crucially different. Since females are the heavily investing sex, they require resources for successful reproduction: resources with which to feed the growing embryo and to produce milk for the newborn, resources to get them through a period of relative vulnerability in the later stages of pregnancy and while the baby is young, and so on. Since males are the low investing parent, they have much smaller resource needs. How are these differing needs translated into preferences? We can expect females to be very choosy about their partners, demanding evidence of good genes, of the possession of resources, and of the ability and the disposition to stay and assist with the tasks of child-rearing. Since men invest much less, we can expect them to be relatively undiscriminating in the choice of a sexual partner, but if they are considering whether to invest in an ongoing relationship, we should expect their standards to rise considerably. So this is the prediction Buss tested: that females will value resources in a potential mate much more than will males.

To test his hypothesis, Buss and his associates surveyed men and women in thirty-seven cultures, which represents a fair sampling of the different kinds of extant human groupings. In every culture, they found that women value financial prospects in a potential mate more than men do. On average, women value resources roughly twice as much as men, though there were significant variations across cultures. Nowhere, however, was the prediction falsified: in every culture women placed more weight on resources than men did.[77] Buss revealed many other systematic mate-choice preferences of women, and gave them an evolutionary explanation. In almost every culture, women value older men, presumably because age is strongly correlated with the possession of resources. Women value intelligence in a partner more than men do, for the same reason. Less predictably, women prefer tall partners. Why? Buss speculates that male tallness would be correlated with ability to protect partners and children. And so on. In general, women have just the kinds of preferences one would expect, on the basis of the facts about their biology and their degree of parental investment.[78]

Though Buss says that he finds women much more mysterious than men, and therefore in greater need of scientific examination, he also investigated, and attempted to explain, male preferences. He paid particular attention to male judgments of female attractiveness. Men place much greater emphasis on attractiveness than women do. Accordingly, they value those traits that we regard as attractive: youthfulness, symmetrical faces, clear and smooth skin, and so on. Why are these features universally regarded as attractive, and highly valued by men? Buss argues that it is because they are cues to lifetime fertility. A young woman is obviously capable of bearing more future children than an older one; moreover, she is less likely to come with already existing children, who would represent a drain on male resources for no good end (in genetic terms). Clear skin is a sign of a low parasite load and current health. Bodily and facial asymmetries are the result of environmental and developmental insults – injuries and diseases that afflict a growing embryo or a young child – and therefore are indicative of poor health or low genetic quality.[79] Buss also explains men's preferences in body shape. It's often suggested that our current preoccupation with feminine slenderness is historically unique. As a glance at a Rubens' painting will confirm, at earlier stages in Western history men preferred rather larger women. It's reasonable to think this preference was a response to the relative scarcity of food before the industrial revolution: only wealthier women could afford to have excess weight. Today, at least in Western countries, it seems harder to remain slim than to gain weight. Our preferences have changed accordingly.

This explanation seems thoroughly cultural and historical. Moreover, Buss does not deny that it contains more than a grain of truth. But, he insists, its truth is not evidence against evolutionary psychology. Evolutionary psychology holds that our behavior is the result of adaptive modules and preferences, but it does not claim that our behavior is programmed, in the sense that we always act in the same way, no matter what the circumstances. Instead, our behavior is *facultative*, which is to say that different strategies are triggered in different circumstances. Men do not have an evolved preference for a certain percentage of body fat in prospective mates: "Rather, they have an evolved preference for whatever features are linked with status,"[80] and this preference leads them to prefer women with whatever degree of fat is linked with status in their culture.

However, though male preferences can be shaped by culture, inasmuch as they will prefer whatever body shape a culture selects as high status, there are evolutionary constraints that ensure that only some body shapes are potential candidates for this position. Beneath the variations in body fat across cultures, one preference remains fixed. In all cultures, men have a strong preference for women with a particular waist-to-hip ratio (WHR). Here Buss relies upon a well-known, and much repeated, experiment by Dev Singh.[81] Singh found that, given a range of different body types to choose from, some of which were heavier than is considered attractive in our culture, some normal, and some underweight, men always preferred a WHR of around 0.7. Further studies show this preference to be quite robust; in almost all cultures, no matter what amount of fat that culture considers attractive, the same WHR is preferred (I shall examine apparent exceptions, and the kind of explanations evolutionary psychology advances for them, later).

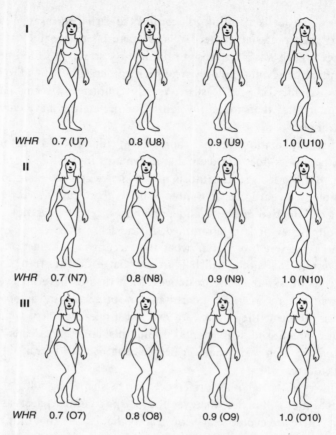

Figure 4: Male subjects in Singh's study were presented with these sketches of underweight (I), normal weight (II) and overweight (III) women. The subjects exhibited a consistent preference for the figure with a WHR of 0.7 across the weight ranges. From Devendra Singh, "The Adaptive Significance of Female Attractiveness: Role of Waist-to-Hip Ratio," *Journal of Personality and Social Psychology*, 65, 1993, p. 298. Reproduced with the permission of Devendra Singh and the American Psychological Association.

Why the preference for this particular WHR? WHR might be a reliable indicator for a great variety of reproduction-relevant information. It is primarily the result of the distribution of adipose tissue, which is directed by the sex hormones (estrogen and testosterone). Thus, WHR is an indicator of the health of the endocrine system, of whether the individual possesses the optimal amount of sex hormones, and so is correlated with fertility. Moreover, a higher WHR might be indicative of pregnancy; if our judgments of attractiveness are keyed to the extent to which potential partners might aid us in increasing the representation of our genes in the next generation, a female who is already pregnant is a liability to a male. She cannot become pregnant with his child until she has given birth and stopped breast-feeding; and, from the gene's eye view, channeling resources to the child of another man is wasteful.

Infanticide

What, though, if a man marries a woman who is already pregnant with another man's child, or if two people who already have children marry? The "blended family," formed when relationships that have produced children break up and new relationships form, is increasingly common. Obviously, when such families form, at least one of the adults becomes a step-parent. For evolutionary psychologists, this is alarming; a little thought soon shows why. From an evolutionary point of view, children of previous relationships are a liability for the new partner. Therefore, we might expect sexually reproducing organisms to be strongly motivated to rid themselves of such children, or at least to refuse to channel their resources to them. Indeed, in many animal species, males are likely to kill the young of rivals. Among those animals in which a single male (or a small coalition of males) controls a harem, a new dominant male will frequently kill all the young animals. This has the dual function of limiting the number of mouths to be fed, and of bringing the females into estrous, therefore ensuring that they are capable of falling pregnant to the newcomer. This behavior is found in lions and in langurs and other primates; infanticide of the offspring of rivals outside the context of "harems" is found in mice and rats, and some bird species.

It appears that human beings do not have an evolved disposition to kill the offspring of rivals, but why might this be true? It might seem obvious that infanticide cannot be adaptive, since it is difficult to see how anyone who engages in it could find their reproductive success thereby enhanced. They are likely to end up in jail, or worse. However, recall that a behavior counts as an adaptation if it would, on average, have boosted inclusive fitness *in the EEA*. Its effect on fitness today is irrelevant. Our evolved preference for high-calorie food is an adaptation, despite the fact that in the changed environment in which we – the inhabitants of the developed countries – live, it is dysfunctional. So, infanticidal behavior would be adaptive, and possibly selected for, if it boosted inclusive fitness in the EEA. However, on the best evidence we have, which stems largely from the study of hunter-gatherer groups, it fails to be adaptive. Such groups impose heavy punishments on those who engage in this behavior, and because females who have had their children killed are hardly likely to warm to the killer, it seems that, in the EEA, infanticide would usually have detracted from inclusive fitness. However, just because infanticide is not an adaptation, we ought not to conclude that evolutionary psychology will have nothing illuminating to say about it. Despite the fact that it is not adaptive, an evolutionary perspective might be able to explain its occurrence. How can this be? The answer lies in the fact that many aspects of animal behavior are not direct targets of natural selection, but are instead *by-products* of adaptations.

Martin Daly and Margo Wilson are the champions of the by-product theory of infanticide. Their analysis of the available cross-cultural data on infanticide reveals a striking fact: step-children are at a much higher risk of being abused, injured, or killed by their step-parents than are biological children. In the United States, a child living with at least one step-parent was approximately one hundred times more likely to be seriously injured or killed than a child living with both its genetic parents.[82] Similar – or worse – findings were reported for other societies: hunter-gatherer, agricultural and industrial. Even if we control for other risk factors, such as income and education levels, being a step-child remains an independently significant risk. Moreover, abusive step-parents are selective: they tend to spare their own children who live in the same household.

If infanticide and abuse are not adaptive, what explains the fact that its victims are precisely those children who, if it were adaptive, we might expect would be harmed? Daly and Wilson argue that the behavior in question is a maladaptive by-product of a true adaptation: the adaptation that leads parents to feel overwhelming and unconditional love for their offspring. It is the *absence* of this adaptation, the fact that these feelings are not typically triggered by step-children, which explains the pattern of abuse, not the presence of any actual adaptation. For isn't it the case that, in the absence of these feelings, parents would harm their children far more often than they do?

> Little children *are* annoying after all: they cry and soil themselves and sometimes refuse to be consoled. A caretaker with a heartfelt, individualized love for a squalling baby is motivated to tenderly alleviate its distress, but a caretaker who is simply playing the part without emotional commitment – and who might even prefer that the child had never been born – is apt to respond rather differently.[83]

Thus, evolutionary principles explain an important feature of human behavior, present and past, and this despite the fact that the behavior is acknowledged not to be an adaptation.

Rape

In a similar manner to the way in which, by reference to an evolutionary explanation of normal family interactions, evolutionary psychology claims to be able to explain abnormal family behavior, so it has offered to explain rape, by reference to normal sexual desire. The best representative of work in this area is that of Thornhill and Palmer.[84] The pattern of argument should be familiar. Since rape is a sexual activity, it is clear how it is directly relevant to reproduction, and therefore to inclusive fitness. On the one hand, the disposition to engage in rape might be a facultative adaptation: under the right conditions, males might be disposed to rape because being so disposed boosted the inclusive fitness of their ancestors. On the other, it might be that rape is not itself an adaptation, but a by-product of other aspects of male sexuality that are, themselves, adaptive: for example the propensity of males to be easily sexually aroused (adaptive since males, unlike females, can benefit from a large number and great variety of sexual encounters). Thornhill and Palmer disagree on this question: Thornhill favors the view that rape is a facultative adaptation, and Palmer argues that it is a by-product of other adaptations, not itself an adaptation. However, they do agree that it is one or the other, and that therefore rape can best be explained using the tools of evolutionary psychology.

What is the evidence that rape is either an adaptation or a by-product of adaptations? Thornhill and Palmer proceed in the same manner as other evolutionary psychologists. Firstly, they adduce what we might call sociobiological evidence: they give examples of coerced sexual activity in other animals. In some species, the circumvention of female mate choice by males is quite common. Some species of duck, engage in it, as do orang-utans. But the most suggestive animal model is provided by the behavior of the scorpion fly. Male scorpion flies seduce females by offering them a "nuptial gift": either a mass of hardened saliva they have produced, or a dead insect. Female scorpion flies willingly accept the advances of males who bring them such gifts, and reject those who cannot provide them. But male scorpion flies also have a clamp on their abdomen, the only purpose of which seems to be to hold reluctant females immobile. When they cannot or will not produce nuptial gifts, they use this clamp to circumvent female mate choice. Since the clamp has no other purpose, it seems that it is an adaptation specifically for "rape."

There is good evidence, therefore, that at least in some species "rape" is an adaptation. What about human beings? Thornhill and Palmer claim that if we examine patterns of rape, we see evidence that it is adaptive. The evidence concerns both the conditions under which men are likely to rape, and the effects of rape on its victims. Men are most liable to rape, they argue, when the costs of doing so are likely to be low, and the (reproductive) benefits relatively high. The cost for rapists is, typically, the risk they run of injury or death, either at the hands of a successfully resisting victim, or of the victim's kin group or society. These costs are eliminated, for all practical purposes, in certain circumstances: for example, in time of war the social networks that normally ensure rapists are punished break down; in these circum-stances, soldiers can rape with impunity, and that is exactly what many of them do. Moreover, Thornhill and Palmer claim, young women – at the peak of their fertility – are far more likely to be raped than older women, and their rape is more likely to be vaginal, so more likely to result in pregnancy.

Even more striking, and surprising, is the effect that rape apparently has on its victims. If rape were a male adaptation, then *women's* sexual behavior would itself have evolved in a context where rape was an ever-present threat. If rape were a reproductive strategy that (on average, and in the EEA) enhanced the fitness of males who employed it, then this benefit to individual men would come at the expense of women. If rape is adaptive, then raped women pay a cost, not only in emotional and physical trauma, but also in the currency of inclusive fitness. As we have seen, women choose their mates by reference to cues which are guides to fitness: the health of prospective partners, their genetic prospects, their ability to support them and their children when they are vulnerable, and so on. Rape prevents women from making these choices, thereby ensuring that their children are fathered by men with possibly less than optimal genes and who will not provide them with the resources they need. From this perspective, rape might best be understood as the best reproductive strategy employed by men who, for one reason or another, would not be chosen by women as partners.

Thornhill and Palmer therefore hypothesize that we shall find evidence of female counter-adaptations to male rape. In particular, the degree to which different women find rape traumatic suggests to them that female responses evolved in a context in which rape circumvented reproductive choices often enough to exert selection pressure on women. The evidence suggests that women of reproductive age experience more trauma than girls or post-menopausal women.[85] Thus, the trauma associated with rape is not caused only by the violence and coercion it involves. Indeed, the greater the level of violence employed by rapists, the *lower* the degree of psychological distress the victim reports. We can explain this surprising finding, Thornhill and Palmer suggest, by invoking the evolutionary function of expressions of trauma. Women in the EEA who were the victims of rape faced not only the immediate consequences of the attack, but also the possibility of rejection by current or potential partners. Men seek faithful partners, to minimize the chance that they will invest in the offspring of another man. They will therefore seek assurances that a raped woman was indeed raped, did not consent, and that she will take every step within her power to ensure that it never occurs again. Genuine and heartfelt expressions of distress signal to partners that the woman did not consent, and reassure him that she will do all she can to avoid a recurrence of her pain. But if she sustained physical injuries, then these are signaled for her. Hence, the apparently counter-intuitive fact that the victims of violence suffer less, not more, psychic distress.

Empathy and systemizing ability

Let me present one final example of an evolutionary explanation of human psychological characteristics. In a recent, highly successful, book, Simon Baron-Cohen argues that, as a result of their respective biological heritage, men and women have substantially different brains. His thesis, stated starkly on the very first page of *The Essential Difference* is that "*The female brain is predominantly hard-wired for empathy. The male brain is predominantly hard-wired for understanding and building systems.*"[86] Empathy, as Baron-Cohen uses the word, is the ability to understand the mental states of others and, by producing similar feelings in oneself, to react appropriately. This allows the empathizer to respond easily and naturally to the distress of others. A good empathizer will know, intuitively, what to say to someone in emotional pain, how to put a tense person at their ease, what to do to settle disputes, and how to get everyone at a party relaxed and talking.

Systemizers find all this difficult because they take a rule-based approach to understanding the world. They attempt to formulate rules that govern the behavior of everything they confront. But this approach, which serves them so well when it comes to understanding and controlling the physical world, leaves them at a loss when it comes to negotiating the trickier world of social interaction. Human behavior just isn't rule-governed in any sense that would be useful to someone trying to understand it. True, we are able to formulate many rules of thumb to predict human actions and emotions. But there are just too many exceptions to these rules for them to be very helpful as a guide to action. Consider the rule "if people get what they want, they will be happy." Now suppose you gave Hannah what she wanted for her birthday. Will she be happy? She might, but that depends on many other facts about her. Is she upset about getting older? What else is going on in her life? How does she feel about you? Perhaps she doesn't want a present from you at all. Systemizers, Baron-Cohen argues, "just cannot get a foothold into things like a person's fluctuating feelings."[87]

Baron-Cohen's primary area of expertise is autism, and it is his studies of autistic people, especially those with the less severe Asperger's syndrome, which have revealed to him the severe limitations of an exclusively rule-based approach to social life. Sufferers of Asperger's syndrome are often highly intelligent people, yet they lack even the most minimal understanding of the social world of human interaction. They cannot see what is appropriate in a social situation, and are forced to substitute their rule-following, systemizing ability for empathy. They often "struggle to work out a set of rules concerning how to behave in each and every situation, and they expend enormous effort in consulting a sort of mental table of how to behave and what to say, from minute to minute."[88] But their brilliance at rule-formulating invariably proves insufficient. They cannot have rules for all eventualities, and sooner or later they are caught out by the unpredictability of social life.

Autism and Asperger's syndrome are primarily found in males. Baron-Cohen believes that this is significant. Systemizing is predominantly a male ability and empathizing a female ability. Autism and Asperger's syndrome, Baron-Cohen suggests, represent the male brain in an extreme form, lacking almost all empathizing ability. People with the extreme male brain are at a disadvantage in many ways, but if their systemizing ability is intact, or even enhanced, as it may be in Asperger's syndrome, they are nevertheless able to make important contributions to areas of inquiry in which systemizing is the most important skill. Baron-Cohen believes that it is no accident that many areas of science are male-dominated. It is no coincidence, he says, that we refer to the products of technology as man-made, or that only three of 170 living Nobel Prize winners in science are women.[89] Systemizing brains are much better at physics, engineering and mathematics than empathizing brains, and far more males than females have systemizing brains.

So, males and females typically have very different abilities. Males are good at understanding the world, at making and repairing things. They are also good at understanding and raising their status in social hierarchies, since these, too, are systems. Females, on the other hand, are typically good at understanding people, and responding to them: "There are things that most women can do that most men cannot do as well. Hosting a large party tactfully, making everyone feel included, is just one example of something that many men may shy away from."[90]

But why do these sex differences exist? The explanation is evolutionary. Baron-Cohen claims that systemizing abilities would have been useful to males in the EEA. Systemizing gave them an advantage in the tasks males typically performed: tool-making, hunting and fishing, navigating, trading, and fighting for status in the social hierarchy of the group (which would allow them to command more resources, and therefore to attract more female partners). High empathizing ability would not merely be unnecessary for engaging in such tasks, it might actually be counter-productive. An ability to feel others' emotional states, and respond with similar emotions, would interfere with the efficient performance of such tasks. If one cares about the feelings of others, one will find it more difficult to treat them as rungs on the ladder of success.

In contrast, females in the EEA needed the skills that allowed them to be, above all else, effective mothers. Here, the crucial skill is the ability to read the emotional state of their baby, even before it is able to articulate its needs in language. Hence, females needed high empathizing skills. Such skills would also have proved useful in constructing alliances of females, who may have found they needed to rely upon one another when the adult males were off hunting or at war. So, females typically evolved quite a different psychological profile to males. Females will be good empathizers; males will be good systemizers. We see the consequences today, in the tendency of males and females to gravitate toward certain occupations and to shun others. Males become scientists, engineers, and plumbers – occupations that require good systemizing skills. Females become nurses, primary school teachers and social workers – occupations that require good empathizing. It is not culture, but evolutionary biology, which explains the patterns of social life.

We now have before us four examples of evolutionary psychological explanations, stemming from major figures in the field and widely hailed as having, for the first time, put the study of human beings on a truly scientific footing. Before we evaluate the successes and failures of evolutionary psychology as an explanatory method, we need to pause to examine its moral implications. Evolutionary psychology has been accused of almost every crime that could conceivably be committed by an intellectual theory: of offering support to racists and sexists, of supporting elitism and inequality, and of cultural imperialism. Naturally, its practitioners deny these charges, arguing that evolutionary psychology is a neutral scientific enterprise, not a political program. Its only relevance for morality, they argue, is its ability to provide accurate accounts of phenomena of moral concern, thereby enabling us to better predict and control aspects of social life that matter to us. We need to discover where the truth lies in this debate. Is evolutionary psychology truly a morally significant, or even a dangerous, enterprise, which changes the terms upon which moral debate ought to be conducted, or is it merely a scientific discipline, whose findings we can and ought largely to ignore, when it comes to framing our moral principles and social policies? In the next chapter, we assess evolutionary psychology, and discover what implications its claims might have for our evolved morality.

4

A clean slate?

Railing against men for the importance they place on beauty, youth, and fidelity is like railing against meat eaters because they prefer animal protein. Telling men not to become aroused by signs of youth and health is like telling them not to experience sugar as sweet.

David Buss, *The Evolution of Desire*

To its opponents, evolutionary psychology is not merely wrongheaded; it is downright dangerous: an attempt to give a quasi-scientific *justification* to the inequalities that have, to a greater or lesser degree, hitherto characterized all societies. These critics argue that even if its advocates are not racist or sexist, their work offers support to racism and sexism. Its implicit message, they claim, is that the male domination of professional and political life, their propensity for infidelity and rape, and the systematically disadvantaged place occupied by women are not facts to be deplored or altered. Rather, they are the products of our in-built preferences and desires. They are fixed. We must accommodate ourselves to them, not rail futilely against them. Not surprisingly, the practitioners of evolutionary psychology reject these accusations. They invoke two separate defenses against the charges: firstly, the repudiation of genetic determinism, and secondly, the invocation of the naturalistic fallacy.

Genetic determinism

The foes of evolutionary psychology and sociobiology often accuse their opponents of the sin of genetic determinism. What do they mean? In philosophy, determinism refers to the thesis that all events are necessitated by prior events, in such a manner that if we had sufficient knowledge of the initial conditions and the laws of nature, we could, in principle, predict precisely what would happen in the future. Events that are determined are *caused*.

Genetic determinism is therefore the thesis that the phenotype of an organism is entirely caused by its genotype, so that, if we had sufficient knowledge of the genotype and understood the mechanisms by which genotypes build phenotypes, we could predict every aspect of a phenotype, from its height to its intelligence to its personality (if it's the kind of organism that can have one). It is easy to see why genetic determinism might appear threatening. If it is true, then attempts to alter society by altering the behavior of people are doomed to failure. Opponents of evolutionary psychology accuse it of attempting to provide a justification of the *status quo*, and therefore of being politically conservative. They argue that if genetic determinism is true, then our fondest hopes – of improving society, and eliminating endemic racism, sexism, and inequality – must inevitably come to nothing.

But, although incautious advocates of evolutionary psychology occasionally write as if they believe that genetic determinism is true, none of them really hold this view. A little thought reveals that it *must* be false. Many things beside our genome affect our morphology. If we are malnourished during childhood, we will be shorter and probably less intelligent than we might otherwise have been. If we are abused, then we can expect it to have some effect on our personality. No respectable evolutionary psychologist denies these obvious points. They are not, in this crude sense, genetic determinists.

Instead, evolutionary psychology is committed to a view we might describe as *interactionism*. Phenotypes, it holds, are always the product of interaction between a given genotype and its environment. Once we recognize that interactionism is correct, we see that evolutionary psychology cannot be guilty of the grievous charges laid at its door. If evolutionary psychology was committed to genetic determinism, then,

for example, its evolutionary explanation of rape would indeed provide an excuse for rapists. But an interactionist perspective provides
neither excuses nor justifications for behavior.[91]

Ought we to find evolutionary psychology not guilty of the charge
of genetic determinism? If we construe the charge narrowly, then
clearly we must acquit. But perhaps we should construe it more
broadly. It might be useful to cast the question in the terms of the
"nature – nurture" debate: the debate over the extent to which important human traits are the product either of our innate biological inheritance or of our environment and upbringing. "Nature" and "nurture"
are most usefully seen as endpoints of a continuum. At one extreme is
the view that human traits are entirely in-built, the absurd position we
have allocated to genetic determinism. At the other is the equally
absurd view that biology does not shape human traits at all. No
rational person holds either of these two positions. The real debate
does not concern whether it is nature *or* nurture that shapes our traits,
but rather the *extent* to which each is responsible.[92]

Seen in this light, the charge that evolutionary psychology is committed to genetic determinism recovers much of its force. There is a
real debate to be had. Evolutionary psychologists are making the substantive (and controversial) claim that the influence of biology on our
phenotypic traits is much greater than is usually believed, and they
explicitly cast this claim as a rejection of the views of what they con-
temptuously refer to as the "standard social science model" (SSSM).
Genes certainly don't shape human behavior all by themselves, but
evolutionary psychologists claim that, in a very wide range of environments, they produce very predictable effects, and that we understand
human behavior better by focusing on genes, mental modules, and
evolved desires, than by looking at cultures and social norms.

Consider the evidence, as discussed in chapter 3, that men have
evolved to have strong preferences with regard to the waist-to-hip ratio
of prospective partners. If, as suggested, WHR is a good indicator of
fertility, then men with a preference for a WHR in a certain range would
tend to have, on average, more offspring than those who did not have
this preference. The genetic basis for the preference is therefore passed
on, and will eventually become very common in the population. This
preference is certainly not genetically determined: no one claims that,

no matter what environment they are raised in, boys will inevitably grow up with this preference. Indeed, there is empirical evidence that this is not so. One group of men, belonging to the Yomybato tribe, who live in the Peruvian rain forest, has a markedly different preference.[93] There, men presented with Singh's original sketches preferred women with the highest possible WHR. Evolutionary psychologists do not regard this finding as a refutation of their claims about WHR, but argue that precisely the same evolutionary perspective that generated Singh's original prediction will explain the preferences of the Yomybato. In the harsh environment in which their ancestors lived, obesity was all but impossible. As a consequence, the preference for women with a higher WHR was itself adaptive: "A male preference for the largest available women would in the past have encouraged males to have sexual liaisons with women with relatively large fat reserves and relatively high fertility *in the ancestral Yomybato environment.*"[94] Thus, male preferences are not in-built, in any simple sense. It is perfectly possible for the mechanisms that lead most of us, in normal environments, to have a certain preference, to lead us to quite different preferences in a different environment.

If this view is right, and the explanation Alcock offers for the deviant preference of the Yomybato is correct, then male WHR preferences are facultative. They are not determined by the genome, but are the result of interaction between it and the environment in which it finds itself. Nevertheless, it should be clear from this example that, if evolutionary psychology is right, the extent to which we can alter our preferences is severely constrained. Thanks to our new knowledge of the mechanisms that underlie male preferences, we know that we could alter the normal preference for a WHR of 0.7, but only in one direction, and only by taking steps which would be disastrous and immoral: that is, by causing widespread famine.

Thus, it is not true that the preferences identified by evolutionary psychologists are literally inevitable. They can be altered; in this sense, evolutionary psychology is not genetic determinism. But they are altered only through great effort, and at great cost.[95] This is a view evolutionary psychology inherits from sociobiology, and which is made explicit by its doyen, in a warning against moves designed to change the position of women in society: "There is a cost, which no one yet can measure, awaiting the society that moves either from juridical equality of opportunity between the sexes to a statistical equality of their performance in the professions, or back toward deliberate sexual discrimination."[96]

These costs could take many forms. Most obviously, they would include limits to our freedom. We can alter our in-built preferences, but if not by altering the environment very much for the worse by starving people, then only by an intensive program of indoctrination or other interferences in people's lives. Human nature – our repertoire of innate preferences, emotions, and desires – stands in the way of Utopian plans for the transformation of human society into a harmonious and peaceful commonweal. Our human nature ensures that implementing Utopian plans would impose costs greater than the supposed benefits of the program:

> Inborn human desires are a nuisance to those with utopian and totalitarian visions, which often amount to the same thing. What stands in the way of most utopias is not pestilence and drought but human behavior. So utopians have to think of ways to control behavior, and when propaganda doesn't do the trick, more emphatic techniques are tried.[97]

The charge of genetic determinism, construed narrowly, is false. Nevertheless, it is disingenuous of evolutionary psychologists and their supporters to dismiss it, as though they did not make claims about the robustness of human preferences, about the difficulty of altering them, and about the costs such attempts inevitably impose. We cannot dismiss the debate, as they are wont to do, as though it were based on a crass misunderstanding of their scientific claims. There is a great deal at stake, for morality and for human social life, in the assertions of evolutionary psychologists. If they are right, they are identifying significant and perhaps (for all practical purposes) immovable obstacles that stand in the way of some of our most cherished hopes for peace, equality, harmony, and happiness.

The naturalistic fallacy

However, evolutionary psychology has a second line of defense against the claim that it has dubious political implications. Its advocates often deny that it has political implications at all, on the grounds that it is a purely factual enterprise. They claim it is a mistake to believe that factual findings have moral implications. To attempt to draw moral conclusions from such findings is to commit the naturalistic fallacy. Thus, for instance, Thornhill and Palmer deny that their claim that rape might be adaptive does anything either to justify rape or excuse rapists. Though we often make the mistake of thinking that if something is natural, it must be good, this is a fallacy. Nature contains many things, some of which are, by our standards, wonderful, and others that are deplorable. As scientists, evolutionary psychologists are in the business of understanding human phenomena, not of justifying them.

As we saw in the first chapter, there is no naturalistic fallacy. However, we also saw that no one has, as yet, proposed a plausible analysis of goodness that would allow us to reduce it to purely natural properties. In so far as evolutionary psychology is concerned with the natural, its advocates seem to be right in claiming that it is a mistake to see them as engaged in an enterprise with moral overtones. The demonstration that rape is, in some sense, natural, does not justify it, any more than the naturalness of death and disease shows that they are good things. However, evolutionary psychology does not entirely escape the charges leveled against it. In their zeal to defend their work against political accusations, its practitioners make something of a fetish of the gap between "is" and "ought" and thereby absurdly overextend its reach. Consider Steven Pinker's recent defense of the biologists of human nature against the charge of dangerous political consequences, by reference to the naturalistic fallacy:

> We should not concede that *any* foreseeable discovery about humans could have such horrible implications. The problem is not with the possibility that people might differ from one another, which is a factual question that could turn out one way or the other. The problem is with the line of reasoning that says that if people do turn out to be different, then discrimination, oppression, or genocide would be OK after all. Fundamental values (such as equality and human rights) should not be held hostage to some factual conjecture about blank slates that might be refuted tomorrow.[98]

In this view, moral values are totally cut off from scientific discoveries. No matter what evolutionary psychology – or biology, or physics – tell

us at ⟨…⟩ is an absurd
posit ⟨…⟩ iman beings,
were ⟨…⟩ cant impacts
upor ⟨…⟩ hand that we
acco ⟨…⟩ it in central
dom ⟨…⟩ f our factual
belie ⟨…⟩ cated on the
belie ⟨…⟩ s. They must
be, re ⟨…⟩ . The right to
vote ⟨…⟩ children or
chim ⟨…⟩ iter cognitive
reso ⟨…⟩ en or chim-
panz ⟨…⟩ n identifiable
grou ⟨…⟩ w their right
to vc ⟨…⟩ if a group of
Mar ⟨…⟩ cognitive and
emotional capacities; that is, we would gather facts about them. So facts cannot be morally irrelevant, as Pinker claims.

Indeed, Pinker himself must realize that his position is absurd, for he soon backs away from it. He continues to insist that biological discoveries could not justify discrimination, but gives a different rationale: "The case against bigotry is not a factual claim that humans are biologically indistinguishable. It is a moral stance that condemns judging an *individual* according to the average traits of certain *groups* to which the individual belongs."[99] Thus, Pinker claims, discoveries about the average properties of groups ought not to influence our treatment of individuals who belong to these groups, because such discoveries will not mean that every individual has that property. The discovery that Martians are, on average, too stupid to make sensible judgments concerning the policies of political candidates would not imply that a particular Martian might not be a brilliant political analyst. We ought not to denigrate all Martians, just because most of them are dull.

The first thing we should note about Pinker's view is that it certainly does not establish that morality is independent of factual claims. It is a factual matter whether any Martian possesses the cognitive resources to be given the right to vote. Perhaps none do. And the right to vote is not the only one predicated on the possession of certain characteristics. Philosophers often claim that though it is wrong to inflict unnecessary pain on any sentient being, only those with a conception of themselves as existing over time are entitled to the respect due to people. That is why killing a cow is, at minimum, less wrong than killing a person. We do not distinguish between the two kinds of killing on moral grounds alone, without references to the actual properties of cows and people, and we would be irrational if we did.

Pinker's radical individualism is untenable, because we cannot, as he presupposes, hope to isolate the cognitive capacities of individuals from the characteristics of the groups they belong to. Intelligence and knowledge is not something that we develop on our own. Instead (as the interactionist perspective emphasizes) to develop the requisite abilities, we must be treated in certain ways. Chimpanzees, for example, do not normally develop a signed language, but when they are exposed to one, some become quite adept at it (though they never achieve anything like the fluency of even young human children). Similarly, human infants acquire a language only if they are exposed to it at the critical age; if this window of opportunity is missed, they will never attain fluency, and their entire cognitive development will be retarded. It is for this reason that deafness has been described as a preventable form of mental retardation.[100] Since the development of the cognitive capacities that underlie the possession of certain moral rights requires that individuals be treated in certain ways, we cannot wait until development is well advanced before we identify potential candidates for rights possession. Instead, we shall have to make a decision as to how we are to treat them, and we must do so *before* they develop the relevant abilities. So, we make that decision on the basis of the kinds of characteristics they are likely to develop, that is, on the basis of group membership.

Moreover, if there is any substance at all to the claims, often made by feminists and members of minorities, that aspirations play a powerful role in shaping what people can achieve, and that the achievements of women and minority members have therefore been limited by what they believe themselves capable of, then we shall have another important reason to treat people, at least partly, on the basis of group membership. What we aspire to is often limited by what those around us, who are relevantly similar to us, have been able to achieve. Thus, girls often believe themselves incapable of filling certain roles, because few women have occupied these positions. This provides one of the most important rationales for affirmative action policies, which treat people on the basis of their group membership. If instead we treat people exclusively as individuals, as Pinker suggests, then we shall inevitably and inadvertently favor members of certain groups over others: those which have already done well.

None of this is meant to settle these difficult and important questions. It may be, for instance, that affirmative action is wrong, in spite of these considerations. All we need learn from this discussion is that, though it is certainly a mistake to identify what is natural – in one or another sense of that multiply ambiguous word – with what is good, it is equally a mistake to think that the (supposed) naturalistic fallacy insulates morality from factual discoveries, and that evolutionary psychology can therefore proceed as if its claims had no moral implications whatsoever.

Clearly, many factual claims are morally irrelevant. If we were to discover a group of human beings who usually had six toes, instead of five, we should draw no moral conclusions from the finding at all. Let's turn to some of the actual claims of evolutionary psychology, to find out whether its (alleged) findings are insulated from morality by the gap between "is" and "ought." As we have seen, many of its most controversial claims concern sex differences. Setting aside the more obvious biological differences between men and women, one of the most strikingly gendered features of most societies is the division of labor. In almost all societies, past and present, men have been far more prominent in those activities and occupations that are public, and highly valued. Feminists typically regard this as the outcome of a history of injustice, and aim to change this state of affairs. Evolutionary psychology has a rather different explanation for the disparity.

Evolutionary psychologists claim that the gendered nature of social life is a consequence of sexual selection. Given that men are highly motivated to seek sexual partners, and that women reserve their sexual favors for men who possess certain characteristics, men strive to acquire these characteristics. Women want men who can channel resources to them and to their offspring, and who can protect them when they are vulnerable. As a consequence, men are highly motivated to seek power and wealth, and so are much more strongly driven to succeed in professional life.[101] It has even been suggested that the theory of sexual selection explains the origins of human intelligence, because, for whatever reason, women evolved a preference for brainy men, which resulted in a process of runaway sexual selection and the evolution of much higher intelligence than would be required merely to solve the problems that confronted our ancestors in the EEA.[102]

This does not imply that men are more intelligent than women. Males might have high intelligence because women preferred brainy men, but to be able to assess the intelligence of potential partners, women needed to keep up.[103] Where men and women will tend to differ, according to the theory of sexual selection for intelligence, is not with regard to their levels of intelligence, but with regard to their penchant to use that intelligence in creative display. Knowing that women prefer intelligent, dominant, males, men will take every opportunity to parade their verbal brilliance in front of women:

> Men write more books. Men give more lectures. Men ask more questions after lectures. Men dominate mixed-sex committee discussions. Men post more email to Internet discussion groups. To say that this is due to patriarchy is to beg the question of the behavior's origin [...] The ocean of male language that confronts modern women in bookstores, television, newspapers, classrooms, parliaments, and businesses does not necessarily come from a male conspiracy to deny women their voice. It may come from an evolutionary history of sexual selection in which the male motivation to talk was vital to their reproduction.[104]

Men talk more than women because men who talked in the EEA had more descendants. As a result, men dominate the professions in which talking is an essential skill.

As Pinker and Baron-Cohen insist, if this hypothesis is true, it does not follow that particular women should be excluded from the professions. However, a great deal of moral significance does follow. Feminists see injustice in the current distribution of positions of power and prestige. But evolutionary psychologists typically insist that though the bias in distribution might be exaggerated by cultural factors that are unjust, a marked bias is not itself unjust but is to be expected,

from the differing motivations ⌐f   men to succeed in the
public sphere. This i⌐   ludes.[105] And if mainstream f⌐   liffer in the extent to
w   ⌐y will differ corres-
                                                     ⌐tionary psycholo-
                                                     (since there is no
                                                     ⌐d (since people's
                                                     ⌐ range of envir-
⌐   ⌐anging cultural
e⌐   ⌐lly think that
afı   ⌐ver, feminists
typ   ⌐sychologists
disn   ⌐ieve equal
repre   ⌐tions, but
evolu⌐   ⌐king that
statistic   ⌐ıce of systematic
injustic⌐   ⌐ıs of the freedoms and legitimate asṛ   ⌐ perhaps women too).[106]

Simila⌐   ⌐ṗe ıs a facultative adaptation, this will have implications for what policies could play a role in reducing it. If rape is adaptive,
then, under the right conditions, men will have the desire to rape. We
can reduce it either by avoiding those conditions, or by ensuring that
men do not act on their desires. We could accomplish these goals by
avoiding anything that might arouse men sexually, or by removing the
opportunities for them to act upon their desires. Thus, Thornhill and
Palmer have a series of prescriptions to prevent rape – aimed at *women*,
not men: don't wear revealing clothes, or excessive makeup (you risk
arousing male desire); don't date unchaperoned (you provide opportunities for rape). If the adaptation hypothesis is true, then maybe this
is the best we can do. But we must not pretend that the theory has no
implications for what we can hope to achieve, and what means we have
to employ to these ends. Feminists hope to transform society, in such a
manner that women do not have to be eternally vigilant, so that women
can have as few restrictions on their movements and their actions as
men. If rape is an adaptation, that goal is likely forever out of reach.

Finally, though it is a fallacy to equate "natural" with "good," it is
not far-fetched to equate "natural" with "conducive to happiness,

other things being equal". It is quite likely that forcing people to attempt to do things that do not come naturally will make them miserable. George Will, the conservative American columnist, makes this connection explicit in his review of Danielle Crittenden's book advising women to marry and begin families early: "Crittenden sides with the anthropologist, Lionel Tiger, who says, dryly, that if biology is not destiny, it certainly is 'good statistical probability.' Ignoring probability brings punishment. Feminism, having established that women are human, forgot they are women, with distinctive desires, the ignoring of which causes unhappiness."[107]

Women who ignore the facts about their gendered nature, who aspire to lifestyles for which they are not suited, pay the price in unhappiness. This is only a statistical prediction: some women will turn out to be very well fitted to the life of power and politics. But if we hold this out as an aspiration for all, if we suggest to our daughters that these are the kinds of lives that women ought to lead, we risk rearing generations of unhappy women. Feminism, conservatives often allege, is responsible for just such misery. It tells women that they can have it all, thereby encouraging them to delay childbearing, often until it is too late. But for most of them, nothing will be more satisfying than childbearing, since this is the task for which they are best adapted, physically and emotionally. Evolutionary psychology thus seems to have policy implications: we should encourage people to pursue the lives for which they are evolved.

It is, therefore, false to claim that evolutionary psychology has no political implications. Only a very simplistic, not to say self-deceptive, view of morality could lead anyone to think otherwise. The naturalistic fallacy cannot insulate scientific claims from moral consequences, not when those claims concern the capacities of human beings. Some evolutionary psychologists have countered their critics by charging them with a fallacy of their own devising, the "moralistic fallacy." Someone commits the moralistic fallacy when they infer from the (supposed) fact that something is good that it is therefore found in nature.[108] I am not committing the so-called moralistic fallacy. I am not claiming that, because some of the claims of evolutionary psychology have consequences that I regard as pernicious, they must be false. We shall discover how much truth they have in them, not by assessing their consequences for morality, but by examining them as sets of empirical claims; that is, by assessing the degree to which they are coherent, supported by evidence, have considered and eliminated alternative explanations, and so on. The fact that, as I claim, they have undesirable implications does not make them false. It simply makes examining them all the more important.

Assessing the claims of evolutionary psychology

The sworn enemy of evolutionary psychology is the standard social science model, which claims that human behavior is very largely the product of culture and socialization. According to the SSSM, behavior is learned, and therefore can be changed by environmental intervention. Evolutionary psychologists have nothing but contempt for this view, and devote many pages to refuting it. Only if they succeed in this enterprise will their alternative explanations be credible.

Unfortunately, they spend much of their time tilting at a straw man. The version of the SSSM they attack is actually a parody of the view advocated by mainstream social scientists. Pinker dubs this straw man "the blank slate." Someone who believes in the blank slate believes that *nothing* is innate in the human mind: that human beings do not have evolved preferences or dispositions, or modules which make learning some tasks more difficult. *No one who has reflected deeply upon human behavior believes in the blank slate*, not even behaviorists like Skinner. Even he believed that animals have an innate desire for food, a desire that he put to work in his schedule of reinforcements for the behaviors he wished to condition. The debate between evolutionary psychology and the SSSM is not between people who believe that there are some evolved dispositions and propensities and those who deny that there are any. Instead, it concerns the *relative* malleability of human behavior, the *extent* to which it is open to alteration by environmental interventions that are practically and morally accessible to us. If social scientists do not mention our evolved propensities in their explanations, it is not because they deny that they exist, but because they deny that calling attention to them is illuminating.

The view that Pinker spends so much time excoriating, that there is no reality and that everything is "socially constructed," is indeed confused but it does not follow that *nothing* is socially constructed (indeed, few evolutionary psychologists would claim this). Thus, devoting page after page to attacks on the blank slate is irrelevant to the real debate. The real dispute concerns the explanation of particular behaviors, and must be conducted at this level. We shall therefore re-examine each of the central claims of evolutionary psychology, and test them against alternative explanations which are more in the tradition of the SSSM. We shall then adduce some general considerations, which suggest that evolutionary psychology can never hope to replace the more traditional social sciences (though it might prove to be a useful addition to the repertoire of social scientific skills and approaches).

Evolutionary psychology and human sexuality

Evolutionary psychology claims that men and women are disposed by nature to have different desires and preferences, as a consequence of differences in the extent of their parental investment. Because women are destined to invest far more heavily in their offspring – since eggs are more costly to manufacture than sperm, and since women must provide children with nutrition, both before and after birth – we can expect women to be far more choosy about their sexual partners than men. Women will be motivated to seek men with good genes (so as to maximize the quality of their offspring), with plentiful resources and with the willingness to commit them to a partner and offspring. Men, on the other hand, will be motivated to seek variety in their sexual partners, since they are able to maximize the number of their offspring by having sex with as many women as possible.

Buss claims that the preferences of men and women today, across all cultures, support this prediction. Men and women really do have the preferences that the theory predicts. This might seem a stunning vindication, except for one thing: *we all knew, beforehand, that this was so.* It is common knowledge that, on average, men seek greater variety in sexual partners than do women. For all its supposed scientific methodology, we are better off treating the claims of evolutionary psychology as inferences to the best explanation than as deductive arguments. Given a set of data, evolutionary psychology fabricates an evolutionary story that apparently explains it. It receives relatively little support from the careful testing of hypotheses.

The appropriate way to contest its claims, then, is to offer alternative explanations of the same data. The most common alternative explanation, the one which evolutionary psychology needs to refute if its own hypotheses are to be vindicated, is the *patriarchy explanation*. According to this view, women are motivated to seek men with higher status and more resources because there are systematic barriers to their acquiring these resources in other ways – barriers that are a result of a history of discrimination, not importantly due to differences in the brains of men and women. From this, all the other observed differences in the behavior of men and women follow. Since women have fewer resources with which to attract mates, they are forced to treat sex as a resource, and to limit its availability. Since men have less to gain from long-term relationships, they are less strongly motivated to pursue them.[109]

I believe that the patriarchy explanation makes better sense of the data than does the evolutionary psychological explanation. For a start, it does a much better job of explaining apparent exceptions to the predictions of evolutionary psychology. Buss predicted that men would prefer younger women as long-term mates, since such women would be just beginning their reproductive life. Conversely, women would prefer older men, because age is correlated with control of resources. Indeed, just as we should expect *on either theory*, women tend to marry older men. But there are exceptions:

> Not all women, however, select older men [...] A study of a small Chinese village found that women who were seventeen or eighteen sometimes married "men" who were only fourteen or fifteen. The contexts in which this occurred, however, were highly circumscribed in that all the "men" were already wealthy, came from a high-status family, and had secure expectations through inheritance.

Other exceptions occur "among women who already have high status and plentiful resources of their own."[110]

Buss explains the exceptions by invoking that old evolutionary psychological stand-by, the facultative adaptation. That is, women are not simply motivated to prefer older men, but have a conditional preference, which responds to the circumstances in which they find themselves. We know that there really are such things as facultative adaptations, so we cannot criticize the psychologists for invoking them. However, we can legitimately demand high standards of evidence when they resort to such claims. Philosophers of science have often pointed out that it is possible to hang on to any theory even in the face of apparently refuting evidence, if we are willing to adjust our background assumptions and invoke *ad hoc* hypotheses. What we require from evolutionary psychology is evidence that it is not engaged in adjusting its theory to fit the facts in an *ad hoc* manner. The danger here is that the invocation of facultative adaptations could be used to make the theory invulnerable to criticism, and render its hypotheses untestable. Without this constraint on acceptable hypotheses, no theory could be falsified. I might claim, for instance, that people are adapted to wear their underpants on their head, yet, when it is pointed out to me that people rarely wear their underpants there, simply shrug and say "it's a facultative adaptation."

Remember the form of explanation that is at issue here. Evolutionary psychology claims that we have modules or preferences that dispose us to act in ways that, in the EEA, would have been adaptive. In this case we are concerned with explanation by way of preferences: women are claimed to have a preference for older males. We need to be careful here concerning the *content* of that preference. Women are not hypothesized to have a preference for *resources*, but for older men; that is the content of their proximate preference, though its ultimate explanation will invoke resources (just as we have a proximate preference for sweet-tasting foods, not for calories, though it is because sweet-tasting foods are high in calories that we have this preference). Indeed, Buss claims that the preference for age is robust, even when access to resources is controlled for statistically. That is why he needs to claim that the adaptation is facultative when he is confronted with apparent exceptions. Under the right conditions, women must lose their preference for older men.

Our preferences come to be facultative only under certain conditions: if our ancestors in the EEA had to deal with situations which varied in systematic ways, so that different types of behaviors were rewarded in different conditions, and these different kinds of conditions recurred. If our ancestors had regularly encountered situations in which eating high-calorie foods was maladaptive, *as well as* situations in which eating such foods was adaptive, we might have evolved facultative food preferences; preferences which were sensitive to our environment, so that in some circumstances the sweetness preference would not be expressed (so we might today have a preference for broccoli over chocolate). We do not have such a facultative preference, because it is only very recently that the desire for high-calorie foods has become maladaptive.

Similarly, women could have evolved a facultative proximate preference, which is sensitive to the possession of resources, only if was the case that in the EEA resources were sometimes correlated with youth rather than age, or sometimes controlled by women, or that the link between the age of men and control of resources was broken in some other way, and that this situation recurred fairly frequently. Only under these conditions would such a preference have been adaptive. Buss adduces no evidence that the EEA was ever like that, nor, to my knowledge, has anyone else. Without such evidence, it is completely mysterious why women usually prefer older men, but sometimes prefer younger.

Let's consider the alternative explanation of this preference, offered by the patriarchy explanation. We might sum it up as: *women are rational* (this is a shocking hypothesis, I know, but bear with me for a moment and let's see how far it will take us). Women will be motivated to employ whatever mating strategy is in their, and their offspring's interest. Thus, when they know that, economically, boys are better prospects than men, they will choose to marry boys (other things being equal). Notice that this rival explanation does not invoke the blank slate. There is no claim that women will have whatever preferences they are socialized to have. On the contrary, if it were spelt out fully it would definitely mention innate desires: to provide for their offspring, to live comfortable lives, and so on. The claim is not that culture is everything and biology nothing, but that the constraints of biology are fewer and looser than evolutionary psychology suggests.

Buss himself has considered and dismissed the patriarchy explan-ation, which he calls "the structural powerlessness hypothesis," for pat-terns of human sexuality. We must consider his arguments against the view, if we are to vindicate the suggestion that it is more promising than its rival. The evidence he considers most telling comes from a study of American women that showed that:

> Successful women place an even greater value than less successful women on mates who have professional degrees, high social status, and greater intelligence [...] Perhaps most tellingly, these women express an even stronger preference for high-earning men than do women who are less financially successful [...] Taken together, these results not only fail to support the structural powerlessness hypothesis, but directly contradict it.[111]

Buss's claim is that if women simply had a rational preference for resources, then women who already possessed sufficient resources would not care about the wealth of potential mates and would make their mating decisions on other grounds. However, women who are wealthy have an even stronger preference for successful mates. Therefore, the patriarchy explanation is false.

There are several reasons to be skeptical of Buss's claim that this result invalidates the patriarchy explanation. Firstly, we ought to expect *some* degree of robustness in the preference of women. If culture has a role to play in explaining our preferences – and, to repeat, no one denies that it has *some* role – we ought to expect those preferences to be difficult to shed. Just as our taste for sugar stays with us today, in the modern West, long after it has ceased to be adaptive, so women's culturally derived preference for wealthy males may linger long after it is rational, especially if this preference tends to be taught, explicitly or implicitly, to children. It is a commonplace that feelings can remain with us long after we reject the beliefs that made our acquiring them rational. The child who is brought up in a religious family can feel guilty about her failure to attend church many years after she becomes an atheist. Similarly, the woman who, as a child, was surrounded by a culture that impressed on her the importance of landing a good "catch" may find the preference for a wealthy partner hard to shake off.

Secondly, when we examine the actual content of the reported preference, the claim that it is an innate disposition, rather than a response to the conditions in which women find themselves, becomes less plausible. Suppose that the preference is innate, so that, like our taste for sweet things, it is not responsive to changes in the environment which would make pursuing it irrational. Then, we would expect all women to have much the same preference, regardless of their own access to resources. But they don't: wealthier women have a *stronger* preference for resources in a mate. This is a puzzle for the evolutionary explanation, not a confirmation of it.

How do we explain the fact that wealthier women have a stronger preference for resources than the less wealthy? There are several factors that go toward explaining it. For one thing, possession of resources is strongly correlated with social status: it comes as no surprise that women with high social status want to marry men of a similar status. We all want our spouses to feel at ease and to fit into the circles we move in. Moreover, wealthier women are accustomed to a higher standard of living, and, rationally, may seek a mate that will enhance that standard (remember our working hypothesis: *women are rational*). There is no mystery here.

The patriarchy explanation, which is a specific hypothesis in the tradition of the SSSM, seems to do just as a good a job as evolutionary psychology in explaining the usual patterns of female preferences, and a better job of explaining at least some deviations. Does this give us a decisive reason to prefer the SSSM to evolutionary psychology? Better, I think, to say that it gives us good reason to integrate the two. The SSSM does a very good at explaining cultural variation, but it has no explanation for our most basic desires, those preferences which all cultures express in one form or another, however varied. For these basic preferences – our taste for sugar, our desire for comfort, companionship, and for sex, and our aversion to pain, isolation, humiliation, and many other things beside – evolutionary explanations seem to be the only credible contenders. But when it comes to explaining the fine details of behavior – the ways in which we pursue our basic desires and goals, how we balance them against each other, and the specific content of these general preferences – the SSSM does better. So, the major goals of psychology are better pursued in the traditional way: against a taken-for-granted background of human nature, broadly conceived.

I suggest that this view becomes even more convincing when we examine other aspects of human sexual behavior. Let's briefly consider two other, allegedly innate, sexual preferences. Men, Buss tells us, value attractiveness in women much more than women value attractiveness in men, and men value virginity in women much more than vice versa. Both of these have evolutionary explanations: female attractiveness is held to be a good indicator of fertility, while a virgin cannot be carrying another man's child, and her lack of sexual adventure might indicate that she is more likely to be faithful. Hence, men are likely to have a strong preference for both of these qualities. Women, however, have less reason to prefer virginity: since the resources women invest in children are (largely) biological, they don't run the risk of diverting their resources to an illegitimate child. They value fidelity, not because extramarital sex is a threat to them, but because they fear that their mate might begin to channel resources to another woman. So, they value emotional loyalty and possession of resources, not sexual inexperience or attractiveness.

What do we find when we test the preferences of men and women? This is one area in which, for the United States, historical as well as contemporary data exists: data which, for Buss, confirms his hypothesis. Subjects were asked to rate the importance of attractiveness in a marriage partner on a scale from 0.0 to 3.0. In 1939, men gave attractiveness an average rating of 1.50, while women rated it at 0.94. In 1989, men rated attractiveness at 2.11, while women rated it 1.67. Buss takes this as confirming his hypothesis, since "the sex difference remains invariant," with men placing more emphasis upon attractiveness, just as he predicted.[112]

But it is simply not true that the sex difference has remained invariant. In fact, the gap between men and women's ratings has narrowed, from 0.56 in 1939 to 0.44 in 1989. More strikingly, the emphasis that women placed upon attractiveness in 1989 was *greater* than that placed by men in 1939! Buss takes these expressed preferences as evidence that our desires are innate and relatively inflexible, but they seem to indicate instead the degree to which they are malleable. Once again, something akin to the SSSM does a better job of explaining the observed facts than does evolutionary psychology.[113]

Consider the evidence on male preferences for female virginity. Do we find that this preference is fixed, like our preference for sugar, or facultative, so that, depending on the environment, it switches from one state to another? The evidence does not support either hypothesis. In traditional societies, a high premium is still placed on virginity, but in the United States its importance has declined markedly. In much of western Europe, "virginity is largely irrelevant" in a mate.[114] What explains this alteration in male preferences? Buss himself notes that it may be "traceable in part to variability in the economic independence of women."[115] Since women are less economically dependent upon men in Europe and America, they are in a better bargaining position than elsewhere. Consequently, men are less able to make demands of them. The availability of effective contraception is certainly also part of the explanation. Men's preference for virgins is simply rational, in a society in which every act of sexual intercourse can lead to pregnancy (*men are rational too*). The fact that this preference has largely disappeared when it no longer serves a function suggests that it was a social norm, based upon a reasoned response to prevailing circumstances, not an innate disposition.

From what we have seen so far, we have little reason to abandon the SSSM, though we may indeed have reason to integrate evolutionary considerations into it. However, I don't expect to have convinced anyone yet. Perhaps some of the other evolutionary explanations I sketched in the previous chapter will prove more convincing than Buss's story of the evolution of desire. Let's turn now, from male and female desires, to male and female brains.

Baron-Cohen's male brain

According to Baron-Cohen, the relative success of men and women in the sciences and engineering can be explained in terms of their – innate – differences in systemizing and empathizing ability. But there are very good reasons to doubt that he succeeds in demonstrating his conclusion. There are a great many things wrong with Baron-Cohen's claims, ranging from flaws in the design of his studies to serious mistakes in his conceptions of intelligence. I will briefly sketch both kinds of problems.

Let's begin with Baron-Cohen's studies and the ways in which they are flawed. His claim that a higher degree of empathy is innate in women is supposed to be demonstrated by a study which shows a correlation between sex (and sex hormones independently of sex) and the degree to which neonates are interested in human faces, rather than in mechanical objects. But there are at least two things wrong with the facile assumption that a greater degree of interest in faces demonstrated by female infants equates with a higher degree of empathy in women (quite apart from the fact that the design of this study was flawed, as the researchers were frequently aware of the baby's sex).

Firstly, it is far from obvious that an interest in faces is a sign of, or a marker for, empathy. It might be an entirely unrelated trait. It is surely possible that a person might find faces fascinating without caring in the least what the person whose face it is thinks and feels. Secondly, it might be that there is a link between neonate interest in faces and adult empathy, but that this link is merely causal. Female babies might find faces more interesting, and therefore be better placed to learn about the emotions that faces express. On the latter hypothesis, it is the interest in faces, and not empathy itself, that would be innate. Finally, it could be the case that Baron-Cohen is correct in his surmise that empathy is innately stronger in female neonates, and yet still be true that, if women have more empathy (on average) than men, this is more importantly a product of culture rather than biology. It just doesn't follow that because infant A has a higher degree of trait x than infant B, infant A is more likely to develop into an adult with better developed x-ing ability. We cannot conclude that because one child learns to walk, or talk, earlier than another that it will be a better walker or talker later in life, not even on average. For some traits this might be true, for others, false. Only detailed empirical work will establish if there is a link between neonate empathy and adult empathy, independent of the culturally entrenched ways in which we treat girls and boys. Baron-Cohen has not carried out that work; indeed, he doesn't even seem to realize that it is needed.

More importantly, however, Baron-Cohen's implicit equation of "systematizing" ability with the kind of intelligence needed by scientists reflects a view of intelligence that looks increasingly implausible today. The idea that the essence of intelligence is the ability to formulate the rules that govern the behavior of systems is the central hypothesis of the research program that has come to be known as GOFAI (Good Old-Fashioned Artificial Intelligence) among computer scientists. Researchers in this tradition hold that building an intelligent machine is merely a matter of designing a computer that will manipulate sensory inputs by following rules of sufficient complexity. After forty years of GOFAI, the results have been far from impressive, and most researchers now look elsewhere in the search for thinking machines. The fundamental problem seems to be that the very definition of intelligence with which GOFAI worked was fatally flawed. Intelligence, including the intelligence of the scientist, consists of far more than the ability to systematize.

The primary obstacle to progress in GOFAI comes from what has come to be called the frame problem: the problem of specifying what rules and what information are relevant in a particular situation. When a human being is confronted with a changing situation, she usually grasps which changes are important and which trivial without needing to reflect upon the matter. If we are trying to understand a physical system, for example, we (typically) ignore the movements of shadows across it. But defining how we distinguish relevant from irrelevant information has so far eluded scientists. Attempts to formulate rules that tell us what to ignore and what to regard as salient run into two problems. Firstly, there seem to be so many exceptions to any useful rules that they soon become too unwieldy to apply (it is not just understanding social interactions, as Baron-Cohen thinks, but also understanding the physical world, which proves too complex for rules). Secondly, we need to know when to apply the rules, and for this we require higher-order rules: rules about rules. But then we need to know when to apply the higher-order rules, which requires yet higher-order rules. And so on. Hence, it seems impossible to capture the essence of intelligence in a rule-based system.

Given our inability to describe, in a rule-based way, what we do when we think intelligently, it seems unlikely that our intelligence is merely a systematizing ability. Scientists, it seems, need an analog of empathy: an intuitive ability to grasp what matters, as well as a highly developed systematizing ability.[116] But if this is so, then even if it is true that men and women have opposite cognitive profiles, in that males are better systemizers and females better empathizers, we have no reason to think this would give men an advantage in the sciences. Balanced brains, not "male" or "female" brains, would be best here. What explains the statistics on the domination of the sciences by males that Baron-Cohen quotes? Once again, I suggest that the patriarchy explanation is likely to prove true here. These statistics have their roots in a history of oppression of women. We explain these differences in terms of prejudices and culture, not genes and evolution.

Rape as an adaptation

Let's turn now to the suggestion that rape is either itself an adaptation, or a by-product of adaptations. If rape is adaptive, then it must be true that, in the EEA, the benefits of rape (measured in the currency of inclusive fitness) were greater than the costs. But all the evidence we have (from the study of hunter-gatherer societies, which are presumed closely to resemble the earliest human groups) is that the costs are high. Rapists risk injury or death, from their victims, from their victim's kin, and from the wider group. What benefits might outweigh these costs? Thornhill and Palmer suggest that males who have no other chance of reproducing might be willing to run these risks, since rape might be their only chance of passing on their genes. Thus, if rape is an adaptation, it is likely to be facultative, triggered by lack of access to willing partners and the knowledge that this state of affairs may be permanent.

On this hypothesis, we ought to expect that rapists will be single men who lack the resources to attract willing partners. And indeed, Thornhill and Palmer claim, "rape is disproportionately committed by males with lower socioeconomic status."[117] However, as they themselves point out, such males are disproportionately responsible for a wide range of crimes, not just rape. Moreover, economically disadvantaged men are not necessarily men without access to consenting women. Indeed, as they themselves point out, "self-report studies of men have found a positive correlation in normal unincarcerated men between sexually coercive tendencies and high level of sexual access to females."[118] Rapists do not seem to be the lonely strangers the theory predicts.

Thornhill and Palmer therefore need to find some way of accommodating this data, in order to rescue the rape-as-adaptation hypothesis. Their effort to reconcile the facts with their theory would be truly heroic, if it weren't so appalling. Their reasoning runs thus: men with multiple partners will tend, on average, to be more attractive to women, which explains why they have been so successful sexually. But though women desire to mate with physically attractive men, they know that the likelihood that such men will display fidelity toward them is low, given that they will receive frequent offers from other women. Thus, women who wish to retain such prize catches will have to make themselves especially attractive. They know that men value chastity in their long-term mates, so they can attempt to raise their value in the man's eyes by displaying an unwillingness to mate. Now, "if a woman's display of reluctance is truly effective, a man who achieves copulation with her will perceive that he achieved it by force."[119] Attractive men will therefore often think that they have coerced a woman into having sex with them. But they will be wrong: the woman desired the sex all the time. When women say "no," they frequently mean "yes." They thus predict (though they provide no evidence whatsoever) that women who are, apparently, raped by attractive men will experience "significant [...] sexual arousal, including orgasm."[120] Thornhill and Palmer frequently insist that they are dedicated to reducing rape. One way they hope to achieve this, it seems, is by redefining it out of existence: in their theory, some acts of coerced sex will not count as rape.

Unless we accept this bizarre and repugnant hypothesis, the evidence that rapists belong primarily to the group to which Thornhill and Palmer assign them is weak. Worse is to come for their theory: there is little or no evidence that the reproductive benefits of rape would, in the EEA, have outweighed its costs. On Thornhill and Palmer's own evidence, the reproductive benefits of rape are small – only about two percent of rapes result in pregnancy.[121] As they point out, however, natural selection can work effectively with very small margins: "Even traits that confer a seemingly trivial net reproductive benefit (say, one percent) relative to alternative traits increase in frequency very rapidly as a result of evolution by selection."[122] This is perfectly true. In evolutionary terms, a one percent advantage is significant, other things being equal. But this is only the case if the advantage is *net*: if it is not outweighed by costs – and a one percent advantage is easily outweighed by costs. Moreover, Thornhill and Palmer probably overestimate the reproductive benefits of rape, since they forget to factor in infanticide and neglect, which were common in the EEA, and which, probably, were directed at the children of rape victims more frequently than at other children. Given the fact that the benefits of rape are, on average, probably non-existent in the EEA, when weighed against the costs of punishment to the rapist, it is extremely unlikely that rape can be an adaptation.

Thornhill and Palmer reject this line of reasoning. Though they apparently admit that the reproductive benefits of rape are probably outweighed by its costs, they will not accept that this shows that rape is not an adaptation. They point out that "the coevolutionary battle of the sexes is ongoing, and which sex is ahead at any time is largely unpredictable."[123] If men had evolved an adaptation that benefitted them at the expense of women, this adaptation would exert selection pressure on women, who might well evolve counter-adaptations. Thus, they argue, we cannot infer from the fact that rape has no net reproductive benefits that it is not an adaptation.

However, this line of argument is illegitimate. It is *possible* that rape might once have been adaptive, but conceding that it was probably not adaptive in the EEA is conceding that there is no evidence that rape has *ever* been adaptive for human beings. Daniel Dennett argues that "reverse engineering" is central to evolutionary methodology, in all its forms. To reverse engineer a trait, we postulate a function for it, and then try to discover how it works and perhaps imagine a selection history for it on that basis. If the trait fulfilled a particular adaptive function in the EEA, it is a safe bet that it was selected for that function. But if it turns out *not* to fulfill that function, we ought to abandon the hypothesis that that was its original purpose (unless we have some other evidence for the claim).[124] Certainly it is possible to imagine that rape once served a function that, so far as we can tell, it has not served in the recent evolutionary past. But it is equally possible to dream up functions for any other trait. This is idle speculation, and when the topic is one as inflammatory – and important – as rape, it is both pernicious and reprehensible. It is not bad science *because* it has objectionable implications (the objection to it that Pinker and other defenders of Thornhill and Palmer attribute to advocates of something more like the SSSM). It is objectionable, in part, because it is bad science.

So we must abandon the claim that rape is an adaptation. But of course Thornhill and Palmer do not claim that rape is an adaptation. They claim that *either* rape is an adaptation, *or* it is a by-product of adaptations. Might we yet be forced to concede that rape is a by-product of adaptations? I think we ought. *Of course* rape is either an adaptation or a by-product of adaptations: that exhausts the possibilities, so far as behavioral traits and characteristics are concerned. Whatever we are able to do, we can do either because in doing so we exercise physical and psychological traits which were selected in the EEA (at least in part) because they allowed our ancestors to act similarly, or because we are able to put to some new use characteristics which were selected for some other purpose. To say that a behavior is an adaptation or a by-product of an adaptation is simply to say that we are products of natural selection.

This is not to say, however, that all by-product explanations are necessarily uninformative. Daly and Wilson's hypothesis, that patterns of child-abuse are (in part) a by-product of other adaptations, is informative, if it is true. However, the burden of providing a content for the explanation must be shouldered, and the only way to make a by-product explanation substantive is by providing good evidence for the adaptations, of which the behavior is alleged to be a by-product, and tracing the path whereby the behavior is a by-product of that adaptation. This Thornhill and Palmer do not do. They simply mention alleged features of male sexuality (greater sex drive, greater visual sexual arousal, desire for numerous partners) that they claim are adaptations, and which might facilitate rape. But without detailed work showing that these features are innate and adaptive, and demonstrating how they come into play in rape, this is completely empty speculation. We knew before Thornhill and Palmer began their research that rape was either adaptive or a by-product of adaptations. Nothing in their work adds to our knowledge, neither of the cause of rape, nor of the means whereby its incidence could be reduced.

Evolutionary psychology and social norms

I have provided relatively detailed, alleged adaptation specific, rebuttals of particular evolutionary psychological claims. But the weaknesses I have identified are specific to those explanations, not general features of evolutionary psychology. Some evolutionary hypotheses are more carefully formulated and tested: Daly and Wilson's work is a case in point. In this section, I want to step back from the details of particular hypoth-eses and look at the broader picture. If I am to vindicate the suggestion that evolutionary psychology cannot replace the SSSM, but ought instead to be integrated with it, we must defend the continuing usefulness of a social scientific approach against charges that it is unable to explain the very social norms it regards as its home territory.

The problem, according to evolutionary psychologists, is that the social norms that are thought of as the special subject of anthropologists and sociologists do not vary greatly from time to time, or across geographical regions. Instead, they are universal, and universality is good evidence of innateness. It is surely no accident that (almost) all of us are born with two arms and two legs. The explanation for the universality of this trait, of course, is that it has gone to fixation: it is inscribed in the human genome.[125]

Certainly, evolutionary psychologists argue, the universality of a trait is decisive evidence against the SSSM view: against the view that that trait is "socially constructed," merely the result of arbitrary norms and conventions. It is precisely by invoking the (alleged) universality of sex differences in psychology that Pinker, for instance, argues against such views:

> Things are not looking good for the theory that boys and girls are born identical except for their genitalia, with all other differences coming from the way society treats them. If that were true, it would be an amazing coincidence that in every society the coin flip that assigns each sex to one set of roles would land the same way (or that one fateful flip at the dawn of the species should have been maintained without interruption across all the upheavals of the past hundred thousand years).[126]

The SSSM has to meet this challenge: explain the existence of cultural universals, or cede its place as the best available theory of social behavior.

The SSSM could simply *deny* the existence of such universals. Evolutionary psychologists do tend to exaggerate their number and significance. Moreover, some universals are probably what Dennett calls "good ideas": obvious, or optimal, solutions to recurrent problems, which we can expect to be "routinely rediscovered by every culture"[127] and which therefore do not require any special explanation. However, some important behaviors and practices, which are not good ideas in this sense, do seem to be universal. Indeed, I have invoked one myself, in arguing against Buss. I claimed that the (near) universal existence of patriarchy was sufficient to explain the data he collected. But in so doing, I was inviting the following response:

> Grant that patriarchy explains the mate-preferences of men and women. But you still need to explain the existence of patriarchy. If it is universal, mustn't we explain its existence by invoking the evolved and gendered nature of human beings? So while your explanation might be an alternative to that offered by Buss and other evolutionary psychologists, it isn't an alternative to evolutionary psychology *per se*. Instead, it is a rival explanation offered from within the same general framework – could you but see it.

Given that the kind of move I have made against Buss's theory and other evolutionary explanations itself seems to require the invocation of cultural universals, if we are to hang on to the SSSM, simply denying the existence of such universals isn't possible. We need to explain them.

Of course, many universals *do* have evolutionary explanations, direct or indirect. We ought to concede that our preferences and desires are, at some level, shaped by evolution. Our quarrel with evolutionary psychology is not on this ground, but concerns the *details* of our desires. Of course we have an aversion to pain because those of our ancestors who ignored traumatic injuries tended to have shorter lives and fewer offspring. The SSSM concedes (or, at any rate, ought to concede) that we are not blank slates, but instead that at the most general level, our emotions and preferences are the products of evolution. It is at the level of the specific content of our behavior that it diverges from evolutionary psychology, not at the level of our basic desires. It holds that this content is provided, for the most part, by culture (though there may be exceptions, like our preference for certain foods, which can be given fairly detailed evolutionary explanations). How, on this basis, might cultural universals have come to exist? These universals, SSSM claims, are *conventions*. To understand conventions, we need to recall a little game theory, the theory we turned in order to understand how morality might have evolved by natural selection.

According to the influential analysis of David Lewis, conventions are solutions to *coordination problems*. Two (or more) people have a coordination problem when they interact regularly in circumstances in which the best course of action for each depends upon the action of the other. For example, in the absence of road laws, two drivers approaching each other from different directions on the same road have a coordination problem. If each drives on the left side of the road, or each drives on the right, then they will pass each other without incident. A convention – "always drive on the left" or "always drive on the right" – will solve their problem.

It is essential to this analysis of conventions that the solution is *arbitrary*, in the sense that there is at least one other option that would have solved the problem just as well. If there is one solution that works much better than the others, then we ought to expect it to be selected, and that solution would not be purely conventional. If different groups of human beings are faced with the same coordination problem at different times, we ought to expect them to hit upon each available solution in equal proportions. If, instead, they repeatedly come up with the same solution, we can be sure that it is not *entirely* a convention. Human beings faced the particular coordination problem of needing to communicate with one another. The solutions they came up with are conventional, at the level of vocabulary: the sheer diversity of spoken languages testifies to this fact. If, instead, they all spontaneously developed the same vocabulary, we would have very good evidence that for some reason this vocabulary is superior to alternatives – or that it is innate.

According to the SSSM, social norms are (at least largely) sets of conventions. Thus, we ought to expect them to vary from society to society. But, as Pinker points out, gender roles do not vary greatly:

All cultures divide their labor by sex, with more responsibility for childrearing by women and more control of the public and political realms by men [...] In all cultures, men are more aggressive, more prone to stealing, more prone to lethal violence (including war), and more likely to woo, seduce, and trade favors for sex.[128]

Indeed, we could easily add to this list of universal, or near-universal, sex differences. I myself have invoked such differences, under the category of patriarchy, in explaining the data Buss collects. But if these differences are near-universal, must we not admit that they are not merely conventional? If male dominance was conventional, then we ought to expect to find it no more widely distributed than female dominance, or equality of the sexes. Since it is near-universal, it cannot be conventional.

This seems to be right, so far as it goes. The near-universality of many social norms suggests that they are not *merely* conventional. But it does not follow from this that patriarchy (for instance) is not *importantly* conventional. The tools developed by John Maynard Smith, the evolutionary biologist who, more than anyone else, is responsible for introducing game theory into biology, will allow us to see how patriarchy might become universal, despite the fact that it is neither innate in the human mind, nor a better solution to the coordination problems faced by our ancestors than others available (such as equality).

Maynard Smith was concerned with explaining a phenomenon which had intrigued biologists for many years: the fact that members of the same species appear to take care to avoid inflicting serious injuries upon one another, even when they are engaged in high-stakes conflict. Earlier biologists had invoked group selection to explain this phenomenon – groups of animals that engaged in ritualized combat, for example, would be likely to out-perform groups whose conflicts took a deadlier form. But the application of game theory to the problem soon showed that this solution would not work. If that was all there was to restraint, then groups that refrained from violence would be vulnerable to invasion by mutants playing the more deadly strategy. In game theory terms, mutual restraint was not an *evolutionarily stable strategy* (ESS) on the group selectionist hypothesis.

Maynard Smith suspected that if game theory revealed the limits of the group selectionist explanation, it was also capable of providing a better theory of the evolution of restraint.[129] Imagine two animals involved in a conflict over some resource that cannot be shared. Each animal has two options: it can escalate the conflict, or it can retreat, leaving the other animal in possession of the resource. Obviously, if it retreats it does not receive any benefit from the resource, but escalation carries risks, both for itself and for its opponent. Either or both may be wounded or killed in a violent confrontation. Maynard Smith represented this conflict as a game between two players. Each player can engage in one of two strategies: it can be a "hawk," and continue to escalate the conflict either until its opponent retreats, or it itself is injured and forced to retreat, or be a "dove," who makes a show of defiance but retreats if its opponent escalates. To calculate the pay-off matrix, Maynard Smith introduced the following variables: the resource is worth V (for value) to each player, a wound reduces the fitness of each by $-W$, and a long contest imposes costs in terms of wasted time, represented by $-T$. We can represent the conflict thus:

	Hawk	Dove
Hawk	1/2(V–W)	V
Dove	0	1/2 (V–T)

When a hawk meets a hawk, each receives (on average) half the value of the resource minus half the value of a wound (on the assumption that each hawk will win the contests half the time, and be wounded half the time); when a hawk meets a dove, the hawk receives the entire value of the resource, and the dove receives nothing (captured in the top right and the bottom left boxes); and when two doves meet, they receive, on average, half the value of the resource, minus the waste of time each expends on the contest.

What happens, of course, depends on the values of these variables, and the proportion of hawks and doves in the population. Here is one possibility, in which W = 6, V = 4 and T = 1:

	Hawk	Dove
Hawk	−1	4
Dove	0	1

Hawks win against doves, but do badly against other hawks. Doves lose against hawks, but, on average, benefit from competing with other doves. Selection here will be *frequency dependent*. If there are mainly doves in the population, hawks will do well – since they meet each other infrequently – and will increase in numbers. But as their numbers increase, their average pay-off will fall, and the number of doves will therefore rise. We should expect a constant oscillation in numbers. To put it another way, there is no ESS here: a population of hawks is vulnerable to invasion by doves, and a population of doves to invasion by hawks.

But, as Maynard Smith noticed, if there is an appropriate asymmetry between the players, an ESS will evolve. One possible asymmetry is first possession – ownership – of the contested resource. To illustrate how this might lead to an ESS, Maynard Smith introduces a third strategy, "bourgeois," to the hawk/dove game. The bourgeois strategy is a conditional strategy: someone who plays bourgeois plays hawk if they are the "owner" of the resources, and dove if they are the interloper. Adding bourgeois to the game gives us the following pay-off matrix:

	Hawk	Dove	Bourgeois
Hawk	−1	4	1.5
Dove	0	1	0.5
Bourgeois	−0.5	2.5	2

A population of organisms playing bourgeois (bourgeoisie?) will do better playing against each other than either hawks or doves do against them. Thus, it is an ESS. In other words, a population in which confrontations between competing animals are purely ritualistic, one in which conflicts typically end before either combatant is seriously hurt, can evolve entirely by individual natural selection. If each organism plays the bourgeois strategy, then interlopers will usually back down after a short display, leaving the established owner in possession of the resource.

Does the bourgeois strategy accurately describe the interactions that actually take place in ritualized combat? At least in some cases, it does. Maynard Smith describes one elegant experiment that illustrates the way that the strategy is used by animals to settle disputes. The swallowtail butterfly is one organism that apparently plays the bourgeois strategy. Male swallowtail butterflies occupy the tops of hills, where they wait for females. But there are more male butterflies than hilltops, so some males miss out on resource possession. When a male flies up to an already occupied hillside, the two males display at each other, until the interloper retreats.

What researchers couldn't know, simply from observing this behavior, is that it was the mere fact of ownership that was doing the work here. Perhaps the occupants of hilltops were invariably stronger than newcomers (maybe because they did not need to expend energy flying from hill to hill), and this fact was perceptible to the interlopers. In that case, it would be strength, and not ownership, that was the proximate cause of the behavior. To discover whether the animals were playing bourgeois or whether some other factor explained their behavior, L. Gilbert allowed each of two male butterflies to occupy the same hilltop on alternate days, for two weeks. He then released them both at the same time on the hilltop. Now both butterflies regarded themselves as the "owner," and neither was willing to back down. A lengthy and mutually damaging contest ensued.[130]

In species in which disputes over the possession of resources are common, we can expect some kind of tie-breaking asymmetry to come to be recognized (since organisms which play by these rules will tend to do better than those that don't). As Maynard Smith points out, this asymmetry can be purely conventional.[131] There is good reason, however, to think that ownership is not a *purely* conventional asymmetry, since if it were we ought to expect the opposite tie-breaking strategy – "paradoxical" – to be just as common as bourgeois. Organisms play "paradoxical" in cases where, as the usual means of settling conflicts, owners relinquish resources to interlopers. It is easy to see why bourgeois has the advantage over paradoxical, since a resource will tend to be more valuable to its owner than to an intruder. Owners will already have gone to the trouble of exploring their territory, and this might give them the advantage when it comes to defending it.

However, the advantage that defenders of territories have over interlopers is likely to be slight. Intuitively, we would think that "bourgeois" would as a tie-breaking strategy, only be slightly more common than 'paradoxical'. In fact, though "paradoxical" has been observed in nature (in a species of spider), it is extremely rare.[132] If the advantage owners have over interlopers is small, what explains the great predominance of "bourgeois" over "paradoxical?"

Brian Skyrms, a philosopher and game theorist, set out to answer this question. Why do the small advantages that accrue to "owners" make bourgeois so much more common than paradoxical? Skyrms argues that the solution lies in what he calls "broken symmetries."[133] He asks us to think of a vertical plank, which is supporting an ever-increasing load. As the pressure upon the plank increases, we would expect it to buckle, either to the left or to the right. But which way will it buckle? If the plank were perfectly symmetrical and perfectly vertical, then there would be no reason for it to buckle to one side rather than the other. If it has no reason to buckle left, rather than right, or vice versa, then we might conclude that it will not buckle at all, no matter how much pressure is exerted upon it! But of course it will. How does this happen? No plank is perfectly symmetrical, though we may not be able to detect the imperfections that make it asymmetrical. As the pressure increases, the asymmetries in the plank will be sufficient to ensure that it buckles upon one side rather than the other. A tiny imperfection will be sufficient to produce the effect.

In the same way, Skyrms argues, a very small advantage accruing to a resource holder will be sufficient to ensure that bourgeois has a decisive advantage over paradoxical.[134] When we model this on a computer, we find that what Skyrms calls the "basin of attraction" – the probability that one ESS rather than another will eventually stabilize – is very much larger for bourgeois than for paradoxical, even if we assign a very small increased weight to resource ownership. Hence, almost all organisms that have a norm for settling conflicts over resources in terms of possession play bourgeois, and paradoxical is almost unknown.

I believe this finding has important lessons for anyone who wishes to understand how and why social norms and conventions arise among human beings. A very small symmetry-breaking ingredient among players who face a coordination problem can be expected to have a decisive effect upon the convention that arises. Coordination problems are pervasive in human life. People are constantly faced with problems to which there are multiple solutions, and which are such that if a solution is in place, no one can do better by unilaterally defecting from it (the technical definition of a coordination problem). For example, relations between the sexes, who need each other for reproduction, can be conceptualized as a set of coordination problems. Responsibility for child-rearing, and for other tasks, has to be allocated. There are, obviously, many solutions to these labor allocation tasks. But if there are natural symmetry-breaking features differentiating the sexes, we ought to expect one set of solutions to these problems to be far more common than others. Are there such symmetry-breaking features? Of course there are, and in the EEA they were far from insignificant. The costs of bearing children and breast-feeding them fall exclusively upon women. Moreover, there are differences in the average strength of men and women, which were probably important in the EEA. These symmetry-breaking features are so conspicuous, and so significant, that it is likely that the basin of attraction for a single set of social norms was very large indeed. We do not need to postulate (even weak) *psychological* differences between men and women to explain the near-universality of traditional roles; the solution is already before us in their physiologies.

Thus, the SSSM can explain social norms without invoking evolutionary considerations. The division of labor which we see in all hunter-gatherer societies, where women stay near the campsite while men roam, is exactly what we would expect, given the different roles men and women play in child-rearing. The exclusion of women from political power and from public forums is most likely to be the consequence of nothing deeper than the fact that males are able, given the relative strengths of the sexes, to impose their will upon women. "Femininity," the norms and behaviors expected of women, is probably no more than the cultural elaboration of these fundamental divisions. Contrary to what the evolutionary psychologists claim, we do not need their theories to explain the near-universality of many social norms.

Let us apply these observations to the work of Daly and Wilson. If their data are to be believed, being a stepchild is the single most important risk factor for abuse, across all cultures.[135] It is a (near) universal norm that one should love one's own children, and exercise patient forbearance in the face of their provocations. But the norm does not extend protection to stepchildren. Can mere convention explain the ubiquity of this norm? Or, as Daly and Wilson argue, are we forced to postulate adaptations for parental solicitude, a by-product of which is the observed pattern of abuse?

If conventions are to do the work, then we need to locate a feature which would break the symmetry between three possibilities: (1) care for all children equally, (2) care for children other than your own more than your own, and (3) care for your own children more than others. It is easy to see that (1) and (2) are highly unstable, if for no other reason than that they frequently would require individuals to care for too many children. In very many social groups, no one person will have the time or the resources to feed, clothe, and house all the children in the group, or even all of those apart from their biological children. Moreover, infants need to be breast-fed, and their mothers will frequently be the only women in the neighborhood who are lactating. Add to this a modest degree of pair-bonding; that is a tendency of males to stay near the women with whom they have fathered children, and also the fact that males will tend to channel resources to their own children, if for no other reason than that they associate with them more and more closely.

Thus, it is easy to see that parental solicitude could become established as a social norm, without needing to postulate any innate tendency to prefer one's own children to the children of others. Of course, that explains only our propensity to care for our own children, not the cross-cultural pattern of child *abuse*. But we can explain the latter in exactly the same way that Daly and Wilson do: as a by-product of this propensity. When the norm is not in place, when a new, unrelated, adult takes over the care of children, abuse is more likely, because there is no internalized norm requiring solicitude for unrelated children.

However, it is unlikely that *all* the work here is done by social norms. As I have been arguing throughout this chapter, evolutionary psychology has a contribution to make to our understanding of human behavior and social life, and this is true here as well. When mammals give birth, a powerful hormone, oxytocin, is released into their brains. This hormone promotes bonding with their new offspring. Oxytocin is unlikely to be wholly responsible for parental solicitude, given that the feelings to which it gives rise are easily transferred to other children, and that oxytocin levels are unlikely to remain high for long (as the phenomenon of post-natal depression shows). However, the release of oxytocin might itself contribute to the establishment of the social norm favoring parental solicitude, since it is itself a symmetry-breaking factor. So, though biological and evolutionary considerations matter, social norms remain an essential part of the explanation for the pattern of child abuse observed by Daly and Wilson.

To say that social norms matter is to say that history and culture matter. This is the true point of contention between evolutionary psychologists and proponents of the SSSM. Evolutionary psychology holds that the differences we observe, between us and our society and those far removed from us in time and space, are relatively superficial. All people share the same human nature, which places significant constraints upon the ways of life available to human beings. Societies that do not respect these constraints, which ignore them in their zeal to establish a Utopia, don't survive for very long, and during their short lives they inflict high costs on their members. Proponents of the SSSM do not (or ought not) deny that we all share a common nature, and that this nature sets limits on the social relations we can hope to achieve. But they believe that these limits are much less constraining than the evolutionary psychologists suggest. The SSSM holds that while our basic desires are the product of our evolved human nature, the specific shape they take varies from society to society and time to time, as a consequence of the way these desires are interpreted. In general, and for many of the most significant aspects of human life, nature only sets boundaries: social norms and history settle what the way of life will be within them.

Which view best captures human life, in all its diversity? I have suggested that, at least in areas surrounding gender relations, something like the SSSM remains the best explanation. The selection of these issues was not arbitrary. Evolutionary psychology has chosen this territory, by devoting a significant proportion of its attention to it. Moreover, it is this work that has, rightly, attracted the most attention, because the conclusions of the evolutionary psychologists with regard to male and female brains and preferences have immediate implications for our morality and for our social policies. If the evolutionary explanations of our social life were true, then we would very likely be stuck with certain forms of inequality. But they are (at best) only partly true, and our future remains open. Existing social norms are not a direct expression of human nature, and we retain the power to transform them for the better.

None of this is meant to imply that evolutionary considerations do not help us understand ourselves. The basic desires that the SSSM presupposes are the products of evolution, and cannot be wished away. They are not "social constructions." Moreover, there are other aspects of human life that are illuminated by evolutionary hypotheses. It may be, for instance, that our "disgust" reactions are triggered by the extent to which an object has characteristics which would, in the EEA, be reliably associated with sources of infection.[136] If this is right, it would be an instance in which our evolved nature can not only explain the constraints on our social lives, but also fill in some of the details.

Evolutionary psychology may yet prove an important and fruitful research program. It goes wrong, not in offering evolutionary explanations of human behavior, but in thinking that its explanations must be exclusive of the more traditional approaches of the social sciences. Every new research program has the tendency to overextend itself: to think that almost everything can best be understood from its viewpoint alone. This is a relatively harmless phenomenon, which, I have no doubt, will soon pass; soon evolutionary approaches will become just one more possible approach to human behavior, often illuminating, but almost never the *whole* story. We ought to welcome the addition of the evolutionary approach. But when its imperialistic urge takes it blundering into politically sensitive territory, and it gets things badly – dangerously – wrong, we ought to combat it.

5

Genetic fallacies

We used to think our fate was in our stars. Now we know, in large measure, our fate is in our genes.

> James Watson, winner (with Francis Crick and
> Maurice Wilkins) of the 1962 Nobel Prize for
> Medicine, for discovering the structure of DNA

In previous chapters, I have traced and analyzed the debates over the importance for morality of our evolutionary past by reference to Darwin's theory of natural selection. There is a sense, however, in which this is a one-sided approach. Darwin's work was certainly one of the most impressive and momentous in the history of science, but it was also critically incomplete. As Darwin saw, the theory of natural selection has three fundamental elements: there must be *differences* between organisms of the same species, as a result of which some are *fitter* than others and therefore tend to have more offspring, and these differences must be *heritable*, so that these offspring tend to possess the traits that made their parents fitter. Without heritability, random differences could not accumulate, and speciation could not occur. Evolution is the story of how life on Earth, in all its fantastic diversity, is descended from very simple organisms. But such descent requires that a fine balance be struck between the preservation of traits from one generation to another – so that offspring tend to resemble their parents, and species can be identified – and slow alteration in traits, so that mutations with differential fitness can arise. Though Darwin saw the need for such a mechanism, he had no credible theory to account for it.

It was largely because of his failure on this score that, though most biologists soon accepted evolution, the mechanisms that Darwin proposed were largely rejected. Scientists looked to other evolutionary explanations. All this changed with the rediscovery of the work of an obscure Austrian monk, Gregor Mendel. Mendel had conducted experiments in the breeding of peas, in which he crossed one variety with another. He noticed that some traits appeared to be *dominant* over others, in the sense that if you crossed a variety with one trait with a variety with another, all the plants in the second generation would have the dominant trait. Upon first inspection, it might seem that the *recessive* (as we now say) trait had been "bred out" altogether. But re-crossing the plants in the second generation with each other showed that this was not the case: the recessive trait reappeared in the next generation! Just what was going on?

Mendel realized that the ratio in which traits appeared was an important clue: the recessive trait appeared in around twenty-five percent of the plants in the third generation. This discovery allowed him to guess at the nature of the underlying process. Somehow, inheritance must involve passing on half the properties of parents to their offspring. That much of course, Darwin had known, but he hadn't been able to explain why traits were not "washed out" in the process. Take Mendel's own subject, the garden pea. The pea comes in round-seeded and wrinkle-seeded varieties, which Mendel crossed with each other. If offspring inherit from each parent equally, then shouldn't we expect the second generation of plants to have had seeds that were half-way between the round-seeded and wrinkle-seeded variety – a little wrinkled, perhaps? But that didn't happen – the entire second generation consisted of round-seeded plants. And the third generation was made up of round-seeded peas and wrinkle-seeded peas in the ratio of 3:1. The traits were not blended, but inherited in stable forms.

Mendel explained the pattern of inheritance by postulating that the appearance of traits was controlled by some heritable element that comes in *pairs*: one from each parent. This, he saw, would explain both why the second generation consisted exclusively of round-seeded plants, and also the ratio in which wrinkle-seeded peas appeared in the next generation. Suppose that the plants in the first generation each had two copies of the same heritable factor (we call them genes), and that one of these factors is dominant over the other, so that even if a plant receives just one, it will possess the trait associated with that factor. In that case, crossing two different *homozygous* plants – plants that possess two identical varieties of a particular gene – would produce the following results. (In this schematic representation, "*R*" represents the allele for rounded seeds, while "*r*" represents the allele for wrinkled seeds. An *allele* is one of the possible variants of a gene – in this case, wrinkled or rounded):

First generation   RR   rr
                          ↓
Second generation Rr   Rr

Since the offspring inherit one gene for seed shape from each parent, and the parents are homozygous for the gene, then no matter which gene they get from which parent, each plant in the second generation ends up with one copy of each allele (the plants are *heterozygous* for that gene). But since the gene for rounded seeds is dominant, each plant *expresses* only that gene: it has rounded seeds.

In the next generation, however, the phenotype for wrinkled seeds reappears:

Second generation   Rr   Rr
                            ↓
Third generation   Rr RR rR   rr

Each plant inherits one allele from each parent. Thus, half the plants get the *R* allele from the parent on the left, and half the *r* allele; half get the *R* allele from the plant on the right, and half the *r* allele. As a result, one of the plants is homozygous dominant (*RR*) for seed shape and two, like the parents, are heterozygous (*Rr*). Since *R* is dominant, all three plants have rounded seeds. But one plant is homozygous recessive (*rr*). Since there is no dominant (*R*) present, the recessive phenotype is expressed – the plant has wrinkled seeds.

Mendel's theory not only explained the ratios in which traits were inherited, but also why heredity did not wash away differences. Since the underlying mechanism was a factor that was passed on as a whole, the trait associated with it either appeared full-blown, or not at all. Mendel's careful experimentation had revealed the underlying mechanism of heredity. When Darwinism made its triumphant comeback in the early years of the twentieth century, it called upon Mendelian genetics to fill the gaps in explaining inheritance. It was not Darwinism, as Darwin himself had elaborated it, which swept biology, but what came to be known as "the new synthesis," or Neo-Darwinism. The genetic perspective allowed biologists to understand a great many phenomena that had been mysterious to evolutionists who lacked the mechanism provided by Mendel.

Indeed, I have invoked the genetic perspective at crucial points in my analysis of the evolution of morality. For example, the notion of inclusive fitness, which underlies kin altruism, only makes sense in the light of Mendelian inheritance. But we need to take fuller cognizance of the role of the gene. When people invoke biology as a means to understand human behavior, to explain, or explain away, ethics and responsibility, it is most often genes they have in mind, not evolution. It is time to examine the other half of the new synthesis, the mechanism of inheritance itself.

The genetics of behavior

What do genes actually *do*? The most common answer is that they are a blueprint, or perhaps a program. They contain the instructions for making organisms. Francis Crick, who, with James Watson, made the breakthrough discovery of the double helix structure of deoxyribonucleic acid (DNA), the substance out of which genes are composed, put it this way, "DNA makes RNA [ribonucleic acid, which carries the genetic instructions to the parts of the cell where proteins are made], RNA makes protein, and proteins make us."[137] Thus, our genome is the blueprint that our cellular machinery follows in constructing us. The genome contains the set of plans for building an organism.

When we are engaged in the project of understanding human behavior and morality, this seemingly technical matter is very important. For the way the blueprint metaphor is usually understood, our genes shape, control, or at very least constrain, what it is we are able to do, think, and desire. Our shared genome explains what we have in common. Equally, our differences are to be explained in terms of the degree to which our genes differ from one another – "it's in the genes," we are often told. More and more, the medical profession looks to the genome to understand disease, and to learn how to fight it. Increasingly, we can test for genes that indicate susceptibility to cancer: for example, possession of the gene BRCA 1 raises a woman's lifetime risk of breast cancer to fifty percent or more. And it is not just our physical characteristics which genes are supposed to explain. Psychological traits and dispositions are also widely held to be under genetic control. In the past few years, researchers have made an astonishing array of claims about the genetic origins of complex behaviors:

1. A disposition to violent behavior is widely believed to have a genetic cause. For example, Terrie Moffitt, from the Institute of Psychiatry at King's College London, claims to have isolated what, on one interpretation, are "genes for violence".[138]
2. A disposition to laziness might have a genetic basis. Professor Susan Ward of Glasgow University predicts that a gene for laziness will be found. She claims that understanding the genetics of laziness should transform our attitude to people who suffer from this condition: "People who don't like exercise are usually seen as lazy, but it may be that it's not their fault. There may be a link between exercise intolerance and genetic make-up which restricts or promotes exercise depending on your genes".[139]
3. Intelligence is very frequently thought to be largely genetic. Professor Gerald McClearn argues that "IQ genes" play a crucial role in determining our cognitive ability.[140] Pinker's *The Blank Slate* is largely devoted to buttressing the case for a genetic basis for IQ.
4. Sexual orientation is in the genes. The discovery of the "gay gene" was widely hailed in the world's newspapers.[141] Dean Hamer, the scientist whose research caused this stir, was himself more careful. He claims only that our genes "influence" sexual orientation, not that they *determine* it. Nevertheless, he describes his search, through linkage studies, for the gene or genes which play this role as "Looking for Gay Genes."[142]

We could continue to multiply examples of claims of genes for phenotypic traits: sporting or artistic ability, dyslexia, autism, psychopathy, depression, binge eating, introversion – all of these, and many more, are sometimes said to be caused (or, at a minimum, influenced) by our genes. The language of the genes, and the message of genetic determinism, has been absorbed into our culture. From *The X-Files* to *The New York Times*, our media repeat to us the message that our destiny is in our genes.

Genethics

If we fail to consider the implications of the new genetics for morality and human behavior, we risk leaving a large hole at the heart of our inquiry. We cannot hope to understand the implications of evolution if we don't explore and account for the role of its principal mechanism, the mechanism that rescued Darwinism from obscurity. Moreover, many of the challenges we have faced thus far, especially under the guise of the evolutionary explanations of human psychology, reappear as more narrowly genetic challenges to our ability to elaborate an adequate account of human morality and freedom. It may be, for instance, that we can puncture the theories of sex differences offered by evolutionary psychology, or counter the claim that there are viable and informative explanations of rape as an adaptation. No matter, critics might claim: whatever the explanations for how certain people come to have "genes for violence," or "genes for nurturing," the fact is that they have them. The evidence is overwhelming: in their desires and their dispositions, people are driven by their genes.

If the more lurid claims of the genetic determinists are true, we shall need to rethink our morality and our politics from the ground up. Recall Susan Ward's contention that a gene for laziness might soon be found, and the implications she draws from its possible discovery. If people have a gene for laziness, then their idleness is "not their fault," she tells us. It's in the genes, and what is in the genes we cannot help (and we are never responsible for what we can't help). On the face of it, this seems a reasonable claim. Some people are born with disabilities that are the result of genetic defects, such as cystic fibrosis, which is caused by a mutation of a gene on chromosome seven. It would be grotesque and immoral to blame someone for being born with cystic fibrosis. They couldn't control their genetic make-up, and we aren't responsible for what we can't control. Similarly, we might think, we cannot blame someone for being born with a gene for psychopathy. And if possession of the gene leads inexorably to the behavior associated with it, then we can't blame them for the behavior either.

Perhaps we can avoid this unfortunate conclusion by recalling that genetic determinism is false. Every reputable scientist working on the genetics of behavior denies that they are committed to genetic determinism. Thus, we might think, the door is opened for the admission of responsibility. Actually, it is not clear that denying determinism admits responsibility. When a scientist repudiates genetic determinism, she has one (or both) of two quite separate and independent claims in mind:

1. The association between the gene and the behavior is statistical: those with the gene have a higher probability of exhibiting the behavior than those without. Thus, not everyone who has the gene will exhibit the behavior, and not everyone who exhibits the behavior will have the gene.
2. Human beings are, sometimes at least, able to resist the influence of their genes upon their behavior. Thus, someone who possessed a hypothetical gene inclining him toward rape could, through sheer will-power, refrain from raping, because he knows that rape is immoral.

Anyone who believes either (1) or (2) holds that genetic determinism (understood as the claim that the presence of gene x invariably leads to the organism exhibiting trait y) is false. But (1) and (2) have quite different implications for human freedom and morality.

All scientists subscribe to (1), or something like it. Every geneticist knows that genes do not cause behavior, or indeed anything else, except in a particular environment, and that the details of that environment can make a crucial difference to the trait shaped by the genes. Thus, Terrie Moffit's research on the genetics of violence, which I previously mentioned, claims that the genetic mutation responsible for making young men violent is triggered by childhood maltreatment. By itself, the gene doesn't cause violent behavior; instead, its effects are crucially mediated by the environment. If a child who has this mutation grows up in a stable and happy home, he may exhibit no unusual propensity to violence. However, if he is mistreated he is more likely to turn violent than is a similarly treated child who lacks the mutation.

Gene–environment interactionism is certainly true. But it does not answer all our questions about the moral and political implications of genetics; it just raises further questions. We can divide these questions into two kinds: questions about free will and moral responsibility, and questions about political and social policy.

As far as the first set of questions is concerned, the problem is this: the fact that our genes do not cause our phenotypic traits by themselves, but require an environment in which they are expressed, doesn't change the fact that our traits are nevertheless caused. *All* causes have their effects mediated in this way. Striking a match normally causes a flame, but this effect is dependent upon the appropriate conditions being present: there must be a high enough proportion of oxygen in the air, the match must not be (too) wet, and so on. The fact that interactionism is true does not make genes any less deterministic causes of phenotypic effects. Interactionism doesn't give individuals any more control over their traits than genetic determinism (narrowly understood) does, since we do not choose our formative environments anymore than we choose our genes. The child who becomes a violent adult as a result of a genetic mutation *and* maltreatment does not seem more responsible for his violence than a (counterfactual) child who becomes violent as the result solely of a genetic mutation.

This set of questions is very, very hard. Fortunately, we can largely ignore them, on the grounds that genetics raises no *special* problems for free will and moral responsibility. Our behavior seems just as much determined whether it is determined by environment alone or by genes alone, so whatever the influence of genes, exactly the same set of issues confronts us. As many philosophers have pointed out, it seems that if our behavior wasn't caused deterministically at all, this would do nothing to restore our freedom. Random behavior, or behavior caused indeterministically (perhaps by the indeterminate decay of quantum particles) seems no freer (perhaps less free) than behavior that is deterministically caused. Genetics is therefore no particular threat to free will: we have or lack it regardless of the truth of genetic determinism.[143]

That is not to say that we can simply ignore genetics when assessing the moral responsibility of particular individuals. We already take into account people's capacities, and the burdens under which they labor, when we assess moral responsibility. We don't blame young children or the insane for crimes, because we believe that they can't sufficiently understand what they're doing. We also excuse, wholly or partially, people who act under duress: the woman who steals a loaf of bread to feed her starving children is dealt with less harshly than the person who doesn't need what she steals. We need to know whether genes can influence our capacities, or (more likely) place special burdens upon us. It might be, for example, that some people find it more difficult to control themselves because, as a result of their genetic endowment, they have lowered levels of serotonin (a neurotransmitter) in their brain. If this turns out to be true, then perhaps it should diminish their responsibility for their actions.[144]

So, despite the fact that genetics doesn't constitute a new threat to human freedom, we still need to understand the precise nature of its influence upon our behavior. This brings us to the second set of questions, concerning social and political policy. Interactionism does not settle any questions here, because we need to know how powerful is the influence of our genes on our traits. It might be, for instance, that the effects of genes (or at least of some genes) are robust, in the sense that they will show up in the same way across almost all environments. Or it might be that we can modify these effects, but not in ways we would like: we can easily modify human intelligence, using crude environmental interventions like drugs or child abuse, but it seems much easier to bring intelligence down than up. Perhaps this is the typical case: perhaps what natural selection gives us is optimal, or at any rate better than the result we could achieve by intervention. We should all be interactionists: we should all recognize that the traits we have are the result of our biological endowment and the environment in which it expresses itself. But recognizing that fact still leaves all the important work to be done. We still need to know the extent to which these traits can be modified, in directions we desire, by environmental interventions.

This question matters, because the extent to which certain types of socially desirable goals are achievable turns on it. If, for example, it turns out that current variation in intelligence is (1) significantly genetic and (2) unmodifiable (for practical purposes) by environmental interventions, then our political choices are greatly constrained. We should only be able to achieve substantial equality by sacrificing goods we value very highly. If we cannot raise the intelligence of the genetically less well endowed, then we might achieve equality by lowering the intelligence of the better off. But that would involve the sacrifice of a very large number of important goods, ranging from the social benefits that the efforts of the talented can bring all of us, to our prized freedom to develop our abilities. If so, perhaps we would be forced to give up on equality. Perhaps, indeed, we should come to think that any attempt even to limit inequalities is illegitimate. But, if we were to discover that the current distribution of intelligence could be altered through interventions which did not carry high costs, then we seem to be obliged to intervene. We cannot rest content with the recognition that interactionism is true. We need to investigate the extent to which intervention is practical and desirable.

There is a second way to deny genetic determinism. We can claim that whatever dispositions our genes may foist upon us, we have the power to resist them. Richard Dawkins sometimes seems to advocate such a view:

> We have the power to defy the selfish genes of our birth and, if necessary, the selfish memes of our indoctrination. We can even discuss ways of deliberately cultivating and nurturing pure, disinterested altruism – something that has no place in nature, something that has never existed before in the whole history of the world. We are built as gene machines and cultured as meme machines, but we have the power to turn against our creators. We, alone on earth, can rebel against the tyranny of the selfish replicators.[145]

In many ways this seems commonsensical. We all have urges that we do not act upon. Just for a moment, you find yourself ready to punch the driver who cuts in ahead of you. But you think better of it, and fight the urge down. Similarly, you might be genetically programmed for violence, or to eat sugar and fat. But you can control these dispositions, learn to recognize the warning signs and take evasive measures, or refrain from getting into situations where you know you will not be able to resist (the prudent dieter does not keep chocolate ice cream in the refrigerator). What does it matter if our genes dispose us to one behavior or another? These dispositions are irrelevant to how we can and ought to act, and what we can realistically hope to achieve.

There are two problems for this view. Firstly, though it certainly seems true that we can often resist our desires, we can do so only as long as we have other resources of rational self-control available, which are equally the product of evolution. It may be that some people have fewer such resources, for reasons that can be traced back to their genes. Secondly, even if we are in the fortunate position of being able to rebel against (some of) our genes, our innate disposition will still impose costs and constraints upon us. We resist many of our urges only through effort and planning. The dieter who plans his day so as to avoid temptation imposes costs upon himself, in the form of forgone opportunities and limited spontaneity. Moreover, there is good evidence that self-control is a resource that can be used up: that even the strong-willed eventually give in if the temptations are repeated too often and too soon.[146] If people have strong, morally relevant, genetic dispositions, then we will need to take account of these desires in building our institutions, in our education systems, and in our courts and legislatures. The mere fact that they can sometimes be resisted (by whom? under what conditions?) does not make them morally irrelevant.

Most of the issues I have just sketched, to do with the extent to which genes influence or control behavior, have a close parallel with the questions raised by evolutionary psychology. In this case as in that, simply invoking the naturalistic fallacy is far from sufficient to prevent the claims of these sciences from being directly morally relevant. But there is also a second kind of problem raised by genetics, which has no parallel among those raised by evolutionary psychology. Genetics offers us unique, and uniquely troubling, opportunities not merely to predict human behavior, but to intervene in it.

This has raised the fear, in many quarters, of inequality of a kind and scale unprecedented in world history. Human genetic engineering, it seems, has the potential not only to cure diseases, but also to enhance a range of desirable characteristics, from intelligence to height. These enhancements are likely to be expensive, and therefore accessible only to the wealthy. As a result, their children will be doubly advantaged over the less fortunate: not only will they have access to all the social goods which money can buy – the best schools, medical care, nutrition, and so on – but they will also begin with a better genetic endowment. If the genetic alterations that their parents provide are of the right sort (technically, if they are the result of germline intervention), then these advantages will be encoded in turn in the genome of *their* children. Generation after generation, the genetic stock of the wealthy might be expected to improve, and their comparative advantage over the less well off increase. Eventually, the purveyors of this scenario fear, the process might lead to the creation of a distinct species, of super-humans.

If this were allowed to occur, critics fear, the bonds of sympathy that connect each of us to every other would be cut or severely weakened. The better off would no longer feel that they have a reason to care more strongly about their fellow human beings than about members of other species; indeed, they might not even believe that they are of the same species. As Buchanan, Brock, Daniels, and Wikler express it, in their important overview of the implications of the new genetics for considerations of justice, "the effectiveness of people's moral motivation to act consistently on universal moral principles may depend significantly upon whether they share a sense of common membership in a single moral community. But whether this sense of moral community could survive such divergence is a momentous question."[147] The fear that genetic engineering could be used not just to cure (what we currently recognize as) diseases, but to create such superior beings, or at very least to exacerbate existing inequalities, seems to be the major impetus behind the widely shared intuition that we should distinguish genetic enhancement from treatment, and ban the former. This is an intuition shared across much of the political spectrum, from egalitarian liberals like Buchanan, to conservatives like Francis Fukuyama.[148] All fear that allowing widespread access to genetic enhancement would lead to massive inequality and social stratification.

The fear must be taken seriously. It may well be, for example, that democracy only works if inequalities in wealth and status are kept within certain limits. Greater inequality might lead to a breakdown of our relatively free, relatively secure, societies. But is the fear realistic? Notice that many of the people who express it are well aware that interactionism is true, that genes have particular effects only within particular environments. They are implicitly suggesting that genetic inequalities are likely to result across the range of practically achievable or foreseeable environments. Are they right? And are they correct in focusing their fears upon genetic interventions? We shall need a much more detailed understanding of the manner in which genes interact with the environment before we can answer these questions, and assess the extent to which genes really constrain our behavior and therefore set the bounds within which our societies must learn to exist.

Genes "for" traits

The extent to which genetic engineering, of the sort that Buchanan et al. and Fukuyama fear, is a live possibility depends upon there being levers which can be manipulated to produce particular phenotypic effects. In the terminology that has pervaded the media, there must be *genes for* those traits. Of course there are such genes – aren't there? Certainly, many scientists believe that there are: for example, Professor Robert Plomin claims to have isolated "the first specific gene for human intelligence." [149] More careful, or more prudent, scientists talk instead of genes involved in, or influencing, intelligence, personality, and behavior. Some of these findings are well confirmed. Genes for cystic fibrosis, or for breast cancer, are well known, their variants are mapped, and the causal role they play in development is slowly being unraveled.

But things are not as simple as they appear. There certainly are "genes" the presence of which is predictive of certain outcomes. But in what sense are they genes *for* those outcomes? Imagine that your new car has a defect in it: it has a mechanical flaw in the axle that causes the front wheels to fall off. Would your mechanic look at the axle and remark that your car has a special feature, the function of which is to make its wheels fall off: a design feature *for* breaking down? Surely not. Analogously, it is unlikely we have genes *for* disease or cancer. Furthermore, in the case of your car, it is easy to see the causal relationship between the defect and the result: the axle breaks and the wheels come off. But with a genetic defect, the relationship might be far more indirect. The gene for breast cancer might play a causal role in bringing about breast cancer. Or it might simply be *correlated* with a high risk of breast cancer. This, too, should make us hesitate before assigning a function to it.

Lenny Moss, a cell biologist turned philosopher, suggests that we can make sense of this talk of a gene for cancer, but only if we accept that it is *just* a useful way of talking, not something that picks out a real object in the world.[150] Moss distinguishes between two, equally legitimate, ways of talking about genes. We can talk about genes as Genes-P (for preformationist), or Genes-D (for developmental).[151] A Gene-P is the kind of thing we have in mind when we talk about a gene for cancer (or for intelligence, or aggression). A Gene-P is a gene for a phenotypic trait. But a Gene-P is *not* a physical entity. In fact, Moss argues, the physical basis of a Gene-P is rather the *absence* of a physical entity. For example, I have the "gene for" blue eyes. But that does not mean that somewhere on one of my chromosomes is a sequence of DNA that has the property of causing me to have blue eyes. Rather, I have blue eyes because I *lack* the molecular structures which, in humans, result in brown eyes, and blue eyes is what we typically get when we don't have brown eyes. Since there are many ways of *not* having a gene – you can have any number of alternative sequences in its place – having blue eyes is not correlated with any particular sequence of DNA. Moreover, the sequences of DNA that I have in place of genes for brown eyes do not necessarily play any sort of role in building my eyes. Similarly, if someone has a gene for breast cancer, she does not have a sequence that other people lack, which causes breast cancer. Rather she *lacks* a sequence, and therefore the ability to make a certain protein, which raises the probability that she will suffer from breast cancer. So a Gene-P, a gene for a phenotypic trait, is not a physical entity. But a Gene-D is a physical entity: it is a particular sequence of DNA. However, Genes-D are not genes for phenotypic traits. They are developmental resources, one set among many in the cell. They work together with the other developmental resources to build organisms, but they do not map on to particular traits.

Both of these ways of talking about genes are legitimate. Genes-P are predictive devices, and their usefulness as such is beyond question.

Genes-D are real sequences of DNA, the stuff which consumes the working lives of molecular biologists. But the gene concept that dominates our culture, the much-hyped notion of the gene, is the result of the illegitimate conflation of these two notions of the gene. *There are no stretches of DNA that are "for" particular phenotypic traits, no Genes-D that are also Genes-P*, Moss claims. Once we recognize this, the hype surrounding the gene should dissipate. Consider the hysteria that surrounded the announcement, in 2000, that the human genome had been mapped. Newspaper headlines around the world announced that "the book of life" (a favorite metaphor) had been decoded, the blueprint of humanity revealed.[152] But all the Human Genome Project did was map the DNA sequences in the human genome. In other words, the genes it lists are Genes-D. We get so excited about this accomplishment only because we (mistakenly) believe that these Genes-D are also Genes-P. But they're not. They might be useful in identifying Genes-P (since a Gene-P may be correlated with many different Genes-D, which occupy the place where a particular sequence is missing), but they are not genes for traits.

As Moss points out, the discovery by the Human Genome Project that we have far fewer genes than expected – about thirty thousand, around the same number as the mouse, with which we share the overwhelming majority of our genes – ought to have led to a deflation of our gene-hyperbole. Given that we have around the same number of genes as much simpler creatures, our great complexity is unlikely to be the product of our genes alone. Rather, it is the result of the modular architecture of organisms as a whole: the entire cellular machinery, as it develops in human beings, is the source of our complexity. Our "essence" is not contained in our genes, but distributed throughout the developmental resources of the organism.

If this deflationary perspective upon the gene is correct, than many of the hopes and fears that surround genetic engineering are misplaced. The enhancements that are so widely seen as inevitable just may not be technically possible. It is likely that complex traits are the result of a great many genes, *in a particular cellular context*. In other words, when we consider the effects that environments have on phenotypes, we must not limit ourselves to the *external* environment. The internal environment – of cellular machinery, of other genes, of the womb – is also crucial. So, we cannot simply "lift" a gene from one organism, splice it into the genome of another, and expect to cause a particular phenotypic trait to develop. Genes just don't work like that. We have an over-inflated view of the power of genes, because the genes(-p) which we have identified so far are genes for gross physical defects, which typically cause their detrimental effects no matter what their environment. But the genes that play a role in the development of desirable traits are not blunt instruments causing traits in simple ways; they work much more subtly, and in a context-sensitive manner. Though we can relatively easily delete a gene, and cause a phenotype to have a defect, improving function will prove much harder. There are no genes for intelligence, if by that we mean genes that are responsible for raised IQs across the range of normal internal and external environments. We are not going to produce designer babies, not now, and perhaps not ever.

Genes and environment

However, the fact that genetic enhancement is likely to prove far harder than is often thought does not stave off many of the threats that genes seem to pose to human hopes. So what if the bases of heredity are far more complex than gene talk seems to suggest? We know that heredity works in *some* manner, after all. Whether we can engineer desirable traits or not, we know that they are passed on. Inability to engineer human enhancements might slow down social stratification, but it will not prevent it. So, for example, Richard Herrnstein claimed. Herrnstein saw this stratification along genetic lines as an inevitable consequence of increasing meritocracy. Pinker summarizes the argument thus:

> As social status becomes less strongly determined by arbitrary legacies such as race, parentage, and inherited wealth, it will become more strongly determined by talent, especially (in a modern economy) intelligence. Since differences in intelligence are partly inherited, and since intelligent people tend to marry other intelligent people, when a society becomes more just it will also become more stratified along genetic lines.[153]

Indeed, as he famously argued in *The Bell Curve*, Herrnstein believed that genetic stratification was already well under way in the United States. Intelligence, he argued, is significantly heritable. But blacks, on average, consistently score lower in IQ tests than whites. Hence, it is likely to be the case that black disadvantage, on a wide range of social indicators, is partly genetic in origin. The existence of a black underclass has many causes, but one of them is the inferior genes of those of African descent.

Herrnstein's thesis, and many others which attribute different traits to different people on the basis of their "genes," does not depend upon any particular theory of how heredity functions. It is enough that it works in *some* way. Darwinian theory also demands that traits be heritable, in some manner. Thus, pointing out the limitations of, and the confusions that surround, talk of genes for traits does nothing to circumvent the dangers for social policy stemming from this particular challenge. It is very clear that these dangers are real. *The Bell Curve* makes them explicit. There, Herrnstein and his co-author Charles Murray argue that, since intelligence is largely inherited, improving the quality of education holds little promise for raising the life prospects of the largely black American underclass. Herrnstein and Murray focused particularly on programs like "Head Start," which aimed to eliminate the social disadvantages suffered by members of low-income households by providing them with access to pre-school education. These programs seemed to offer increases in measured IQ, compared to controls who did not attend them, but these effects were transient. The gains begin to fade shortly after the child leaves the program, and in a few years the effects (on IQ, at least) seem to disappear completely.[154] On the basis of these findings, Herrnstein and Murray argue that pouring resources into remedial education programs for the disadvantaged is a pointless waste of effort. The effects "hardly justify investing billions of dollars in run-of-the-mill Head Start programs." Similarly, they argue, affirmative action, which is based on the false assumption that ethnic groups are equal in intellectual ability, is dangerous: "Affirmative action, in education and the workplace alike, is leaking a poison into the American soul."[155] As Herrnstein and Murray make all too apparent, claims for the heritability of intelligence have direct social and political consequence – not, of course, all by themselves, but when coupled with our other beliefs about society, efficiency, equity, and justice. No matter how many times the naturalistic fallacy is invoked, this remains so.

These are extreme manifestations of the dangers for social policy that lurk in the background – and sometimes in the foreground – of these debates. Less extreme, but perhaps more pervasive, dangers lurk in the inappropriate biologicization of human traits. To the extent to which dysfunctional or undesirable characteristics of human beings come to be seen as "in the genes," in the sense that it would be difficult and costly to alter them, they cease to be felt to be social responsibilities. If depression is caused by an endogenous chemical imbalance, and not by high rates of unemployment; if criminality is caused by a genetic mutation; if low intelligence is inherited; then we must learn to manage, control, or intervene medically in these conditions. We can treat depressives and lock up criminals, but we can't deal with either problem by building a fairer society. However, if these problems are predominantly social in origin, then we might hope to reduce them by social measures. Depression might be treated not (just) by providing anti-depressants, but by providing a sense of hope for a better future (more concretely, by reducing unemployment and alienation).

Of course, we can't build a society upon pious hopes. If depression or intelligence are inherited and beyond our (practical) power to alter, then we need to know. If these claims are true, this is essential information, which we must learn to live with. We cannot reject them simply because they are unpalatable. Rather, we must subject them to scrutiny.

Heredity[156]

What do we measure, when we measure heredity? We measure the extent to which the *variance* in a trait can be attributed to a variable. Thus, if we want to measure the extent to which a trait is "genetic," we place organisms in a controlled environment, and measure the variance of that trait. If the environment is exactly the same for all the organisms, but they differ genetically from one another, then the variation is genetic in origin.

There are enormous practical difficulties in making accurate assessments of the genetic contribution to variation. No matter how hard we try, we cannot control an environment totally; even in the laboratory, there are certain to be minor variations. These problems are magnified many times over in research on human beings, where we cannot conduct controlled experiments at all, for both practical and ethical reasons. For humans, we must rely upon studies of separated identical twins, of identical twins reared together compared to fraternal twins reared together, or of adoptees reared with biological siblings. The limits to the kind of data we can gather pose great problems, problems sufficient to invalidate many of the findings of early studies, which did not put sufficient thought into controlling for these difficulties. But the problems are not insurmountable: careful studies upon very large numbers of people give results that are statistically significant. Hence, I shall not focus on these practical problems but concern myself with the *conceptual* limits upon heredity research.

Herrnstein and Murray, on the basis of their review of many studies on the inheritance of intelligence, estimate that, within the white population, IQ is about sixty percent genetic. That is to say, sixty percent of the *variation* in IQ test scores among whites in the United States seems to be genetic in origin. It is important to understand, however, that the sense of "genetic" here is an artefact of the methodology. To say that a trait is genetic, in this sense, is not to say that it is caused by DNA sequences (or even by DNA sequences plus whatever other cellular and developmental resources combine to build the bodies of organisms). In the sense in which the word is used here, *only significantly variable traits are genetic.* Think, for example, of a trait such as "having two hands." This is, in all probability, an "entrenched" trait, which is to say that its biological bases are laid down very early in the development of an organism, so that any mutation which tended to disrupt this development would almost certainly also have other, far-reaching, and most likely detrimental, effects on the organism. Having two hands is close to invariant in human beings. But what is the heritability of having two hands? You might think that it is close to one-hundred percent, on the grounds that almost every parent with two hands has a child with two hands. But you'd be wrong. Heritability measures the extent to which the *variation* in a trait has a "genetic" cause; since almost everyone is born with two hands, the heritability is in fact close to zero (indeed, a fraction of one percent). Variation in hand number is almost entirely due to *environmental* causes – the effects of drugs on fetuses, or accidents – so hand number is a trait that is almost entirely environmentally caused.

So, in considering claims that a trait is partly or largely genetically determined, the first mistake we have to avoid is to confuse "genetic" in the sense in which it is employed here, with "biological." Hand number is biologically determined, of course, but since it does not vary, it is not genetically caused. Even more bizarrely, using the method of measuring variation to assess the extent to which it is due to genetics counts many traits that are certainly *not* biological in cause as genetic. Consider hair length in the 1950s and 60s, in Western countries. At that time, most women had much longer hair than most men. Thus, variation in hair length was reliably correlated with a real biological difference. Applying the methodology of measuring heritability, we would find that hair length was highly heritable (the female children of mothers with long hair tended to have long hair themselves; the male children of men with short hair tended to have short hair themselves). But the pattern of hair length was entirely explained by fashions and social norms, and its heritability by the fact that these fashions tracked biological features of human beings. It may very well be that a very substantial part of the variance which comes out as genetic on the standard measures is nevertheless rooted in environmental differences, because people who possess certain biological characteristics are systematically treated differently to others who lack these characteristics.

Moreover, as the example of hair length demonstrates, it is a mistake – a most serious mistake, but none the less a very tempting one – to take "genetic" as synonymous with "fixed," or even "difficult to change." Traits might be genetic, and yet easily changed. Mightn't it be objected that though the method of estimating heredity throws up occasional oddities, like the finding that hair length is heritable, this does not undermine the importance of the bulk of its findings? We can see how norms of hair length are maintained, by means that are not biological. Despite the fact that intelligence (for example) is not controlled by social norms, we can see how it can be modified, in certain circumstances, by such norms. If we found that black children scored lower than white, whether they were adopted (by white or black parents) or raised by their biological parents, and that was our only evidence about the heredity of IQ, then we could speculate that racism, perhaps unconscious, is at work in some manner, leading people to treat these children differently, in a way that leads to them scoring lower in IQ tests. But we have a great deal of evidence upon which the social treatment hypothesis apparently gets no grip. Much of the evidence for the heritability of intelligence compares white children with white children, so we needn't worry that racism distorts our results.

We can concede the case that the objector presses here, and continue to insist that "genetic" does not mean "unalterable." Estimates of hereditability, it must be recalled, are always *relative to a context*. We measure heredity by controlling the environment, and our estimate is therefore indexed to that environment. It does not follow, from the fact that a trait is (say) sixty percent heritable in one environment, or even across a range of environments, that its heritability will be about the same in another environment we have not yet examined. It might be the same, or higher, or lower. It might even be zero.

It's useful to construct a graph that represents the extent to which a trait is heritable across a range of environments. Such a graph is known as the *norm of reaction* of that trait. In the following (hypothetical) norm of reaction, the y axis represents the height of genetically identical plants, while the x axis represents an environmental variable (say, the amount of phosphorous in the soil), with all other variables held constant:

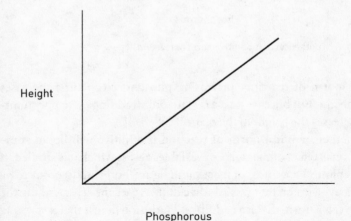

Figure 1: A hypothetical additive norm of reaction

This graph depicts a norm of reaction that is *additive*. That is, the relationship between the variable (in this case, phosphorous) and the phenotype is regular. The more phosphorous we add, the taller the plant. But not all norms of reaction are additive. The norm of reaction sketched above is hypothetical. If we actually tested the relationship between phosphorous and the height of a particular plant, we might discover that the norm of reaction looks something like this:

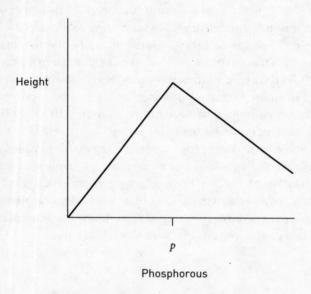

Figure 2: A hypothetical non-additive norm of reaction

In this norm of reaction, increasing phosphorous at first increases plant height. But once we pass a certain point, adding extra phosphorous decreases the height of the plant.

Whether or not a norm of reaction is additive will be, to some extent, an artefact of the range of variables across which it is studied. If we had plotted the norm of reaction in figure 2 only up to point *p*, we would have a graph that was additive. But, as we can see, extending the plot reveals a norm that isn't additive. The lesson here is that it is wrong to assume that the graph will extend at its current angle (or even in the same direction) across new environments. We have to discover the truth empirically, case by case. Figure 1 illustrated an additive norm, but if the graph represented an actual norm of reaction, we could not simply assume that the slope of the graph would extend to infinity at the same angle.

Why does any of this matter? It matters because in the debate about the heritability of intelligence, character traits, and so on, there are some important implied assumptions about their norms of reaction. Indeed, people who claim that these traits are highly heritable typically assume that their norm of reaction is additive. They assume that the norms look something like this:

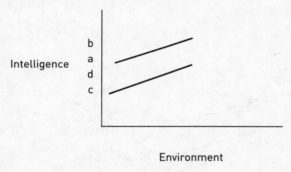

Environment

Figure 3: The norm of reaction for intelligence assumed by those who claim that our potential abilities are fixed at birth

Line *a–b* in figure 3 represents the norm of reaction for the intelligence of Highly Intelligent Helen. Helen was lucky; she was born with lots of genes for intelligence. That is not to say that she will be a genius in any environment: no one believes *that*; rather, it is that in any normal environment, she will be clever. The exact nature of the claim becomes clearer when we compare Helen to Rather Dull Roger (represented by line *c–d*). There is *no* environment in which Roger is smarter than Helen. There may be an environment, way off to the left of the graph, in which Roger is *as* smart as Helen. But that would be an extremely undesirable environment indeed, in which Roger is as smart as Helen only because both have been unable to develop their cognitive capacities to anything like normal levels (perhaps both Roger and Helen are brain-damaged in that environment, as a result of severe malnutrition). Even if environmental intervention can increase Roger's intelligence somewhat (and Herrnstein and Murray's claims about Head Start might lead us to think that they believe that the norm of reaction is even flatter than depicted here), Helen is smarter than Roger across all normal, and all desirable, environments. Genetically speaking, she just *is* cleverer than him.

But if the norm of reaction is not additive, then we cannot speak of the "genetically more intelligent person." Instead, we shall have to talk about the more intelligent person *in an environment.* Consider the following norm of reaction, which depicts the effects of being planted at different altitudes on the height of seven *Achillea* plants:

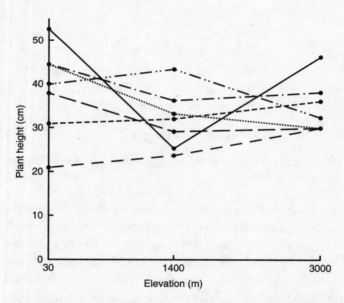

Figure 4: The norm of reaction depicting the height of the plant *Achillea millefolium* as a function of elevation. From David T. Suzuki, et al. *An Introduction to Genetic Analysis* (7th ed.), (New York: W. H. Freeman, 2000), p. 20. Used with permission.

Which of these plants is, genetically speaking, the tallest? Obviously, the question is nonsensical. At different altitudes, different plants are tallest. There is no plant that is tallest, or even relatively tall, across all environments.

Commenting on this example, Francis Fukuyama claims that most human characteristics are not like this.[157] Is he right? What is the shape of the norm of reaction for intelligence? Several studies on laboratory animals have attempted to answer this question. One study examined the effects of impoverished and enriched environments on two strains of rats, one of which had been bred to be dull and the other to be smart (their intelligence was measured by their ability to navigate a maze without making errors). The researchers bred and raised these strains of rats in two environments that differed from that in which their parents had been raised. One was "enriched" with toys and visual stimulation, and the other "restricted"– uniform and mono-chromatic. Then they tested the rats for maze-running ability. The maze bright rats made relatively few mistakes when they were raised in a normal environment – far fewer than the maze dull rats in the same environment. However, when both were raised in an enriched environment, the "maze dull" rats made nearly as few mistakes as the "maze bright" ones (indeed, the difference between the two was not statistically significant). And when both were raised in restricted environments, the (genetically) maze bright rats made just as many mistakes as the maze dull.[158]

A recent study by researchers engaged in the construction of animal models for dysfunctions in human cognition reinforces the point. The research team, led by Professor Colin Blakemore, created transgenic mice (mice into which "foreign" genetic material had been incorporated) to model Huntington's disease – an inherited, and invariably lethal, degenerative neurological condition. The transgenic mice were reared in two separate groups, one in standard laboratory cages, and the other in enriched environments. They found that the onset of the symptoms of brain degeneration was significantly later in the mice reared in the enriched environments, compared to those reared in standard environments. At twenty-two weeks, all the mice in the control group were significantly disabled, but only fifteen percent of the enriched environment mice were experiencing difficulties.[159] Once again, environmental interventions are successful in altering a phenotypic trait that is "in the genes."

The lesson for studies of heritability should be obvious. Even if we assume (for the sake of argument) that findings like those of

Herrnstein and Murray are accurate: certain groups of people are less bright than others *across the environments so far studied*, we can't validly extrapolate from these environments to others as yet unexplored. Heritability is a measure of the extent to which variation is due to genetics *in the environments examined*. In "normal" environments, ability to run mazes is highly heritable, but in enriched and in restricted environments the heritability of the trait drops to near zero. Intelligence *might* be sixty percent heritable in the contemporary United States, but that does not imply that intelligence is fixed unalterably, there or elsewhere. There may be environments, which are accessible to us and not otherwise undesirable, in which its heritability is much lower: perhaps because far more people have a high IQ.

Nor can we assume that, if there are environmental interventions which will be effective in altering phenotypes in desirable ways (making many more humans "maze bright" than is currently the case), these interventions will be difficult to implement or involve restrictions on personal liberties. The story of phenylketonuria (PKU) is instructive here. PKU is a highly heritable disease: sufferers must have inherited a recessive gene from each parent. Until fairly recently, PKU would have been considered an entirely genetic disease, since children of these parents suffered its terrible symptoms (essentially, severe mental retardation) across all known environments. Today, however, we can regard it principally as a product of the environment, because we know how to intervene environmentally to prevent its adverse effects: if sufferers are fed a special diet in the first few years of their life, they escape mental retardation.[160] The heritability of PKU was close to one-hundred percent; now it's close to zero. There is no reason to think that genetic influences – upon behavior or upon physiology – are necessarily harder to alter than environmental influences.

Fukuyama claims that human characteristics are not like this: the norms of reaction for our traits are additive. But there is no evidence for this at all. Norms of reaction are typically not additive,[161] so we have good reason to assume the opposite. Twin studies, no matter how carefully conducted, will not come to the aid of the defender of "nature" over "nurture" here. What is at issue is, in principle, something that these studies cannot reveal, for they are, necessarily, concerned only with a narrow range of environments. No matter the degree to which these studies show intelligence (or any other phenotypic trait) to be heritable in these environments, we cannot extrapolate from them to what might happen in other environments. The only way to discover the effectiveness of environmental interventions of one sort or another is to test them.

It is worth noting, by the way, one other limitation of twin studies. When they discover a pronounced similarity between identical twins reared apart, researchers rightly take this as evidence that innate dispositions play a role in producing phenotypic traits (at least in *this* environment). But we can't conclude that the extent of the similarity is a direct product of "nature," *not even in this environment*. We saw earlier how small asymmetries, which might be due to nature but which might have quite different sources as well, could product large effects. Something similar is true here. Suppose that a child finds music *slightly* more rewarding than most children – perhaps because she is a slightly better musician than average (people enjoy what they find easier, and get pleasure from the praise which comes from being good at something). It is very likely, other things being equal, that the way she is treated and the way she treats herself will enhance that ability. She enjoys playing her instrument, and therefore practices more. As a result she becomes more proficient, and enjoys playing still more. At the same time, she is praised for her abilities and encouraged to develop them further. Her musical ability increases still more, while other tasks she found more difficult (and therefore less rewarding) are abandoned, and her skills in those areas atrophy.

Now suppose that this girl is one of a pair of identical twins who were separated at birth and reared apart. Her twin sister might well also be slightly better than average at music, and as a result of the same kind of processes her musical abilities have been further enhanced in an ever-turning virtuous circle. When psychologists come along and test them, they will find that they have remarkably similar psychological profiles: they are both very good musicians, but bad at sport. They will take this as evidence that abilities are innate. To some extent, it is. But we go wrong if we take this to be evidence of the unimportance of environment. It is largely because the twins had propensities that encouraged certain kinds of treatment that they are now similar. A slight innate similarity causes a quite dramatic effect.

So, twin studies show us the importance of nurture, as much as of nature. People never have their traits as a direct result of nature, but always also as a result of the way in which they have been treated, and in which they treat themselves. Choices, both ours and those of others, matter. Twins reared together are often *less* similar than those reared apart, because they make an effort to differentiate themselves, and once they do so the virtuous circle begins turning, reinforcing those differences.[162] There is nothing inevitable about innate propensities: they remain responsive to cultural and social factors. Biology is not destiny.

We should also note the way in which my remarks concerning heritability are directly relevant to the dispute between the SSSM and evolutionary psychology. Evolutionary psychology is committed to the hypothesis that human psychological traits are inherited and (at least in many versions of it) that they are therefore, practically speaking, unalterable. But now we see that heritability is always relative to environment, so that we cannot extrapolate estimates of it to further environments. A trait that is sixty percent heritable in one environment might be ninety-five percent, or two percent, heritable in another. Conversely, the extent to which a trait is due to environmental factors is always relative to the amount of genetic variation within the population under study. *All* variation in the phenotypes of genetically identical corn (for example) is environmentally caused.

This allows us to state the dispute between evolutionary psychology and the SSSM much more carefully than before. As Philip Kitcher has pointed out, it is essentially an argument about the shape of the norm of reaction of the traits of interest.[163] Those who we regard as being on the side of nature hold that the norm is relatively flat *across the range of environments that are practically accessible.* Though (except for the least sophisticated of them) they do not deny that it is possible to alter the traits in question, they hold that is difficult to alter them in ways that are desirable (to bring Roger's intelligence up to the level of Helen's rather than hers down to his). Moreover, to the extent to which we can alter traits in desirable directions, they hold that we can do so only by altering the environment in highly *un*desirable ways: for example, only by indoctrinating people, or massively restricting their freedom.

In contrast, those on the "nurture" side of the equation do not (or should not) deny that biology is an important influence upon behavior. Instead, they hold that this influence is powerfully mediated by culture, so that we can, at least in principle, alter it in ways of our choosing. They should not deny, either, that sometimes such alterations will be hard to achieve, and that sometimes they will have unexpected costs. But society is not an organism; though it is true that almost all mutations (and by far the overwhelming majority of those that affect entrenched characteristics) are bad for organisms, we have no reason to think the same of societies. Often, if the social changes we make are carefully planned, and informed by all our knowledge of human biology, psychology, and the social sciences, they will bring far more benefits than costs. We can alter society in ways we choose, and in doing so we inevitably alter ourselves. That is the claim made by those who advocate the importance of nurture, and, as we have seen, there is every reason to think it a plausible one.

Remaking ourselves

We saw earlier that genetic engineering arouses a particular horror in many writers. Conservatives and liberals alike see it as threatening to bring about a dystopic "brave new world," as the almost irresistible cliché has it. Genetic engineering has the potential to make the acquired advantages of parents heritable (to make Lamarckism true through technology), and so to create two separate classes of human: one born to rule, and one suited only to be ruled. Moreover, genetic engineering will allow us to choose the characteristics of our children, to transform them from chance "gifts" (perhaps of God) to consciously designed artefacts. In so doing, many fear, it risks stripping human life of its meaning and its dignity. This fear, too, comes in left and right wing forms. Leon Kass, the head of George W. Bush's Council on Bioethics, is one of its better-known conservative defenders:

> Any child whose being, character, and capacities exist owing to human design does not stand on the same plane as its makers. As with any product of our making, no matter how excellent, the artificer stands above it, not as an equal but as a superior, transcending it by his will and creative prowess. [...] Such an arrangement is profoundly dehumanizing, no matter how good the product.[164]

The very fact that we choose the characteristics our children possess dehumanizes us, as well as them.

It should be clear by now that this fear is misplaced. If genetic engineering of human characteristics proves to be possible and practicable – and we have seen that there are reasons to doubt that it will – it will not endow us with powers that we do not *already* possess. If we fear that it will give the rich access to enhancements that are not available to the poor then we need to recall that such enhancements are already available to, and widely used by, the wealthy – in the superior schooling, nutrition, medical care, and other advantages that they can buy. Consider the current life expectancy of a child born today in Sierra Leone, versus that of a child born in the United States: thirty-eight years for the former, and seventy-seven for the latter. This difference is strongly correlated with income. Sierra Leone has a per capita gross national product of just $160, whereas the United States has a per capita GNP of $30,600. Infant mortality figures paint a similarly grim picture.[165] Within countries, the disparities in life expectancy also follow income lines. These stark injustices are not the result of any genetic superiority of Americans over Africans. They are the result of the typical environments in which members of each group are raised. We are already allowing people to use enhancement technologies, and they enhance the only entity that counts: the phenotype.

What goes for life expectancy and for health goes for behavioral traits as well. Recall Terrie Moffit's research upon the genetic bases of violence. Her team found that men who possessed a particular version of one gene *and* were physically or sexually abused as children were far more likely to become violent criminals than were men who possessed the gene, or had a history of abuse, alone. As she pointed out, her research reveals the importance of both elements of the equation, nature *and* nurture: "This is not really the story of a gene that has a risk for anti-social behaviour. It's the story of the interplay between a gene and the experience of maltreatment."[166] Parents already possess the ability to pass on their advantages (or their disadvantages) to their children. So does society at large. We choose our children; design them, at least in rough outline. Better understandings of gene/environment interaction – that is, the construction of more detailed norms of reaction, for more variables and across more environments – will enhance this control, *whether we use genetic engineering or "mere" environmental manipulation* as our instrument.

It might be objected that despite what I have said, genetics will remain a special focus of concern, because enhancements encoded into the genome will be passed on to offspring, in a way in which purely social advantages can never be. This is the real concern: that genetic enhancement by the wealthy could lead to their splitting off from the rest of humanity, becoming a species unto themselves, with a biologically-based right to rule. Once again, though, this ignores the reality of heritability. Since heritability *is* heritability-within-an-environment, the two inextricably linked, we ought to be concerned as much with the environmental as the genetic side of the equation. At present, parents pass on their environmental (dis)advantages to their children as a matter of course, so their children start from significantly different positions. If it is the inheritance of advantage with which we are concerned – the way in which the privileged are able to accumulate it generation upon generation, in ways that are expressed in higher cognitive ability (for instance) – then we ought to be as much concerned with this kind of inheritance as with germline intervention.

It is morally and scientifically arbitrary, not to mention fundamentally confused, to be concerned with *genetic* justice. A concern for justice must be *phenotypic*: it must be focused on the observable characteristics displayed by people, and not on the question of their genetic base, except in so far as the latter is relevant to the former. If we have the intuition that inherited gross inequality is morally impermissible, we ought to be concerned with current inequalities. In principle, the possibilities opened up by genetic enhancement add nothing new to these concerns.

I have no doubt that many people will remain skeptical. The facts about heritability and what it measures – that "heritable" does not necessarily mean "genetic" *nor* vice versa, or that estimates of heritability are always relative to the environments in which they are measured – have been pointed out over and over again for decades, without any discernible impact upon the propensity of apparently intelligent people to invoke heritability claims to show that biology is destiny. The proponents of this view rarely indicate why they believe they can predict what shape norms of reaction will have in new environments. I suggest, however, that, underlying their faith in their predictions, must be the same views about history and cultural variation that divide them so sharply from proponents of something closer to the SSSM. They believe that historically and geographically distant societies differ only superficially from our own, and that *therefore* the capacity of human beings to create social worlds is tightly constrained. Proponents of the SSSM tend to deny the first claim, and insist that the world has seen a great diversity of human societies. From this, it follows that such diversity it possible. Even if they turned out to be wrong about this last claim, however, they might still be right that *future* diversity is possible. One final example, then, to sway waverers, and strengthen the conviction that fundamental alterations in human society – with concomitant changes in gender roles, for instance – are indeed possible.

Human beings are, all sides agree, unique in the degree of their behavioral flexibility. I assume, therefore, that if any species is capable of fundamentally altering their social arrangements in desirable ways, that species will be humans. If any other species has succeeded in such a transformation, it would constitute powerful evidence for the claim that human beings are indeed capable of such a revolution. And at least one other species has altered its fundamental social arrangements, arguably for the better: chimpanzees. Placed in a new environment, which fundamentally differs from their ancestral home, chimpanzee behavior changes radically.

In the wild, chimpanzees live in bands consisting of around fifty members. Chimpanzee society is hierarchical and patriarchal. A single alpha male, aided by allies, monopolizes access to females in estrous, and is deferred to by other members of the group. His allies receive sexual and food privileges in return for their support. Females are not entirely powerless, but because they are, on average, smaller than the males, no female or small group of females is able to override the wishes of the dominant males.

In captivity, the situation is quite different. This is not the result of any direct or planned human intervention to equalize the power of males and females. Rather, it seems to be the unintended consequence of providing the chimps with easy access to food. Freed from the need to forage constantly, female chimps are able to form active coalitions, which play an important role in the "political" life of their group.

This coalition-forming behavior, rare in the wild, has been observed repeatedly in captivity, and has the effect of dramatically increasing the power of female chimpanzees:

> Captive female allies have been able to control certain behaviours of males who are individually dominant over them, and do so in ways that are striking. They usually manage to play 'kingmaker', and they always seem to control which males will be involved with peacemaking [...] a large, well-unified, rank-and-file political coalition is successfully manipulating key behaviours of individuals that are threatening to other individuals.[167]

A change in their environment (the ready availability of food), which, from their point of view, is obviously desirable, leads to an important transformation in chimpanzee social life. Captive chimpanzees do not suddenly transcend their biology. They remain, very recognizably, chimpanzees. But they begin to behave in ways that we would never have suspected, on the basis of observation of their behavior in their own EEA. If "mere animals" that are, we believe, far more tightly constrained by innate behaviors, can have their lives transformed by environmental alterations, then we have every reason to believe that the same is true for human beings. We live in environments that are much further away from our own EEA than do these chimps. Those of us who are lucky are also spared the trial of constant seeking for food. Almost none of us hunt for basic sustenance, or live in nomadic groups. Ten thousand years of agriculture has made us sedentary, and allowed us to live in larger and larger urban conglomerations. It would be very surprising indeed if these changes were not reflected in our behavior and our social lives.

Conclusion: humane nature

How constrained is our future by our past? We are *moral* animals, but we are still *animals*. Our brains allow us to engage in sophisticated reasoning, but they have built-in biases and heuristics of which we are largely unaware. We are not angels, fallen or otherwise, but merely jumped-up apes. Does the legacy of evolution, our Stone Age minds, empty our lives of meaning, and our morality of substance? We are material beings, constrained by physics, and we are animals, constrained by biology. Yet, to a very large extent, indeed to an extent that seems to be ever-growing, we seem able to shape our own futures, to endow our lives with meaning, and to build an ever more adequate morality on the basis of our animal instincts.

We could conclude our story in one of two possible ways: call them the *conservative* and the *radical* views of human nature. The conservative view concedes a great deal to evolutionary psychology: it accepts that a great many of our dispositions are fixed. But it insists – rightly – that nevertheless our future remains open; fixed dispositions do not constrain the possible forms of our social life. The radical view rejects even the claim that there is a large and interesting set of fixed human dispositions. I think the radical view is correct, and I will go on to defend it. But it is important to see that even the conservative view gives us all the freedom and morality we need.

Consider, first, an example that, even upon the conservative view, establishes the extent to which human social life is malleable. The evidence, from a variety of fields, suggests very strongly that human beings are evolved to live in relatively small groups. Robin Dunbar argues convincingly that large brains evolved to enable complex group life. Animals, like monkeys and apes, which live in large and complex societies, with hierarchies that must be respected, need large brains to keep track of group members and to remember the relation in which everyone stands to everyone else. Dunbar has convincingly shown that we can predict the average size of an animal's group just by measuring its relative brain (more specifically, its neocortical) size.

So what size groups are humans evolved for? According to Dunbar, the predicted group size is around 150 members.[168] Further evidence for this figure comes from anthropologists, who tell us that hunter-gatherers (who, we believe, live in conditions quite similar to those prevailing in the EEA) live in groups of around 150, and paleo-anthropologists, who tell us that the archaeological evidence also supports this figure. But of course human beings increasingly live in *much* larger groups, in cities, where populations are measured in the millions. We may have evolved in small groups, and we may still carry around cognitive equipment capable of tracking only a relatively small number of people. But we are not obliged to continue to live in such groups.

Might it be that we are better suited to small group life? Perhaps we would be happier in a small group. Just think of the number of television programs and novels celebrating village life. Doesn't everyone know that life in the city is a rat race, and villages are friendlier places, to which everyone would escape – from the pollution, the noise, the crime, and the pressure – if only they could? Matt Ridley suggests that cities breed crime, because one shot encounters in prisoner's dilemmas encourage the "defect" strategy. If you can melt into the crowd, you can get away with much more.

If cities are so awful, though, why do people continue to move to them, of their own free will? And move they do: around the world big cities are magnets for the surrounding countryside, and the proportion of the world's population that is urbanized is growing ever larger. It may well be true that city living has its costs, but it has its benefits as well. If it can be more alienating, it is also, frequently, wealthier, since industry is usually based in it, and is able to take advantage of the economies of scale that stem from having a large workforce to hand. If it can be isolating, it can also be exciting: it attracts a range and variety of people, together with their traditional food, music and theatre, who would otherwise never mix, and adds the attractions of technology to the mixture. If its anonymity can allow criminals to prosper, it can also allow for a degree of freedom unavailable in the claustrophobic atmosphere of a village. Gay subcultures, artists, intellectuals; all flourish only in cities.

So even if it is true that, in some ways, our Stone Age brains can't adapt to city life, because they can't track social networks bigger than those in which our ancestors lived, and even if that imposes costs on those who choose to live in cities, it still might be rational to make the choice. If there are costs, then there are also benefits, and the latter might outweigh the former. We can transcend our past, which is not to say that we can wish it away, but that we can find ways to work with and even around it, if we so wish. Stone Age minds might be just the tools we need to build our Space Age future.

Even on the conservative view, according to which many of our traits (like the ability to track members of our group) are fixed, and which insists that therefore there are limits to how well we can adapt to new social forms, we can reshape our social lives for the better. We can

turn our in-built dispositions to new tasks and find ways to accommodate what we can't change. Though we might be adapted for small
groups, we might nevertheless be happier, freer, and more fulfilled, in
large ones.

In the course of this book, however, we have seen that there are
many good reasons to think that the conservative view understates the
malleability of the human mind. If, as we have seen, we cannot extrapolate from the heritability of traits at present to the heritability of the
same traits in a future environment, we have little reason to think that
many of our dispositions are as firmly fixed as all that. My guess, for
what it's worth, is that the conservative story will turn out to be true
for *some* dispositions, but far fewer than evolutionary psychologists
generally believe.

According to Matt Ridley, who defends the conservative view, culture adds nothing significant to the human mind: "We human beings
would probably be almost as good at playing, plotting and planning if
we had never spoken a word or fashioned a tool."[169] Radicals like me
reject this view; we think that cultural tools fundamentally change our
cognitive capacities.

In the radical view, too many evolutionary psychologists and proponents of the more simplistic varieties of evolutionary ethics simply
get human beings wrong. They are right in thinking that we need to
understand what kind of animal we are, but they do not see the ways in
which human beings are unique: uniquely unique. We are a kind of animal who can – who *must* – rebuild ourselves, using the tools of our culture. We come into the world relatively undeveloped and helpless, and
require a lengthy childhood before we can take care of ourselves. This is
time in which parents take over the task of forming their children,
more or less consciously, and prepare them for a life of continual self-
transformation. We are animals who are incomplete, and are therefore
made to interface with the cultural tools that finish us off. Our minds
are as much outside as inside our skulls.

Andy Clark recounts a wonderful example in his recent *Natural-
Born Cyborgs*, of how access to a system of symbols transforms capacities, even of chimpanzees. Experimenters trained a group of chimps to
associate particular symbols with pairs of objects that were either identical or different, so that any pair of identical objects (say two bananas)

would be associated with a red triangle, whereas any pair of objects that were different (say a banana and a cup) would be associated with a blue square. The symbol-trained chimps, and only those chimps, were able to go on to solve another problem, that of sorting *pairs of pairs* of objects into the right categories. A pair of pairs is the same if both pairs are the same (for example, two bananas and two cups) *or* if both pairs are different (for example, a banana and a cup, and a shoe and a box). A pair of pairs is different if one of the pairs is the same and the other is different. As you can see, the notion of higher-order sameness (difference) is quite hard to grasp, and proved to be completely beyond the grasp of non-symbol-trained chimps. For symbol-trained chimps, however, it was possible: they had only to compare their symbols to get the right answer. Having symbols available transforms a higher-order categorization task into a first-order task, which is much more tractable. Clark suggests that human beings have the cognitive capacities they do because we have an entire system of symbols – language – available to us, which enables us to transform many tasks. But, as he goes on to argue, if this is true, there is every reason to think that further transformations in our symbolic systems will enhance our cognitive capacities even more.[170]

Clark draws the correct moral for our understanding of ourselves in relation to our evolutionary past. Our "cognitive biases are indeed the product of our evolutionary past," but they do not determine the contemporary mind: "Fixed genetic resources [are] one small group of players on a crowded stage. Our self-image as a species should not be that of ancient biological minds in colorful young technological clothes. Instead, ours are chameleon minds, factory-primed to merge with what they find and with what they themselves create."[171] Our minds are products of evolution, and they bear the traces of the past upon them. But we have not yet discovered a limit to their plasticity, and it may be that there is no such limit. We are able to transform our minds by transforming the worlds with which we interact. Our minds create the tools that create our minds.

What of the dispositions that form the basis of our moral system? Are they, too, subject to alteration, through the kinds of social transformations that alter our cognitive capacities? We have no reason to think this set of dispositions is any more immune than any other. This gives us special reason to take extra care in transforming the world and (therefore) ourselves, to ensure that we strengthen those dispositions of which we are justifiably proud and weaken those (equally innate, equally natural) dispositions of which we are ashamed. We have dispositions to care for one another, to empathize and, instinctively, to offer help, and we have dispositions to war, to anger, and to selfishness; we must seek to strengthen the first set and be vigilant against the second. But we have every reason to think that this is a task at which it is at least possible to succeed.

T. H. Huxley, Darwin's bulldog, was right, over a century ago: our moral motives are a product of evolution, but so are our *im*moral motives. We become moral animals not when we obey our evolved dispositions, but when we go to work on them: when we use those which we rightly identify as the most important, the ones which we are obliged to obey, as a template to prune and refine our dispositions. My inclination simply to take what I want, without regard for the feelings of others, is as much a product of evolution as is my inclination to stop and lend a hand. But I am a rational animal (thanks to evolution), and an acculturated one as well (thanks, indirectly, to evolution), and I am able to engage in the ongoing cultural project of distinguishing between evolved dispositions, separating out those which are binding and those to which we ought to accord no weight at all, to work at strengthening some and reducing the power of, perhaps even eliminating, others. Evolution gave us the preconditions of morality, but it is only as a result of the cultural elaboration of this raw material that we come to be moral beings.

Darwin and his followers have been accused of attempting to strip the world, and humanity, of its magnificence, reducing it to no more than a product of blind forces. But the process of evolution, the billions of years long process whereby simple life forms slowly developed into the myriad of animals and plants around us, is awe-inspiring. It allows us to glimpse apparent intelligence in the unexpectedly sophisticated behavior of the simplest microbes, at the same time as it pricks the bubble of pretension of the most complex, showing how they – we – too are the product of blind forces, all too apt to reveal our lowly origins. More magnificent still are the indirect products of evolution: our cathedrals and our philosophical systems, our cities and our morality. Strange to say, these indirect products react back upon their creators, helping to re-create us, to give us new powers and new capacities. We are animals, and we cannot ever free ourselves of our biological heritage. We have no need: it enables all the flexible, rational, and caring behavior that we could want, and allows us to seek to become ever more moral beings.

Further reading

Almost every day brings reports of new findings in evolutionary biology, genetics, psychology, and related fields, which are relevant to the
origins and contours of morality. Fortunately, there are also a number
of valuable books that enable those of us who are not specialists in these
sciences to make some sense of these findings. The following list contains many, though by no means all, of the best work on the topics.
They represent a range of views, from writers defending the autonomy
of ethics against biology, to those arguing that the human sciences need
to be thoroughly "biologicized" (as E. O. Wilson put it). The categories
into which the books are divided are somewhat arbitrary: many of
them could as easily fit into another category. My brief descriptions
of their contents should help readers to locate books on topics that
interest them.

The origins of morality

Matt Ridley, *The Origins of Virtue* (London: Viking, 1996). Ridley's
book is a little unfocused, and his political speculations often go far
beyond the facts he reports. Nevertheless, this is an excellent account of
how morality might have evolved from animal proto-morality.

Frans de Waal, *Good Natured: The Origins of Right and Wrong in Humans and Other Animals* (Cambridge, Mass.: Harvard University Press, 1996). Frans de Waal studies primate behavior, and has published a number of books on (mainly) chimpanzee social organization. He argues convincingly that the building blocks of morality are already present in our closest relatives.

Richard Dawkins, *The Selfish Gene* (Oxford University Press, 1989) (2nd edn.). This is one of the great classics of popular science writing, which itself makes a significant contribution to the science it reports. This is a book that is accessible without sacrificing detail, and deserves its high reputation – even if Dawkins sometimes (perhaps inadvertently) goes too far, and appears to attribute agency to genes. This is an essential reference point in the debates over morality, genetics, and evolution.

Evolutionary ethics

Most writers on the history of evolutionary ethics agree with my assessment of the flaws of Spencer's project. However, some philosophers argue that Spencer is more complex and resourceful than we give him credit for. For a thorough history and interpretation of Darwinian theories of morality, see Robert J. Richards, *Darwin and the Emergence of Evolutionary Theories of Mind and Behavior* (Chicago: University of Chicago Press, 1987). The collection edited by Paul Thompson, *Issues in Evolutionary Ethics* (Albany: State University of New York Press, 1995) contains useful extracts from Spencer, Darwin and T. H. Huxley on its origins and status (as well as a range of valuable recent essays).

Michael Ruse has written extensively and importantly on many topics in the philosophy of biology. His views are well represented by the chapters on ethics in his *Taking Darwin Seriously: A Naturalistic Approach to Philosophy* (2nd edn.) (Amherst: Prometheus Books, 1998).

There has been a recent explosion of interest in evolutionary approaches to morality in philosophy, which has produced a number of relatively technical works that will, nevertheless, repay close study. William Rottschaefer's *The Biology and Psychology of Moral Agency*

(Cambridge University Press, 1998) is an attempt to explain the biological origins of moral agency, and to justify our moral judgments on this basis. My review of Rottschaefer's book can be found here: *http://human-nature.com/nibbs/02/agency.html*.

Richard Joyce, in *The Myth of Morality* (Cambridge University Press, 2001), utilizes evolutionary arguments in an attempt to show that morality is a myth: an illusion caused by our genetic inheritance.

Biology and philosophy of biology

Evolutionary biology has been lucky enough to have two great science writers, themselves both working on the problems they report, keeping us all informed of the progress of the science. One is Richard Dawkins, whose most important book we have already mentioned (though *The Extended Phenotype: The Long Reach of the Gene* (Oxford: Oxford University Press, 1983) also deserves a mention). The other is the late Steven Jay Gould, who was always skeptical of the claim that we could find lessons for morality in biology. On this question, as on so many others, he engaged in a lively, decades-long, debate with Dawkins. Gould published dozens of books, but perhaps the best single volume is his *Wonderful Life: The Burgess Shale and the Nature of History* (London: Penguin, 1991). For a fair-minded and accessible assessment of the Dawkins–Gould debate, see Kim Sterelny, *Dawkins vs. Gould: Survival of the Fittest* (Cambridge: Icon Books, 2001).

Daniel Dennett, in *Darwin's Dangerous Idea: Evolution and the Meanings of Life* (New York: Simon & Schuster, 1995), covers all aspects of evolutionary theory, from the origins of life to morality, and emphasizes the importance of evolutionary styles of thinking for philosophy. Dennett's recent book, *Freedom Evolves* (New York: Viking, 2003) is an attempt to naturalize free will by placing it in an evolutionary perspective.

Kim Sterelny and Paul E. Griffiths, *Sex and Death: An Introduction to Philosophy of Biology* (Chicago: The University of Chicago Press, 1999) is probably the single best introduction to the philosophy of biology. Special mention should also be made of Elliot Sober and

David Sloan Wilson, *Unto Others: The Evolution and Psychology of Unselfish Behavior* (Cambridge, Mass.: Harvard University Press, 1998). This book is an important and convincing attempt to rehabilitate the idea of group selection in evolutionary biology and demonstrate its importance for our understanding of human motivation.

Evolutionary psychology

Evolutionary psychology's precursor, sociobiology, is best represented by the work of E. O. Wilson. Especially relevant here is *On Human Nature* (Cambridge, Mass.: Harvard University Press, 1978). But the discipline really came into its own with the publication in 1992 of an important set of essays: *The Adapted Mind: Evolutionary Psychology and the Generation of Culture*, eds. Jerome Barkow, Leda Cosmides and John Tooby (New York: Oxford University Press). Among other important contributions, this volume includes Cosmides and Tooby's classic essay on the Wason selection task.

For a short and accessible introduction to their work on stepchildren, see Martin Daly and Margo Wilson, *The Truth About Cinderella: A Darwinian View of Parental Love* (London: Weidenfeld & Nicolson, 1998). I have had many critical things to say in this book about Steven Pinker's *The Blank Slate: The Modern Denial of Human Nature* (London: Allen Lane, 2002); nevertheless, this is a wonderful introduction to evolutionary psychology by an excellent writer. More challenging, and probably more defensible, are the classic essays collected in *The Maladapted Mind: Classic Readings in Evolutionary Psychopathology*, ed. Simon Baron-Cohen (Hove: Psychology Press, 1997).

There are several approachable books applying evolutionary psychology to human sexuality. Geoffrey Miller's *The Mating Mind: How Sexual Choice Shaped the Evolution of Human Nature* (London: William Heinemann, 2000), and David Buss's *The Evolution of Desire: Strategies of Human Mating* (New York: Basic Books, 1994) are both interesting, if sometimes a little simplistic. Unfortunately, these are the high-water marks in accessible work on the topic.

For criticisms of evolutionary psychology by writers who (for the most part) think it is entirely intellectually bankrupt, see *Alas Poor Darwin: Arguments Against Evolutionary Psychology*, eds. Hilary Rose and Steven Rose (London: Vintage, 2000). Two books by philosophers of science are worth mentioning here: John Dupré, in *Human Nature and the Limits of Science* (Oxford: Clarendon Press, 2001), has some important criticisms to make of the entire project. Best of all, however, is Philip Kitcher's *Vaulting Ambition: Sociobiology and the Quest for Human Nature* (Cambridge, Mass.: MIT Press, 1985). This book is an attack upon sociobiology, but the faults it finds in the sociobiological program continue to plague evolutionary psychology.

Genetics

There are literally dozens of books on the ethical implications of genetic engineering and cloning. Some are by scientists, who certainly have a good grip on the science but are shaky on philosophy, and some by philosophers and social commentators who have a shaky grip on the science. A recent book by one of Germany's most famous philosophers is representative of many of those opposing genetic engineering and cloning. My review of Jürgen Habermas's *The Future of Human Nature* (Cambridge: Polity, 2003) can be found here: *http://mentalhelp.net/books/books.php?type=de&id=1707*.

The best book on the social and political implications of the new genetics is, without doubt, Allen Buchanan, Dan W. Brock, Norman Daniels, and Daniel Wikler, *From Chance to Choice: Genetics and Justice* (Cambridge: Cambridge University Press, 2000). All four authors are important philosophers, who have written extensively on bioethics and political philosophy. They deal with questions that tend to be neglected by other writers on genetics, but which will probably prove very important, like distribution and social inclusion.

There are a number of useful books available that focus on interpreting the claims made by geneticists, and showing that they just do not have the implications they are often said to have. Jonathan Michael Kaplan, *The Limits and Lies of Human Genetic Research: Dangers for Social Policy* (New York: Routledge, 2000) is an excellent recent overview of the claims of population geneticists, and the way in which these claims are misused for political purposes. Lenny Moss, *What Genes Can't Do* (Cambridge, Mass.: The MIT Press, 2003) is more technical and difficult, but essential reading for anyone who wants to sort through the confusion surrounding claims that there are genes for traits. My review is here: *http://mentalhelp.net/books/books.php?type= de&id=1446.*

Other resources

There are a number of excellent websites that provide useful guides to further reading and links to relevant new stories and research. Best of all by far is *The Human Nature Review* (*http://human-nature.com*). *The Human Nature Review* is a forum for book reviews and articles, largely on evolutionary biology and psychology, and human behavior. Excellent though the *Review* proper is, however, the website has much more to offer. I find its regularly updated new links service (*http://human-nature.com/nibbs*) especially useful – it provides links to recent reports, both popular and scientific, of relevant research, and links to book reviews on other sites. The site also has links to *Evolutionary Psychology*, a refereed journal, and to the evolutionary psychology discussion group, and much more.

The *Talk.Origins Archive* (*http://www.talkorigins.org*) is another excellent resource. It is devoted to providing resources to rebut pseudo-scientific creationism.

Two other websites are worth mentioning. The Edge (*http://www. edge.org*) is devoted to intellectual inquiry, but tends to focus on naturalistic and evolutionary thinkers. Past editions have featured Matt Ridley, E. O. Wilson, Andy Clark, Steven Pinker, Daniel Dennett, and many other important thinkers who bring a biologically informed perspective to moral and philosophical questions. Another useful website is the book reviews section of *Metapsychology Online* (*http://www.mentalhelp.net/books*). A drop-down menu enables visitors to limit their search to books in genetics or philosophy.

Biology and Philosophy is a refereed journal devoted to philosophical reflection on the life sciences, and to understanding their implications for all branches of human inquiry. Full text is available to subscribers only, but the contents and text of one free sample issue are freely available at the following address: *http://www.kluweronline.com/issn/0169-3867/contents.*

Notes

1. Jared M. Diamond, *The Third Chimpanzee: The Evolution and Future of the Human Animal* (New York: HarperCollins, 1992).
2. The phrase "Darwinian fundamentalism" is due to Stephen Jay Gould. See his "Darwinian Fundamentalism," *New York Review of Books*, June 12, 1997.
3. David P. Barash, "Evolutionary Existentialism, Sociobiology and the Meaning of Life," *Bioscience*, Nov. 2000, p. 1013.
4. In describing evolution as a gradual process, I do not mean to take sides in the debate over Stephen Jay Gould's theory of "punctuated equilibrium," according to which evolution is characterized by long periods of stasis interrupted by sudden change. Even on Gould's account, evolution is a gradual process *in human terms*, with speciation occurring in a mere ten thousand years. It is this slowness when measured on the human timescale, not the geological, which concerns us here.
5. Dean Hamer, *The God Gene: How Faith is Hardwired into Our Genes* (New York: Doubleday, 2003).
6. Paraphrased from the version of events recorded in J. R. Lucas, "Wilberforce and Huxley: A Legendary Encounter," *The Historical Review*, 22, 1979.

7. T. H. Huxley, "Evolution and Ethics," in *T. H. Huxley's Evolution and Ethics with New Essays on Its Victorian and Sociobiological Context,* eds. James Paradis and George C. Williams (Princeton: Princeton University Press, 1989), p. 138.

8. Ibid., p. 141.

9. George C. Williams, "Huxley's Evolution and Ethics in Sociobiological Perspective," in *Issues in Evolutionary Ethics,* ed. Paul Thompson (Albany: State University of New York Press, 1995).

10. Herbert Spencer, *The Study of Sociology* (London: Williams & Norgate, 1874), p. 346.

11. Cited in Richard Hofstadter, *Social Darwinism in American Thought* (Boston: Beacon Press, 1955), pp. 45–46.

12. Ibid., p. 45.

13. See Michael Ruse, *Taking Darwin Seriously: A Naturalistic Approach to Philosophy* (2nd edn.) (Amherst: Prometheus Books, 1998), p. 74.

14. See Mike Hawkins, *Social Darwinism in European and American Thought, 1860–1945* (Cambridge: Cambridge University Press, 1997). In his book *The Evolution Wars: A Guide to the Debates* (Rutgers University Press, 2001) Michael Ruse argues that Social Darwinist political views were more diverse than is usually appreciated.

15. See Gary Wills, *Under God: Religion and American Politics* (New York: Simon and Schuster, 1990), p. 109.

16. Quoted ibid., p. 102.

17. Ibid., p. 104.

18. Hawkins, *Social Darwinism in European and American Thought,* pp. 6–7.

19. Ibid., p. 222.

20. Ibid., p. 242.

21. Allen Buchanan, Dan W. Brock, Norman Daniels, and Daniel Wikler, *From Chance to Choice: Genetics and Justice* (Cambridge: Cambridge University Press, 2000), p. 34.

22. Ibid., p. 38.

23. Hawkins, *Social Darwinism in European and American Thought,* p. 279.

24. Elliott Sober, *Philosophy of Biology* (Boulder: Westview Press, 1993), p. 109.

25. Charles Darwin, *The Descent of Man, and Selection in Relation to Sex* (2nd edn.) (London: John Murray, 1885), pp. 133–134.

26. Richard Dawkins, *The Extended Phenotype: The Long Reach of the Gene* (Oxford: Oxford University Press, 1983).

27. James Rachels, *Created From Animals: The Moral Implications of Darwinism* (Oxford: Oxford University Press, 1991), pp. 68–69.

28. Ibid., p. 65.

29. Ruse, *Taking Darwin Seriously*, pp. 75–77.

30. Elliot Sober and David Sloan Wilson, *Unto Others: The Evolution and Psychology of Unselfish Behavior* (Cambridge, Mass.: Harvard University Press, 1998), p. 122.

31. Gregory Stock, *Redesigning Humans: Our Inevitable Genetic Future* (Boston: Houghton Mifflin Company, 2002), p. 3.

32. Lee M. Silver, *Remaking Eden: How Genetic Engineering & Cloning Will Transform the American Family* (New York: Avon Books, 1998), p. 277.

33. Francis Fukuyama, *Our Posthuman Future: Consequences of the Biotechnology Revolution* (New York: Farrar, Straus and Giroux, 2002), p. 157.

34. Ibid., p. 98.

35. In his recent book *The Future of Human Nature* (Cambridge: Polity, 2003), the prominent German philosopher Jürgen Habermas attempts to articulate a different basis for the intuition that genetic engineering is a threat to human dignity. Habermas argues that engineering a person transforms them into an object, subject to the whims and desires of others, and is therefore incompatible with the autonomy that is the source of our dignity. The problem with this line of argument (as we shall see in later chapters) is that it rests upon the mistaken view that the genetic determinants of our characteristics are more fundamental than the environmental. Parents already choose the characteristics of their children, by feeding, educating and socializing them into a way of life. It is hard to see how this is objectionable; in any case, it is unavoidable.

36. I have in mind the claim that respect for the ownership of property is, at least possibly, a product of natural selection. We shall examine this claim in a later chapter.

37. See Michael Stocker, "The Schizophrenia of Modern Ethical Theories," in *Virtue Ethics,* eds. Roger Crisp and Michael Slote (New York: Oxford University Press, 1998), pp. 66–78.

38. See J. L. Mackie, *Ethics: Inventing Right and Wrong* (Harmondsworth: Penguin Books, 1977).

39. Darwin, *The Descent of Man*, p. 130.

40. Richard Dawkins, *The Selfish Gene,* (Oxford: Oxford University Press, 1989) (2nd edn.), chap. 2.

41. Darwin, *The Descent of Man*, p. 132.

42. Sober, *Philosophy of Biology*, pp. 101–102.

43. Dawkins, *The Selfish Gene*, pp. 169–170.

44. More precisely, parents pass on fifty percent of the genes that *vary* in the population to their children. Most genes don't vary: all of us share almost all of our genes. I ignore this complication in what follows.

45. Not all the organisms in which castes of sterile workers are observed have haplo-diploid reproductive systems. Among termites and naked mole rats, the same kinds of effects are achieved through interbreeding. The main point is the same: a high degree of genetic relatedness encourages apparently altruistic behaviors, ranging from refraining from breeding to laying down one's life for others.

46. Gerald S. Wilkinson "Food Sharing in Vampire Bats," *Scientific American*, February 1990, pp. 76–82.

47. Rather than say that it is rational to be irrational, it would perhaps be better to say that what the prisoner's dilemma and related situations show is that there is more to rationality than weighing up the costs and benefits of our actions. A long-standing philosophical tradition, long absorbed into common sense, opposes rationality to emotions. But if the evolutionary explanation of the origins of the moral emotions is correct, then the emotions are actually themselves important elements in a wider notion of rationality. Certainly, they can lead us to act irrationally, on occasions, in the wider sense of that term. But so can rationality itself, narrowly construed, lead to (all things considered) irrationality.

48. Matt Ridley, *The Origins of Virtue* (London: Viking, 1996), pp. 134–135.

49. Robert H. Frank, *Passions Within Reason: The Strategic Role of the Emotions* (New York: Norton, 1998), p. 5.

50. Robert Trivers, *Social Evolution* (Menlo Park, CA.: Benjamin/ Cummings Publishing, 1985), pp. 415–418.

51. Ridley, *The Origins of Virtue*, p. 82.

52. Richard Joyce, *The Myth of Morality* (Cambridge: Cambridge University Press, 2001).

53. Ruse, *Taking Darwin Seriously*.

54. See Hamer, *The God Gene*; David Sloan Wilson, *Darwin's Cathedral: Evolution, Religion and the Nature of Society* (Chicago: University of Chicago Press, 2002).

55. Michael A. Persinger, *Neuropsychological Bases of God Beliefs* (New York: Praeger Publishers, 1987).

56. Quoted in Shankar Vedantam, "Tracing the Synapses of Our Spirituality," *Washington Post*, June 17, 2001.

57. This is not to deny that there are significant and relevant differences between color perception and moral responses. Most importantly, there seems to be much greater disagreement in the correct application of moral terms across cultures then there is in the correct application of color terms (though there is some, rather equivocal, evidence for the culture-relativity of color perception). However, the evidence is strong that there is cross-cultural agreement upon the shared core of morality, and this seems sufficient to rescue morality from the charge that its evolutionary history renders it illusory. On the extent to which cultures do – and *must* – share a common concept of morality, see my *Moral Relativism: A Short Introduction* (Oxford: Oneworld, 2002).

58. Ruse, *Taking Darwin Seriously*, pp. 252–255.

59. Ibid., p. 241.

60. Bruce N. Waller, "Moral Commitment without Objectivity or Illusion: Comments on Ruse and Woolcock," *Biology and Philosophy*, 11, 1996, p. 253.

61. See, for instance, Elizabeth Allen et al., "Against 'Sociobiology'," in *The Sociobiology Debate*, ed. Arthur L. Caplan (New York: Harper & Row, 1978). This famous response to E. O. Wilson was signed by

many of Wilson's Harvard colleagues, including such important and influential biologists as Steven Jay Gould and Richard Lewontin.

62. Richard Dawkins, quoted in Hilary Rose, "Colonising the Social Sciences?" in *Alas Poor Darwin: Arguments Against Evolutionary Psychology*, eds. Hilary Rose and Steven Rose (London: Vintage, 2000), p. 114.

63. Christopher Badcock, *Evolutionary Psychology: A Critical Introduction* (Cambridge: Polity, 2000), p. 243.

64. Quoted in Lawrence Weiskrantz, *Consciousness Lost and Found: A Neuropsychological Exploration* (Oxford: Oxford University Press, 1997), p. 187.

65. It would be wrong to place too much emphasis on the degree to which brain functions are localized. It is certainly true that particular regions of the brain usually carry out particular tasks, but, if that region is damaged or missing, the task may be delegated to other parts of the brain instead. Depending on how extensive the damage is, and how early it occurs, the task may be carried out by a new region of the brain almost as well as by the old. Nevertheless, brain function certainly becomes highly localized. The thesis that the brain is compartmentalized must be distinguished from the hypothesis that it is highly *modular*. Brain modules are not necessarily physical parts of the brain at all: they may instead be more akin to specialized software than to hardware.

66. Jack A. Palmer and Linda K. Palmer, *Evolutionary Psychology: The Ultimate Origins of Human Behavior* (Boston: Allyn and Bacon, 2002), p. 68.

67. John Alcock, *The Triumph of Sociobiology* (Oxford: Oxford University Press, 2001), pp. 163–164.

68. Palmer and Palmer, *Evolutionary Psychology*, p. 68.

69. The psychology of the Müller-Lyer illusion is a little more complex than this brief description suggests. There is some evidence that susceptibility to this illusion, among others, is culturally specific. See M. H. Segall, D. T. Campbell, M. J. Herskovitz, *The Influence of Culture on Visual Perception* (Indianapolis: Bobbs-Merrill, 1966). People who do not live in cultures in which straight lines and corners (especially inside houses) are common show reduced or

no susceptibility to the illusion. But though this complicates the picture, it doesn't detract from the main point: that our brains are designed by evolution to make sense of our environment, and to this end they possess rules for interpreting perceptions. These rules work almost all the time to give us an accurate representation of reality, but they are susceptible to producing systematic illusions under certain conditions.

70. Kim Sterelny and Paul E. Griffiths, *Sex and Death: An Introduction to Philosophy of Biology* (Chicago: The University of Chicago Press, 1999), p. 326.

71. Adapted from Leda Cosmides and John Tooby, "Cognitive Adaptations for Social Exchange," in *The Adapted Mind: Evolutionary Psychology and the Generation of Culture*, eds. Jerome Barkow, Leda Cosmides, and John Tooby (New York: Oxford University Press, 1992).

72. For this criticism, see Badcock, p. 110. Cosmides and Tooby, together with Laurence Fidick, reply to this criticism in "No interpretation without representation: The role of domain-specific representations and inferences in the Wason Selection Task," *Cognition*, 75, 2000.

73. John Dupré, *Human Nature and the Limits of Science* (Oxford: Clarendon Press, 2001), pp. 60–61.

74. Martin Daly and Margo Wilson, "Evolutionary social psychology and family homicide," in *The Maladapted Mind: Classic Readings in Evolutionary Psychopathology*, ed. Simon Baron-Cohen (Hove: Psychology Press, 1997), p. 116.

75. At first glance, these examples might appear difficult to explain from a Darwinian perspective. After all, bright plumage, or the ability to construct an attractive bower, has no obvious survival value. So it seems mysterious that females would select males with just these characteristics. The puzzle is solved when we realize that bright plumage and other attractors are indicative of qualities more directly related to survival. For instance, the ability to construct an elaborate tail, as male peacocks do, is indicative of general health since it is so costly to grow and to carry. In addition, the ability to grow it seems to be indicative that the animal has few parasites, perhaps because it is especially good at resisting them

(Geoffrey Miller, *The Mating Mind: How Sexual Choice Shaped the Evolution of Human Nature* (London: William Heinemann, 2000), pp. 63–64; 118). Moreover, once the trait has been chosen by females, for whatever reason, it becomes self-reinforcing. Given that most females prefer brightly colored plumage, for instance, no female can afford to ignore this preference. If she does, her male offspring will tend to be less brightly colored than average, and therefore will have fewer and lower quality partners than average. Even the choice of a partner with plumage that is averagely bright carries risks, since we can expect the brightness to increase in the next generation. Thus, females will choose the brightest colored birds, and the brightness of plumage will increase from generation to generation. This process, known as *runaway sexual selection*, explains such magnificent but useless ornamentations as the peacock's tail. It is the result of peahen preferences across many generations.

76. David M. Buss, *The Evolution of Desire: Strategies of Human Mating* (New York: Basic Books, 1994).

77. Ibid., 24–25.

78. Ibid., 28, 34, 39.

79. Ibid., 19, 51, 54.

80. Ibid., 56.

81. Dev Singh, "Body shape and women's attractiveness: the critical role of the waist-to-hip ratio," *Human Nature*, 4, 1993, pp. 297–321.

82. Daly and Wilson, "Evolutionary social psychology and family homicide," p. 118.

83. Martin Daly and Margo Wilson, *The Truth About Cinderella: A Darwinian View of Parental Love* (London: Weidenfeld & Nicolson, 1998), p. 34.

84. Randy Thornhill and Craig T. Palmer, *A Natural History of Rape: Biological Bases of Sexual Coercion* (Cambridge, Mass.: MIT Press, 2000).

85. Ibid., p. 89.

86. Simon Baron-Cohen, *The Essential Difference: Men, Women and the Extreme Male Brain* (London: Allen Lane, 2003), p. 1.

87. Ibid., p. 5.

88. Ibid., p. 141.
89. Ibid., pp. 64, 72.
90. Ibid., p. 12.
91. Alcock, *The Triumph of Sociobiology*, p. 193.
92. It is for this reason that the claim of some evolutionary psychologists that the principle of parsimony supports their view is mistaken. It is a well-established principle, in science and philosophy, that when two rival explanations seem to explain the phenomena in question equally well, we ought to prefer the more parsimonious (that is, the one that is simpler in that it postulates fewer kinds of entities). In this case, however, evolutionary psychology and the more traditional social sciences postulate exactly the same number of entities: a mind with some innate dispositions and modules, and a cultural and physical environment to which that mind reacts.
93. Alcock, *The Triumph of Sociobiology*, p. 141.
94. Ibid., p. 143.
95. On this point, see Philip Kitcher, *Vaulting Ambition: Sociobiology and the Quest for Human Nature* (Cambridge, Mass.: MIT Press, 1985), pp. 126–127. As Kitcher would himself acknowledge, this is something of a simplification. It would be more accurate to say that, *so far as we know* our innate preferences are alterable only with difficulty. It is certainly possible, as Richard Dawkins points out, that we might discover a quite easy way to alter any particular preference. Dispositions that are normally hard to reverse may suddenly become easy to alter if just the right agent is applied (Dawkins, *The Extended Phenotype*, p. 11). This agent might be chemical, or genetic, or even, quite conceivably, environmental. Evolutionary psychology is not committed to the view that environmental changes will not make any differences to the preferences it identifies, just to the view that the preference will be robust across a wide range of environments, and that effective environmental interventions are very likely to be costly.
96. Edward O. Wilson, *On Human Nature* (Cambridge, Mass.: Harvard University Press, 1978), p. 147.
97. Steven Pinker, *The Blank Slate: The Modern Denial of Human Nature* (London: Allen Lane, 2002), pp. 169–170.

98. Pinker, *The Blank Slate*, pp. 141–142.

99. Ibid., p. 145.

100. On the way in which deafness can lead to cognitive impairment, if it prevents a child from acquiring a language (that is, in the absence of any language, spoken or signed), see Oliver Sacks, *Seeing Voices: A Journey into the World of the Deaf* (London: Pan Books, 1991).

101. Buss, *The Evolution of Desire*, p. 46.

102. Miller, *The Mating Mind*, p. 106.

103. Ibid., p. 93.

104. Ibid., pp. 376–377.

105. Pinker, *The Blank Slate*, pp. 351–357.

106. The implications of Baron-Cohen's view are even less palatable. He insists, like Pinker, that we ought to treat people as individuals, without reference to the group to which they belong. We ought not, therefore, assume that the woman would be a better parent than a man in a child custody case, or that a male applicant to a mathematics department is a better candidate than a female (Baron-Cohen, *The Essential Difference*, p. 12). Yet if the figures he provides, both of actual success of men and women in the professions, and from his studies of the abilities of males and females are accurate, then we are indeed entitled to make these assumptions, especially the latter. Extremely few women score highly in his test for the systemizing quotient. (See Simon Baron-Cohen, Jennifer Richler, Dheraj Bisarya, Nhishanth Gurunathan and Sally Wheelwright, "The Systemizing Quotient: An Investigation of Adults with Asperger Syndrome or High-Functioning Autism, and Normal Sex Differences," *Philosophical Transactions of the Royal Society, Series B*, 2003, pp. 361–374.) On his figures, we are entitled to assume that female candidates will perform relatively poorly, unless there is very good evidence to the contrary.

107. George Will, "A Radical Proposition," *Washington Post*, February 4, 1999.

108. Pinker, *The Blank Slate*, p. 162.

109. Notice that this explanation utilizes several elements that might profitably be understood in an evolutionary framework. For instance, the desire of women (and men) for resources is best

understood as a product of evolution, as is the desire of men (and women) for sex. This is only to be expected: as I have repeatedly emphasized, no coherent explanation of human social behavior can dispense entirely with evolutionary considerations, nor with social and cultural considerations.

110. Buss, *The Evolution of Desire*, pp. 28, 29.

111. Ibid., p. 46.

112. Ibid., p. 58.

113. Why do men place a greater value on attractiveness than do women, according to the SSSM? To say that this preference is cultural might be true, but cannot suffice as an explanation. For we will want to know why *this* particular preference has been culturally reinforced, and not another. This preference, along with other sexual preferences, is most probably the result of the gender disparity in resource control characteristic of almost all human societies. Women prefer older men – and as a consequence put less of a premium on beauty, which of course is correlated with youth – since such men are more likely to control substantial resources. This leaves male preferences unexplained. I don't think a directly evolutionary explanation will prove useful here, but I do have a suggestion modeled on a Darwinian hypothesis. The theory of sexual selection tells us that any characteristic whatsoever can become the target of selection: it is sustained simply by the fact that the preference for that characteristic is widely shared, so that any female who does not take it into account will have male offspring who are at a disadvantage. Analogously, socially maintained preferences can be sustained simply by community agreement, regardless of their rationality or lack thereof. Since social status is, as Buss correctly notes, bound up with mate-choice (Buss, *The Evolution of Desire*, p. 59), it is irrational for each individual to deviate from the social consensus on attractiveness. To deviate just *is* to risk a fall in social status. Finally, we need to note that the marked emphasis on female beauty is somewhat of an embarrassment for the evolutionary approach. From the differences in parental investment, you will recall, evolutionary psychology predicts that males will compete with one another for access to females, while females choose from among the

competitors. But the emphasis on female beauty is obviously a sign of female–female competition for male attention. This comports better with the patriarchy theory, which makes resource possession by males critical to sexual strategies, than it does with evolutionary psychology.

114. Buss, *The Evolution of Desire*, p. 68.

115. Ibid., p. 68.

116. On the extent to which intelligence is far more than a mere rule-based ability, but requires an empathy-like intuition, see Hubert Dreyfus's classic critique of GOFAI, *What Computers* Still *Can't Do* (3rd edn.), (Cambridge, Mass.: MIT Press, 1992), and Andy Clark's *Being There: Putting Brain, Body, and World Together Again* (Cambridge, Mass.: MIT Press, 1997). Clark amasses evidence from cognitive science, neurobiology, computer science, and robotics for the thesis that intelligence is essentially an embodied ability.

117. Thornhill and Palmer, *A Natural History of Rape*, p. 67.

118. Ibid., p. 68.

119. Ibid., p. 70.

120. Ibid., p. 70.

121. Ibid., p. 100.

122. Ibid., p. 121.

123. Ibid., p. 113.

124. It is certainly possible that we might have evidence that a trait is an adaptation, even though it brings no advantage to the organisms that possess it. Sometimes, we can find traces of a history of adaptation and counter-adaptation, the result of which is to leave the organisms involved in much the same relative position now as they were before they developed the adaptations in question. For instance, there is good evidence that human fetuses evolved traits designed to allow them to maximize the resources coming to them from their mother's body, so as to ensure that the pregnancy continues and the child will be as well nourished as possible, even in environments in which food is short. Thus, the fetus attempts to hijack the resources of the mother's body. But women have evolved counter-adaptations, such as mechanisms which lead to a fall in her blood sugar levels early in pregnancy, which limit the

availability of resources to the fetus (Palmer and Palmer, *Evolutionary Psychology,* pp. 145–146). It may be that these adaptations and counter-adaptations cancel each other out, leaving the parties in the same relative position as previously. But the mechanisms themselves only make sense in the light of a history of maternal–fetal conflict and adaptation. If Thornhill and Palmer are to vindicate the suggestion that rape is an adaptation, despite the fact that it fails to confer a fitness benefit on rapists, they must show evidence of similar counter-adaptations. They provide only one piece of evidence. The function of the female orgasm, they allege, is to increase the probability of fertilization. Thus, the absence of orgasm in women who are the victims of rape might be a counter-adaptation, to allow women to choose the males who will father their offspring (Thornhill and Palmer, *A Natural History of Rape,* p. 99). But of course this is nonsense. Unlike the drop in pregnant women's blood sugar early in pregnancy, absence of orgasm in rape victims does not require any kind of explanation. Orgasm is the result of sexual pleasure, and – Thornhill and Palmer's bizarre and offensive speculations aside – we already know that raped women do not experience such pleasure.

125. Indeed, the insistence upon the universality of traits goes to the heart of the debate between evolutionary psychology and the SSSM. Philosophical defenders of evolutionary approaches, like Janet Radcliffe Richards, point out that there is no reason, in the abstract, to believe that traits which are adaptations are any more difficult to alter or to eradicate than traits which are the result of socialization (Janet Radcliffe Richards, *Human Nature after Darwin: A Philosophical Introduction* (London: Routledge, 2000), pp. 120–123). This is true, in the abstract. But evolutionary psychology constructs a detailed empirical case for particular, robust, adaptations. Its central claim, as we have seen repeatedly, is that these traits have proved impossible to eradicate across all environments so far, including environments in which the elimination of the trait has been an explicit aim, like kibbutzim (Pinker, *The Blank Slate,* pp. 257, 346). The evidence of universality is explicitly advanced as evidence that the preferences in question are hard to alter.

126. Pinker, *The Blank Slate*, p. 350. Baron-Cohen lays down the same challenge to cultural explanations of the gendered patterns of social life: "If it is just a matter of culture, why should most cultures be producing the same pattern?" (Baron-Cohen, *The Essential Difference*, p. 74).

127. Daniel C. Dennett, *Darwin's Dangerous Idea: Evolution and the Meanings of Life* (New York: Simon & Schuster, 1995), p. 487.

128. Pinker, *The Blank Slate*, p. 346.

129. John Maynard Smith, *Did Darwin Get it Right? Essays on Games, Sex and Evolution* (London: Penguin Books, 1988), pp. 204–215.

130. Ibid., p. 214.

131. Ibid., p. 212.

132. Brian Skyrms, *Evolution of the Social Contract* (New York: Cambridge University Press, 1996), p. 78.

133. Ibid., pp. 67, 68.

134. Ibid., pp. 78, 79.

135. Daly and Wilson, "Evolutionary social psychology and family," p. 118.

136. On evolutionary explanations of disgust, see Valerie Curtis and Adam Biran, "Dirt, Disgust, and Disease: Is Hygiene in Our Genes?" *Perspectives in Biology and Medicine*, 44, 2001, pp. 17–31.

137. Quoted in Evelyn Fox Keller, *The Century of the Gene* (Cambridge, Mass.: Harvard University Press, 2000), p. 54.

138. "Nurturing Nature," *The Economist*, August 1, 2002.

139. "Couch potatoes may be able to blame the 'laziness' gene," *Daily Telegraph*, August 25, 1999.

140. "Intelligence is mostly in the genes study finds," *Daily Telegraph*, June 6, 1997.

141. See, for example, "Research Points Toward a Gay Gene," *Wall Street Journal*, July 16, 1993.

142. Dean Hamer and Peter Copeland, *Living With Our Genes: Why they matter more than you think* (London: Pan Books, 1998), p. 192.

143. What is the answer? Do we have free will? Part of the difficulty in answering this question is that most of us have no clear idea what we mean by the phrase. It may be that we are conceptually confused, asking for something that is simply an impossibility

(perhaps an ability both to weigh reasons, and simultaneously decide without reference to them). If by free will we mean the ability to respond in a flexible manner to the changing challenges of our environment, then the answer is yes, we have free will. But it is not clear that this kind of free will is sufficient to underwrite all our moral practices of praise and blame. The best defense of free will in an explicitly evolutionary context is Daniel Dennett's recent book, *Freedom Evolves* (New York: Viking, 2003).

144. On this question, see the essays collected in *Genetics and Criminal Behavior*, eds. David Wasserman and Robert Wachbroit (Cambridge: Cambridge University Press, 2001).

145. Dawkins, *The Selfish Gene*, pp. 200–201.

146. Here I have in mind the work of Roy Baumeister and his colleagues on the phenomenon they call "ego depletion." See, for example, Mark Muraven, Dianne M. Tice, Roy Baumeister, and F. Roy, "Self-Control as Limited Resource: Regulatory Depletion Patterns," *Journal of Personality and Social Psychology*, vol. 74(3), March 1998.

147. Buchanan et al., *From Chance to Choice*, p. 95.

148. Fukuyama, *Our Posthuman Future*, pp. 156–157.

149. "Scientist finds first gene for intelligence," *Boston Globe*, March 11, 1997.

150. Lenny Moss, *What Genes Can't Do* (Cambridge, Mass.: MIT Press, 2003), pp. 44–50.

151. Preformationism was the seventeenth-century school of biology that argued that the adult was contained, in miniature but complete, in the "seed" from which it grows. Preformationists defended the notion of *emboitement*, according to which each "seed" contained the adult, and each miniature adult in the seed itself already contained seeds which each contained even smaller miniature adults, which each contained seeds, and so on. Preformationists were opposed by defenders of *epigenesis*, according to which the traits of an organism were acquired in a context-sensitive manner during development. Moss's point, in labeling his genes "Gene-P" and "Gene-D," is to highlight the fact that the preformationist/epigenetic conflict continues to this day,

now transformed into a battle over the right way to understand the gene.

152. "They've got your number," *The Observer,* June 11, 2000, is representative here. The author asks whether the Human Genome Project will lead to scientists "privatizing the human soul."

153. Pinker, *The Blank Slate,* pp. 106–107.

154. Incidentally, this is an effect that we might be led to predict on the basis of Pinker's work. Pinker claims that adopted children tend, when young, to have IQs similar to those of their adoptive parents, but as they age their IQs come increasingly to resemble those of their biological parents (Pinker, *The Blank Slate,* p. 375). Environmental alterations can only disguise underlying IQ for a relatively short period, after which its real – innate – nature is revealed. Pinker claims that his position has no moral implications, so long as we remember that this is a statistical, group level, effect: we can avoid discrimination against individuals by treating them on their merits. To this end, Pinker advocates much wider use of intelligence testing (ibid., p. 147). IQ tests, he tells us, are really predictive of a child's life prospects and ability to take advantage of educational opportunities (ibid., p. 150). But it is difficult to see how to reconcile his beliefs that (1) IQ tests are reliable indications of the abilities of children, and (2) the results of IQ tests can be distorted by environmental alterations, such that less intelligent children score significantly higher than they ought to.

155. Richard Herrnstein and Charles Murray, *The Bell Curve: Intelligence and Class Structure in American Life* (New York: Free Press, 1994), p. 405.

156. The following discussion of heritability draws liberally upon Ned Block and Gerald Dworkin, "Heritability and Inequality," in *The IQ Controversy: Critical Readings,* eds. Block and Dworkin (Pantheon Books, 1976); Ned Block, "How Heritability Misleads about Race," *Boston Review* XX, January 1996; and Jonathan Michael Kaplan, *The Limits and Lies of Human Genetic Research: Dangers for Social Policy* (New York: Routledge, 2000).

157. Fukuyama, *Our Posthuman Future,* pp. 136–137.

158. Kaplan, *The Limits and Lies of Human Genetic Research,* p. 30.

159. van Dellen, Anton, Blakemore, Colin, Deacon, Robert, York, Denis, Hannan, Anthony J., "Delaying the onset of Huntington's in mice," *Nature*, April 13, 2000, pp. 721–722.

160. Kaplan, *Limits and Lies of Human Genetic Research*, pp. 13–21.

161. Sterelny and Griffiths, *Sex and Death*, p. 16.

162. Matt Ridley, *Nature Via Nurture: Genes, experience and what makes us human* (London: Fourth Estate, 2002), p. 257.

163. Kitcher, *Vaulting Ambition*, p. 25.

164. Leon Kass, "Preventing a Brave New World," *The New Republic*, May 17, 2001.

165. Source, *The New Internationalist*, April 2000.

166. "Genetic test may identify boys who will grow to be violent," *The Independent*, August 2, 2002.

167. Christopher Boehm, "Conflict and the Evolution of Social Control," *Journal of Consciousness Studies*, 7, 2000, p. 91.

168. Robin Dunbar, *Grooming, Gossip, and the Evolution of Language* (Cambridge, Mass.: Harvard University Press, 1996).

169. Ridley, *Nature Via Nurture*, p. 226.

170. See Andy Clark, *Natural-Born Cybogs: Minds, Technologies, and the Future of Human Intelligence* (Oxford: Oxford University Press, 2003). The chimp and higher-order sorting example is on p. 70.

171. Ibid., p. 141.

Index

Note: page numbers in **bold** refer to diagrams.